GONE ASTRAY

Cornelie Holzach
Ellen Maurer Zilioli
Editors

The Art of
Gold- and Silversmithing
on the Edge of Reason

Hollowware
Jewelry
Utensils

Yet names and things have
become estranged. […]
That things no longer do
what they always did, and that this
can no longer be changed.
It has simply come to a
general strike of the things.

Aber Namen und Dinge
sind sich abhanden gekommen. (…)
Daß die Dinge nicht mehr tun mögen,
was sie immer taten, und daß dies
nicht mehr zu ändern geht.
Es ist eben zum Generalstreik
der Dinge gekommen.

Erhart Kästner*

The Pipe Wrench Lanyard
The Châtelaine
Alltagslöcher 1
Fernglas
BRILLE – LE CLUB OPTIQUE
Ohrschützer
Telefonhörer
Don't Forget the Voice of Peace
Für die kleine Messe
Kelch
Casted Salt Glasses
Salt Necklace 09
Salt Vessels
Salt Shakers
Belly
Black on Black
Graphite Head
The Toolness of Things
See no Evil (Tryptich)
9th Inning
Poppy
BEYOND REPAIR / LILIES VASE
Ohne Titel / Untitled (Kino 12)
Ohne Titel / Untitled (Kino 13)

Ohne Titel / Untitled (Kino 11)
SOAP HANDLE
TEXTILE HANDLE
STASH
Singing in the Void (Green)
Niche
Shalo boli duge
circle 02
circle 01
Roségoldblech mit Griff
Deckel mit Pins 1–3
Ensha
Entität
Things 21
Things 23
Ohne Titel / Untitled (Vessel / Hanging container)
Things 2
Gefäß / Vessel
Spectacle Bread and Mother-of-Pearl
Soap
Teapot
Vine Glass
oOOo
Very Practical Necklace

Shadow
Extraordinary Piece No. 2
Darkness Falls
Preciouses
Space of Home
ingrown
box
empty
box
Ohne Titel / Untitled (oval)
Ohne Titel / Untitled (rund / round)
pawn
Nadel und Box / Pin and box
Blown up
Ebb #4
Bag beneath #3
Timeline
Handled #4
Lure of Space Collection—space sketches
WITHIN
Double Cylinder Slide
Antique White
Penguin
Taped Pitcher

Freistehende Bratpfanne / Freestanding skillet
Apron, Mittens and Mask
Sleeves and Skirt
Gefäß / Container
innen#7
innen#5
innen#2
Klobrille / Toilet seat
Nudelholz / Rolling pin
Fleischhammer / Meat tenderizer
Hammer
Pfanne / Pan
Bügeleisen / Flat iron
KNELL – The Gender Bell#29
KNELL – The Gender Bell#3X
KNELL – The Gender Bell#2
HOME#33
HOME#17
Hot Mess
Woods Baroque 2
A Dutch Encounter VII
String Theory – ST2
Creation
Off Balance

Hein-Ecken
Hommage to Hannah Höch
About Ornament II
Baking Pin
Table
Zuckerdose / Sugar bowl
Rhythmus
I Am Hungry Nr. V
Presse
Ich bin keine Vase

The beautiful is (thus)
not something that can be
grasped but a state of
reflective awareness.

*Das Schöne ist (demnach)
kein Etwas, das es zu erfassen
gilt, sondern ein Zustand
reflektierender Wahrnehmung.*

Monika Leisch-Kiesl*

Preface 10
Vorwort 11

Gone Astray? 14
Auf Abwegen? 15
Cornelie Holzach

A Different Logic of Things 22
Eine andere Logik der Dinge 23
Ellen Maurer Zilioli

Katalog / Catalogue 41

Werkverzeichnis / List of Works 129
Biografien / Biographies 159

PREFACE

Art does not suffer constraints gladly, refuses to be categorized, and usually defies ultimate definition. The situation is similar with jewelry. More and more silversmiths and goldsmiths are pushing the boundaries of conventional genres, exploring new materials, and making daring objects. The exhibition Gone Astray – Jewellery and Utensils on the Fringe of Reason, which will open at Pforzheim Jewellery Museum (October 6, 2023, to January 14, 2024) and then grace CODA Museum in Apeldoorn (May 19, 2024, to September 22, 2024), features unusual exhibits, thus opening our eyes to new ways of seeing and looking at things.

VORWORT

Kunst lässt sich nicht einengen, nicht kategorisieren und meistens nicht abschließend definieren. Ähnlich verhält es sich mit Schmuck. Immer mehr Silber- oder Goldschmiede sprengen die Grenzen herkömmlicher Gattungen, erkunden neue Materialien und fertigen gewagte Objekte. Die Ausstellung Auf Abwegen – Schmuck und Gerät am Rande der Vernunft, *die zuerst das Schmuckmuseum Pforzheim (6. Oktober 2023 bis 14. Januar 2024) und anschließend das CODA Museum in Apeldoorn (19. Mai bis 22. September 2024) bereichert, zeigt ungewöhnliche Exponate und öffnet den Blick für neue Betrachtungsweisen.*

We are grateful indeed to Ellen Maurer Zilioli for choosing this exciting subject with all its many new ramifications. She has made an interesting selection of some 150 exhibits that are the work of twenty-nine artists from a wide range of countries and different generations, including both well-known and new talents. All exhibitors occupy a marginal zone with their various stances. They all think on multiple levels about forms, material, and fundamental concepts such as tableware, vessels, and jewelry, and their adventurous journey takes them into new territories that must be explored. Experimenting with materials is an important aspect of such. The creations presented consist of not only familiar materials such as silver and gold but also sugar, soap, shells, salt, and textiles. The vessel as a utilitarian object is a common theme in the applied arts, yet here it is charged with political awareness and ironic or critical commentary. Complex and seriously fresh thinking on utensils, vessels, and jewelry has begun, and the exhibiting artists are conducting a dynamic ongoing dialogue with material. Craft is transformed into art. A new artistic idiom is being invented and, in the process, is casting traditions in a new light. Making a piece of jewelry is increasingly resulting in autonomous artworks or, on the other hand, implements for daily use.

Very Practical Necklace, to take one example, is the title Nils Hint has given to one of his pieces of jewelry. And wrenches of various sizes as well as bicycle tools do indeed dangle from this wrought-iron chain. Karen Pontoppidan transforms mundane objects into valuables by hollow casting a rolling pin, a toilet seat, and an iron. Definitely not wearable, nor taken from any known jewelry tradition—on the contrary, with them she is exploring the field en route to design. Anna Rikkinen links historic ornaments with new forms: she strings painted wooden objects along with found objects on a black cloth band into neck jewelry reminiscent of Dutch Old Master portraits. Ute Eitzenhöfer makes pin objects from pieces of shampoo or shower-gel bottles. She transmutes what is thrown after use into the trash as plastic garbage into appealing pin objects. Nowadays not all jewelry artists are moving in the same direction; rather, different stances exist, all equally valuable and interesting. We are above all indebted to the participating artists for this diverse ›tour de plaisir‹. To them we are very much obliged, and would like to give them a big thank you for their trust in us and for making it possible for us to view their special works, indeed on a permanent basis, in this sumptuous publication.

Cornelie Holzach, Director of Pforzheim Jewellery Museum,
and Carin E.M. Reinders, Director General of CODA Museum Apeldoorn, the Netherlands

Für die Wahl dieses überaus spannenden Themas mit vielen neuen Aspekten sind wir der Kuratorin Ellen Maurer Zilioli sehr dankbar. Sie hat eine interessante Auswahl von rund 150 Exponaten 29 internationaler Künstler und Künstlerinnen unterschiedlicher Generationen zusammengestellt, darunter bereits bekannte wie auch neue Talente. Alle bewegen sich mit ihren unterschiedlichen Positionen in einem Zwischenraum. Alle denken vielschichtig und ganz neu über Formen, Material und fundamentale Begriffe wie Gerät, Gefäß oder Schmuck nach. Diese abenteuerliche Reise führt in neue Gebiete, die es zu erkunden gilt. Das Experimentieren mit Materialien gehört als wichtiger Faktor dazu. Die vorgestellten Kreationen bestehen nicht nur aus bekannten Materialien wie Silber oder Gold, sondern auch aus Zucker, Seife, Muscheln, Salz oder Textilien. Das Gefäß als Gebrauchsgegenstand ist ein gängiger Topos des Kunsthandwerks, doch hier wird es mit politischem Bewusstsein und ironischen oder kritischen Kommentaren aufgeladen. Ein komplexes und höchst frisches Denken über Utensilien, Gefäße und Schmuck hat begonnen, und die Künstler führen einen dynamischen Dialog mit dem Material. Handwerk verwandelt sich in Kunst. Eine neue künstlerische Sprache wird erfunden und wirft damit ein neues Licht auf Traditionen. Die Anfertigung eines Schmuckstücks tendiert immer mehr zum selbständigen Kunstwerk oder aber zum Werkzeug für den täglichen Gebrauch.

Very Practical Necklace *nennt beispielsweise Nils Hint eines seiner Schmuckstücke. Und in der Tat hängen an dieser geschmiedeten Eisenkette unterschiedlich große Schraubenschlüssel sowie Fahrradwerkzeug. Karen Pontoppidan verwandelt Alltagsgegenstände in Preziosen, indem sie Nudelholz, Toilettenbrille und Bügeleisen hohl abformt. Definitiv nicht tragbar und auch keiner Schmucktradition entlehnt – vielmehr lotet sie das Feld Richtung Design aus. Anna Rikkinen verknüpft historische Ornamente mit neuen Formen: Bemalte Holzobjekte fädelt sie neben Fundstücken auf ein schwarzes Textilband zu Halsschmuck, der an Porträts niederländischer Meister erinnert. Ute Eitzenhöfer schafft Ansteckobjekte aus Teilen von Shampoo- oder Duschgelflaschen. Was als Plastikmüll nach Gebrauch achtlos in die Tonne wandert, verwandelt sie in ansprechende Ansteckobjekte. Schmuckkünstler bewegen sich heute nicht nur in eine Richtung, vielmehr existieren unterschiedliche Positionen, alle gleichermaßen wertvoll und interessant. Diese vielfältige »Tour de plaisir« haben wir vor allem den beteiligten Kunstschaffenden zu verdanken. Wir sind ihnen sehr verbunden und bedanken uns herzlich für das Vertrauen und die Möglichkeit, ihre besonderen Arbeiten betrachten zu dürfen, sogar dauerhaft in dieser wertvollen Publikation.*

Cornelie Holzach, Leiterin des Schmuckmuseums Pforzheim
und Carin E.M. Reinders, Generaldirektorin des CODA Museums Apeldoorn, Niederlande

GONE ASTRAY?

Cornelie Holzach

Where have we ended up? What is going on here? How come?
What's that supposed to be? So, it's all right after all? Why is that so? What?
And what's what here? And that's supposed to be beautiful now?
And why is everything here so different? What? Is that even possible? But why?
No, really, why that of all things? Strange, what's the meaning of that?
Now where are we supposed to go? Is anything else forthcoming? Do you
go up or down here? And there's no way back? Has anyone ever been here?
Where is the right path in fact? Can't you rely on anything anymore?
Is that the way it's supposed be? Well, it's all gone astray!

AUF ABWEGEN?

Cornelie Holzach

Wo sind wir denn da gelandet? Was ist denn hier los? Wie? Was soll das denn sein? Ach, geht das denn? Warum ist das so? Wie? Und wo geht's hier lang? Und das soll jetzt schön sein? Und wieso ist das hier alles so anders? Was? Geht das denn? Aber warum? Nein, wieso sowas? Komisch, wie ist das gemeint? Wo sollen wir jetzt hin? Kommt da noch was? Geht's hier rauf oder runter? Und zurück kommt man nicht mehr? War hier schon mal jemand? Wo ist eigentlich der richtige Weg? Kann man sich denn auf gar nichts verlassen? Soll das so sein? Ach, das ist ja alles völlig abwegig!

That's the way it is with straying from the straight and narrow; you usually distrust what comes at you, often reject it, and if you stumble across it yourself without having chosen this path, you sometimes lose the courage to go further astray off the beaten track. On the other hand, this is still a path, not unexplored terrain, not uncharted territory on which you are the first person to set foot; hence it might perhaps at some future time be a track that will later become a way—whether it will be off the beaten track at that point is not yet certain. In fact, what is perhaps the most frightening thing about going astray is the unpredictable, the not-unambiguous, and non-pigeonholeable aspect of it. We are acting outside the normal, the known, and the classifiable. There is much to be said for normality: you don't have to worry about whether something is right or wrong, suitable or unsuitable. Many people do, undoubtedly, manage to live their lives without ever having gone astray, and lives lived like that are not in the least unhappy. On the contrary, taking the foreseeable, straight path guarantees security and self-validation. Living your whole life in the same place, having the same friends from kindergarten to nursing home for the elderly, vacationing for decades in the same place at the same time of year in order to meet the same people each time can be profoundly satisfying. When changes do occur, they take place in gradual, virtually imperceptible cycles. It is simply time passing and external influences that cause changes rather than any wish to change. Uniformity may occasionally seem dreary and dull and can even lead to fundamentally questioning the meaning of life, yet it also has something tremendously comforting about it. A corset, especially one you choose yourself, provides stability and engenders self-assurance; a creeping feeling of being boxed in tends to be ignored: there is no room for doubt. You never step out of line, but if you do, such brief escapades are over quickly since you realize that behaving differently does not hold a candle to the familiar and habitual. Still, slight doubts may linger, something that eludes definition, something you don't want to encounter on the one hand but, on the other, exerts an increasingly strong pull. Something that, no matter how hard you try, doesn't simply vanish into thin air. It feels like a vague unease that is difficult to grasp, at times timidly nagging at you, at others hitting you in the face. You don't really succeed in ignoring it altogether. It is ultimately up to you to decide on whether you should invest more time and energy in not letting yourself be thrown off kilter or, alternatively, daring to take the step and go astray by leaving the beaten track.

And then you just do it? That rarely happens without a hitch. On the contrary, it is a protracted process that creeps up on you and catches you almost unawares but nonetheless advances inexorably; whether in fits and starts or whether you return for a while to what has served you so well in the past changes nothing about the

So ist das also mit den Abwegen, man begegnet ihnen meistens misstrauisch, oft genug ablehnend, und gerät man selbst darauf, ohne sich diesen Weg ausgesucht zu haben, verlässt einen schon mal der Mut, ihn, den Ab-Weg, weiterzugehen. Andererseits, es ist immerhin ein Weg, kein noch nicht betretenes Gebiet, kein Neuland, auf welchem man erste Schritte tut, damit vielleicht irgendwann ein Pfad, später ein Weg daraus wird – ob dieser dann abwegig sein wird, steht noch nicht fest. Überhaupt, das vielleicht Erschreckende an den Abwegen ist das Unvorhersehbare, das Nicht-Eindeutige und Nicht-Zuordenbare. Wir bewegen uns außerhalb der Norm, dem Bekannten und Eingeübten. Das Normale hat viel für sich, man macht sich keine Gedanken, inwieweit etwas richtig oder falsch, passend oder unpassend ist. Vielen gelingt es sicherlich, ihr Leben zu führen, ohne jemals auf Abwege geraten zu sein, und dieses Leben ist keinesfalls unglücklich. Im Gegenteil, der überschaubare, gerade Weg schafft Sicherheit und Bestätigung. Ein ganzes Leben am selben Ort zu wohnen, dieselben Freunde vom Kindergarten bis ins Altersheim zu haben, Jahrzehnte zur selben Zeit am selben Ort Urlaub zu machen, um immer dieselben Menschen zu treffen, kann zutiefst befriedigend sein. Veränderungen stellen sich in langsamen, kaum merkbaren Zyklen ein. Es ist die Zeit, die vergeht, und es sind äußere Einflüsse, die Änderungen bewirken, nicht der Wunsch danach. Gleichförmigkeit mag einem bisweilen öde und trist erscheinen und zu grundsätzlichen Fragen nach dem Sinn des Lebens führen, sie hat aber auch etwas ungemein Tröstliches. Ein Korsett, zumal ein selbstgewähltes, gibt Halt und schafft Selbstgewissheit, das vielleicht leise Gefühl des Eingeengt-Seins wird dabei gerne ignoriert, Zweifel sind unerwünscht. Niemals tanzt man aus der Reihe und wenn doch, werden die Eskapaden schnell beendet, genährt durch die Erkenntnis, dass dieses andere nicht an das Bekannte und Eingeübte heranreicht. Möglicherweise bleibt aber ein leises Rumoren, irgendetwas nicht genau zu Taxierendes, dem man einerseits nicht begegnen will, was andererseits eine zunehmend starke Anziehungskraft hat. Etwas, das bei allen Bemühungen nicht verschwindet. Es lässt sich als ein wenig fassbares, indifferentes Gefühl ausmachen, das mal zaghaft, mal vehement auftritt. Ihm keine Beachtung zu schenken, gelingt mehr oder weniger schlecht. Letztlich bleibt nur die Entscheidung, mehr Kraft und Zeit zu investieren, um sich nicht aus seiner Bahn zu bewegen, oder aber den Schritt zu wagen und sich auf Abwege zu begeben.

Und dann macht man es einfach? Selten geschieht das einfach, es ist vielmehr ein langer schleichender und fast unsichtbarer Prozess, der aber unaufhaltsam fortschreitet. Ob dabei Pausen gemacht werden oder man zeitweise zum Altbewährten zurückkehrt, ändert nichts an der Tatsache, dass die Entfernung von der Norm immer größer wird, dass gerade, je weiter der Abstand ist, das vorherige

fact that the deviation from the norm continues to widen to the extent that the greater the deviation, the odder your former life comes to seem, and might even appear utterly absurd. There are probably essentially different approaches to stepping off the beaten track to go astray: some people simply happen to go that way; others consciously choose to do so. In either case, both ways it happens have to do with decisions. Decisions you make, sometimes more or less with external pressure being exerted on you, at other times arising from an emotional state or made on a whim. However, we are never inactive participants in the process of taking either the one way or the other. In the first instance, the way not consciously taken, you don't at first perceive it for what it was; it is perceived entirely logically as the outcome of your current life situation, what is known as attendant circumstances, and your personal psychological disposition. Nothing seems unusual, nor is anything abnormal. What we discussed above, consciously experiencing distancing yourself from the life you have previously been living, is scarcely relevant in this connection. You adapt to a new life, which at first might seem disconcerting but becomes increasingly routine without any particular glitches. Your circle of friends may change, or the people you like to be with become fewer and fewer. You rationalize the lack of understanding, questioning glances, or outright rejection directed at you as the inability of others to grasp this way of life, or to have understanding for these views. There is nothing reprehensible about this, let alone deviant in the negative sense: as long as the psychological and physical health of others is not harmed, or the arrangements we have made as a democratic society are not actively rejected and attacked. The point is that the understanding and acceptance which we can show for the deviant paths some of our fellow creatures have taken rest on just that. Everything else—no matter how peculiar it may seem—is left up to the individuals concerned and their comrades in arms. Of course the boundaries between inadvertently going astray and deliberately making the decision to leave what are regarded as normal paths are fluid. What »normal« actually is in this connection must be clarified: acting according to the norm is hardly disputed in the technical sense. As soon as social habits that are deemed normal are in the picture, however, it is not at all clear; what one group views as entirely normal is for others frankly absurd. Normal is, therefore, an ambiguous, polysemic term. If we use it here, then only in connection with deviating from the norm in order to describe deviance as such, any discussion of normality is out of place. Is, however, departing from the ways expected of you even abnormal, or is this just another facet of your personality? If a heavy metal musician

Leben umso seltsamer erscheint, es einem womöglich gänzlich absurd vorkommt. Wohl gibt es entscheidende Unterschiede beim Betreten der Abwege: Die einen geraten darauf, die anderen wählen sie bewusst. In jedem Falle haben beide immer mit Entscheidungen zu tun. Entscheidungen, die man trifft, manchmal unter mehr oder weniger äußerem Druck, ein anderes Mal aus einem Gemütszustand oder einer Laune heraus. Niemals jedoch sind wir nicht aktiv daran beteiligt, welchen Weg wir gehen. Ersteren, den nicht bewusst eingeschlagenen, nimmt man zunächst nicht als solchen wahr, er wird ganz logisch als Konsequenz der aktuellen Lebenslage, der sogenannten Umständen und der eigenen psychischen Disposition, wahrgenommen. Nichts erscheint ungewöhnlich, nichts außer der Norm. Das, worüber wir oben gesprochen haben, die bewusst erfahrene Entfernung vom vorherigen Leben, hat hier kaum Relevanz. Man richtet sich ein in einem neuen Leben, welches anfangs vielleicht befremdlich, mehr und mehr aber zum Alltag ohne besondere Vorkommnisse wird. Eventuell ändert sich der Freundeskreis, oder die Menschen, mit denen man gerne zu tun hat, werden immer weniger. Das Unverständnis, die fragenden Blicke oder die offene Ablehnung erklärt man sich mit dem Unvermögen der anderen, diese Lebensweise, diese Ansichten zu begreifen und zu verstehen. Nichts daran ist verwerflich oder gar abwegig im negativen Sinn, solange nicht die physische und psychische Gesundheit anderer beschädigt wird, die Vereinbarungen, die wir als demokratische Gesellschaft getroffen haben, aktiv abgelehnt und angegriffen werden. Genau damit steht und fällt das Verständnis und die Akzeptanz, die wir den Abwegen, auf die sich manche unserer Mitmenschen begeben haben, entgegenbringen können. Alles andere – und sei es noch so verwunderlich – bleibt den einzelnen und ihren Mitstreitern überlassen. Gewiss sind die Übergänge fließend vom versehentlichen Auf-Abwege-Geraten und der bewussten Entscheidung, sich von den sogenannten normalen Wegen zu entfernen. Es sollte dazu auch geklärt werden, was eigentlich »normal« ist: Der Norm entsprechend in einem technischen Sinne ist wenig zweifelhaft, sobald es sich aber um gesellschaftliche Gepflogenheiten handelt, die als normal bezeichnet werden, ist es keineswegs klar; was die eine Gruppe als völlig normal erachtet, ist für andere geradezu absurd. Normal ist also ein schillernder, vieldeutiger Begriff. Wenn wir ihn hier verwenden, dann nur im Zusammenhang mit einer Normabweichung, um den Abweg als solchen zu beschreiben, die Diskussion über das Normale bleibt hier außen vor. Ist es aber schon abwegig, sich von erwarteten Pfaden zu entfernen, oder ist dies nur eine andere Facette der Persönlichkeit? Veröffentlicht ein Heavy-Metal-Musiker ein

publishes a romantic children's book, has he even deviated from the norm in so doing? Or is the reason why his writing a children's book is regarded as abnormal rather the expectations confronting a musician of this kind? It may, therefore, be that we as observers and judges are the ones to have gone astray in not wanting to accept such seemingly peculiar behavior because it doesn't match the assumptions we have acquired about the type represented by a heavy metal musician. When viewed in this light, deviance takes place in us rather than in the person we assume to be acting in defiance of norms. If we now shift our perspective so as not to look for deviance but instead just let ourselves in for the untrodden path, undreamed-of freedoms open up—provided we aren't too afraid of them. The standard is not set by what has been given the nod of approval, the conventional, and universally acceptable; quite the contrary, the options are incredibly diverse. Being unrealistic is permitted, in fact necessary, pushing the envelope without knowing or even having an inkling of what the outcome of changing lanes like this will be. At the same time, however, decisions have to be made on which direction to set out for, with only the first steps representing deliberate infringement of the norm. You will realize soon enough that deviating from it also changes your viewpoint and that entirely new worlds can open up that now have little to do with your point of departure. Letting yourself in for the freedom to decide and make your own choices regardless of the consequences—taking into consideration the limitations outlined above—makes it possible to discover something really new and develop it. What initially might be unsettling will later prove invigorating because the more practice we have in going astray, the easier it becomes to do so—and, in any case, when are the paths taken entirely normal? Deviating from the norm always calls for new beginnings. Being content with that alone is just the opposite of what we want to achieve by taking refreshingly courageous new paths, and it will not be adequate for designing a future—viewed from this perspective, what is normal is supposed to become »deviant« and what is deviant »normal.«

romantisches Kinderbuch, hat er dann schon etwas Abwegiges getan? Oder ist nicht vielmehr die Erwartungshaltung, die einem solchen Musiker entgegengebracht wird, die Ursache, dass sein Schreiben eines Kinderbuchs als abwegig betrachtet wird? Es kann also durchaus sein, dass wir als Beobachter und Beurteiler auf dem Abweg sind, indem wir diese scheinbar absonderliche Handlung nicht zulassen wollen, weil sie nicht unseren Annahmen entspricht, die wir uns über den Typus des Heavy-Metal-Musikers angeeignet haben. So gesehen findet das Abwegige in uns statt und nicht bei den vermeintlich abwegig Handelnden. Verändern wir jetzt die Perspektive und schauen nicht auf das Abwegige, sondern lassen uns auf den Weg ein, dann eröffnen sich – vorausgesetzt die Furcht davor ist nicht zu groß – ungeahnte Freiheiten. Nicht das Abgenickte, das Gängige und allgemein Akzeptierte wird Maßstab, vielmehr sind die Entscheidungsmöglichkeiten ungemein vielfältig. Es ist erlaubt, geradezu notwendig, unrealistisch zu sein, über die Stränge zu schlagen, nicht zu wissen, noch nicht mal zu ahnen, was bei diesem Spurwechsel herauskommen wird. Zugleich aber müssen Entscheidungen getroffen werden, welche Richtungen eingeschlagen werden sollen, dabei sind nur die ersten Schritte ein bewusstes Der-Norm-Entgegentreten. Ziemlich schnell wird man feststellen, dass sich mit der Abweichung auch die Sichtweise ändert und sich ganz neue Welten auftun können, die nur noch wenig mit den Ausgangspunkten zu tun haben. Sich einzulassen auf die Freiheit zu entscheiden und die eigene Wahl zu treffen, ohne Rücksicht zu nehmen – die oben genannten Einschränkungen berücksichtigend – erlaubt es, wirklich Neues zu entdecken und zu entwickeln. Was vielleicht anfangs verunsichert, wird später stärken, denn je besser wir geübt sind, auf Abwegen zu gehen, desto leichter fällt es – und wann sind es dann ganz normale Wege? Das Abwegige bedarf immer eines neuen Anfangs. Sich zufrieden zu geben, ist genau das Gegenteil dessen, was wir mit den erfrischend mutigen neuen Wegen erreichen wollen, und wird auch nicht für eine Zukunftsgestaltung taugen – so betrachtet sollte das Normale »abwegig« werden und das Abwegige »normal«.

A DIFFERENT LOGIC OF THINGS

Ellen Maurer Zilioli

»Formalism without boundaries is about […]
the operations of a form composed as art, the
aesthetic processes of which begin to break out of it,
fall short of it, overtax it, debase it,—or render it farcical.«[1]

Kerstin Stakemeier

»What am I? A silversmith? Goldsmith?
Creator, designer, artist? Why bother with the
attribution assigned to me?«[2]

Max Fröhlich

EINE ANDERE LOGIK DER DINGE

Ellen Maurer Zilioli

»Der entgrenzte Formalismus handelt (…) von Prozessen einer als Kunst verfassten Form, deren ästhetische Verfahren aus dieser herauszubrechen ansetzen, sie unterschreiten, überfordern, degenerieren oder zur Farce werden lassen.«[1]

Kerstin Stakemeier

»Was bin ich? Silberschmied? Goldschmied? Gestalter, Designer, Künstler? Was ficht mich der Name an, den man mir anhängt.«[2]

Max Fröhlich

A telephone receiver, beer cans, a rolling pin, an iron, knickknacks for the table, a baseball bat—to name but a few of the oddities featuring in our exhibition and the accompanying publication—have crept into the environment of artisanal gold and silver. They serve as set pieces and act complicitly with a critical questioning of traditional standards and aesthetic norms, function as playful »agents provocateurs« in Kerstin Stakemeier's sense in the process of »infringing boundaries,« somewhat off the beaten track and flouting the established rules. Does this mean that the end of an applied arts field has been reached? Certainly not that, but a transformation is taking place. What at first sight might look like nonsense—bunches of pearls from a coffee pot, miniature pieces of furniture arrayed on a necklace, a wreath of cutlery to be worn as a crown, a toilet seat of fine silver, pans and jugs slumping with fatigue, delicate oyster bowls as elements of a small sculptural arrangement, and much, much more—and thus stirs up and parodies the classical canon in the fields of jewelry, vessels, and tableware, uses absurdity, eccentricity, disturbance, shock, and imagination to set knowledge in motion and invalidate time-honored patterns.[3]

When tableware that was once useful mutates, lodging in an act of rebellion as a nuisance factor in the system of »elitist« genres in gold and silver, rules are broken; they undergo a symbolic transfer and are upgraded. A utilitarian object is always part of a complex inventory. It represents—although perhaps imperceptibly—a cultural narrative that causes a paradigm shift via transference in jewelry and vessels/tableware and substantially enriches them. Wrestling with the thing as such, its transformation, derailment, and defamiliarization seismographically reflect epochal disposedness [Heidegger] and form a central theme of modernism.[4]

Viewed in this light, infringements and blurring of »species« boundaries are not so surprising after all. At some point in evolution they are practically inevitable. And now this is happening in gold- and silversmithing circles that are particularly thoughtful and adventurous. Here the disconcerting combination of non-genre-specific materials, trivial quotations, and historic guiding principles serve as the catalyst for creating a changed »raison d'être,« an aesthetic that is neither informed by the art-and-curiosities cabinet nor follows the »rationale,« the stance permissible to its own discipline, which consists in function and adornment. The Silver Triennials of recent years have already demonstrated this. For a long time now it has not been about silver alone but also about making a statement.[5] And a lot more. A »scarcely perceptible nuance« can, according to Eva Linhart, already »represent the step from crafts to art,« for instance, through »the autonomy of the formation processes,« the »complex interrelationship between the creation of a work by both artisanal and artistic means and the aesthetic impact,« hence a tendency to contextualization, staging, performativity: »Inasmuch as purpose leads to definitions of aesthetic form, the handling of the objects becomes an event entailing presentation and performance.«[6] That gets to the heart of the matter with our objects because here a coruscating spectacle is being

Telefonhörer, Bierdosen, Nudelholz, Bügeleisen, Tischnippes, Baseballschläger – um nur einige Wunderlichkeiten unserer Ausstellung und Publikation zu nennen – schleichen sich ein ins Milieu der Gold- und Silberschmiedekunst. Sie dienen als Versatzstücke und agieren als Komplizen einer kritischen Hinterfragung überlieferter Standards und ästhetischer Normen, fungieren als spielerische »agents provocateurs« im Sinne Kerstin Stakemeiers im Prozess der »Entgrenzung«, etwas abseits der Spur und etablierter Regeln. Ist damit das Ende einer Sparte des Kunsthandwerks erreicht? Das sicher nicht, aber es ereignet sich eine Transformation. Was auf den ersten Blick als Nonsens daherkommt – Perlenbündel aus der Kaffeekanne, sich aneinanderreihende Miniaturmöbel am Collier, ein Besteckkranz als Kopfkrone, eine Klobrille aus Feinsilber, erschöpft hinsinkende Pfannen und Kannen, zierliche Austernschalen als Bestandteil eines kleinen skulpturalen Arrangements und vieles mehr – und damit den klassischen Kanon von Schmuck, Gefäß und Gerät aufmischt und verballhornt, nutzt Absurdität, Exzentrik, Irritation, Schock und Imagination, um Erkenntnisse in Gang und bewährte Muster außer Kraft zu setzen.[3]

Wenn das ehemals nützliche Gerät mutiert, sich aufmüpfig wie Störfaktoren einnistet im System des »elitären« Genres von Gold und Silber, dann werden Vorschriften gebrochen, dann erfahren sie eine symbolische Verlagerung und neues Ansehen. Der Gebrauchsgegenstand ist stets Teil eines komplexen Inventars. Er repräsentiert – so ungeachtet er sein mag – ein kulturelles Narrativ, das durch den Transfer in Schmuck und Gefäß | Gerät für eine Verschiebung der Parameter sorgt und diese maßgeblich bereichert. Die Auseinandersetzung mit dem Ding, seiner Verwandlung, Entgleisung und Verfremdung reflektieren seismographisch epochale Befindlichkeiten und bilden eines der zentralen Themen der Moderne.[4]

So gesehen überraschen Übergriffe und Verwischungen zwischen den Spezies weniger. Sie sind an einem Punkt der Entwicklung praktisch zwangsläufig zu erwarten. Und nun geschieht dies in besonders reflexiven und experimentierfreudigen Kreisen der Gold- und Silberschmiedekunst. Hier dient nun die befremdliche Verschwisterung gattungsferner Materialien, trivialer Zitate und historischer Leitideen als Katalysator für die Schaffung einer veränderten »Raison de Vivre«, einer Ästhetik, die weder die Idee der Wunderkammer bedient noch die »Vernunft«, die statthafte Haltung der eigenen Disziplin verfolgt, welche in der Funktion und im Schmücken besteht. Das haben die Silbertriennalen der letzten Jahre bereits bewiesen. Längst geht es nicht um Silber allein, sondern um Aussage.[5] *Und noch sehr viel mehr. Eine »kaum merkliche Nuance« kann nach Eva Linhart bereits »den Schritt vom Handwerk zur Kunst bedeuten«, etwa durch die »Verselbstständigung der Formungsprozesse«, die »komplexe Wechselbeziehung aus handwerklich-künstlerischem Werden und ästhetischen Wirken« und damit den Hang zu Kontextualisierung, Inszenierung, Performativität: »Denn in dem Maße, wie der Gebrauchszweck in künstlerische Formausdeutung übergeht, wird der Umgang mit dem Objekt zu einem*

put on, one that, despite jewelry and vessels being shown, performatively offers confrontations, optical illusions, and fusions that break the rules.

Displacements, delimitations, migrations between what were once presumed to be stable categories and routine are meanwhile the agenda. The thing occupies a strategic position in this process and contributes its specific meaning, its memory, when, for example, Ai Weiwei confronts us in the French Pavilion at the 2013 Venice Biennale with **Bang** (Fig.1), an oppressively convoluted spatial installation of used Chinese wooden stools. Nevin Aladağ interweaves her objects with musical statements; Phyllida Barlow—with respect to the taboos associated with domestic objects from the female life context—subverts this debasement with the textile consistency of her works; Mona Hatoum uses graters and sieves to conjure tactile imprints on wax paper;[7] and Ornaghi & Prestinari from Milan position flasks, bowls, beakers, and other simple, inherently insignificant stuff in bold constructions (Fig.2).[8] Incidentally, the last named artists grate on the same neuralgic points and societal foibles as those preoccupying our artists, if we think— for example—of the **BEYOND REPAIR** series by Beatrice Brovia and Nicolas Cheng (Cat.No.24), or the camouflaged criticism of consumerism voiced by Ute Eitzenhöfer and Luzia Vogt, ennobled in a little silver tower (once plastic bottle stoppers) or the coquettishly colorful aura of mystery surrounding **Shalo boli duge** (once shampoo and body-lotion bottles). What is at stake is always »the relationship between man and objects, and on how this relationship is linked to this history of materials, design, artisanal and industrial production techniques and the consequences related to consumption.«[9] A choreography of this kind between mundane banality and artistic discourse is accepted without question on the global art scene whereas it tends to be met with cluelessness in the field of gold- and silversmithing.

The thing, therefore, is both instigator and companion in a highly complicated and multilayered event. It does not usually refer to »the throbbing great story […] but rather to details, anecdotes,«[10] to illusion, to the usual and the habitual, »missed opportunities and promises not kept.«[11] On the other hand, we can invoke Martin Heidegger. He imputes the character of beingness to the »equipment« [»das Zeug«] and, therefore, an ontological and emblematic dimension that reveals the Being, World, in the artwork. That is what differentiates artists from artisans, »creating« from »making.« The artwork carries »a thrust with it,« shakes the »mundane way of understanding and handling.«[12]

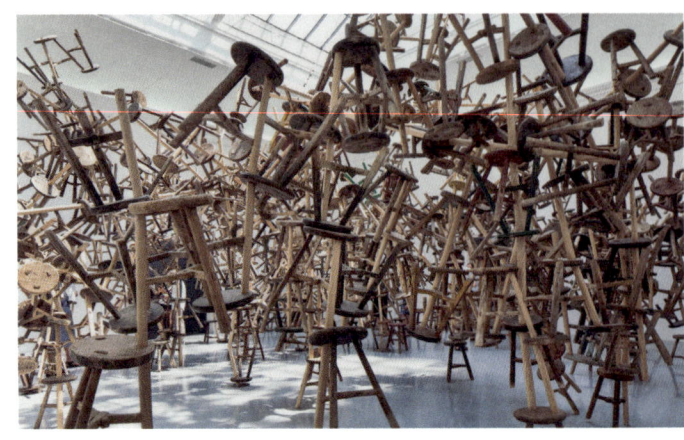

Fig. 1
Ai Weiwei,
installation **Bang**,
Venice Biennale,
2013

Fig. 2
Ornaghi & Prestinari,
Ritrovarsi (2019),
exhibition Fantastic Utopia,
Ala Scaligera, Rocca di Angera,
2020

Ereignis ihres Vor- und Aufführens.«⁶ Das trifft unsere Objekte im Kern, denn hier wird ein funkensprühendes Schauspiel geboten, das zwar Schmuck und Gefäß offeriert, aber regelwidrige Konfrontationen, Täuschungen und Fusionen performativ darbietet.

Verschiebungen, Ent-Grenzungen, Migrationen zwischen ehemals vermeintlich stabilen Kategorien und Alltag sind mittlerweile an der Tagesordnung. Das Ding besetzt dabei strategische Position und bringt seine spezifische Bedeutung, sein Gedächtnis mit ein, wenn uns etwa Ai Weiwei im französischen Pavillon der Biennale von Venedig 2013 mit der bedrängenden Rauminstallation **Bang** *(Abb. 1) gebrauchter chinesischer Hocker konfrontiert. Nevin Aladağ verflicht ihre Objekte in musikalische Statements; Phyllida Barlow – in Bezug auf die mit dem häuslichen Gegenstand aus weiblichem Lebenszusammenhang verbundenen Tabus in ihrer Ausbildung – unterwandert diese Abwertung in der textilen Beschaffenheit ihrer Werke; Mona Hatoum zaubert mittels Küchenreiben und Sieben taktile Abdrücke auf Wachspapier;⁷ Ornaghi & Prestinari aus Mailand positionieren Flaschen, Schalen, Becher und weiteres simples, an sich insignifikantes Zeug in waghalsigen Konstruktionen (Abb. 2).⁸ Übrigens reiben sich Letztere an denselben neuralgischen Punkten und gesellschaftlichen Schwachstellen, die auch unsere Künstler und Künstlerinnen beschäftigen, wenn wir an die* **BEYOND-REPAIR**-*Serie von Beatrice Brovia und Nicolas Cheng denken (Kat. Nr. 24), die camouflierte Konsumkritik von Ute Eitzenhöfer und Luzia Vogt, veredelt im silbernen Türmchen (ehemals Plastikverschlüsse), oder die farbenfrohe kokette Rätselhaftigkeit von* **Shalo boli duge** *(ehemals Shampoo- und Körpermilchflasche) – zum Beispiel. Es geht stets um »(…) the relationship between man and objects, and on how this relationship is linked to this history of materials, design, artisanal and industrial production techniques and the consequences related to consumption«⁹. In der globalen Kunstszene wird eine derartige Choreographie zwischen Alltagsbanalität und künstlerischem Diskurs problemlos hingenommen, während sie im Gold- und Silberschmiedebereich eher auf Hilflosigkeit stößt.*

Das Ding ist also Auslöser und Begleiter in einem höchst diffizilen und vielschichtigen Geschehen. Meist verweist es nicht »auf die trommelnde große Geschichte, (…) sondern mehr auf Details, Anekdoten (…)«¹⁰, auf Illusion, das Gewöhnliche und die Gewohnheit, die »vorübergegangenen Möglichkeiten und uneingelösten Versprechen«¹¹. Andererseits können wir uns auf Martin Heidegger berufen. Er bescheinigt dem »Zeug« Seinscharakter und damit eine ontologische und emblematische Dimension, die im Kunstwerk

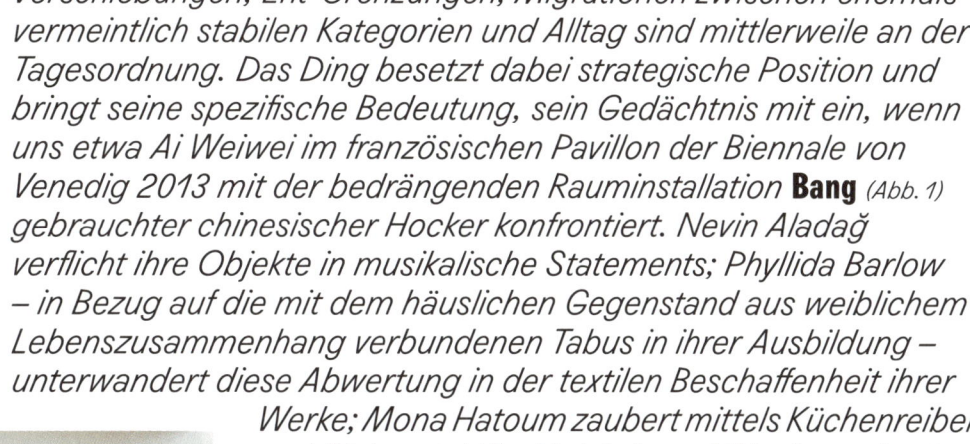

*Abb. 1
Ai Weiwei,
Rauminstallation* **Bang**,
*Biennale von Venedig,
2013*

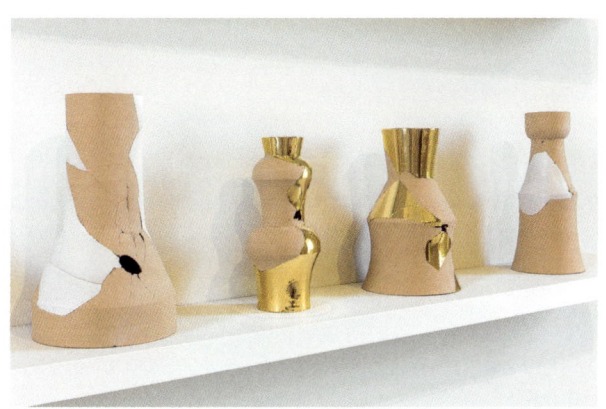

*Abb. 2
Ornaghi & Prestinari,*
Ritrovarsi *(2019),
Ausstellung* Fantastic Utopia,
*Ala Scaligera, Rocca di Angera,
2020*

Our exhibits truthfully demonstrate the above. Our protagonists' thinking sets in at the interfaces between philosophy, aesthetics, and sociological impulses that transcend cultures. By virtue of surprising »crisscrossings and interruptions«[13] of the habitual view of things, they position their works entirely as a matter of course in a gap in which artistic proceeding and artisanal consciousness bear fruit. It entails give and take. Here Karen Pontoppidan's work is to be emphasized as a prime example of this. By interlocking elemental features (paint and canvas on the one hand, embroidery, ornamental quotes on the other), Pontoppidan succeeds in the dialogue between art and jewelry on a small stage. In **KNELL II**—household appliances hollow-cast in fine silver—»high and low« overlap yet again, the noble work of the silversmith and prosaic reality, in which gender-specific allocation generally rules. In Ute Eitzenhöfer it comes to a comparable encounter when a delicate tracery of almost textile quality shows up on a pin object made of plastic waste, thus reconciling coarse refuse and stylish jewelry with one another. The upshot is that several semantic planes overlap.

In fact the collision between disparate substances, props, and destinations from divergent contexts is assigned just as crucial a role as commuting between historical references. Turned decoration from period-style furniture manufacturing is transmuted by Anna Rikkinen into Body Art with volume. Sawa Aso provokes a similar transfer by making a telescope, earphones, telephone receivers, and a stopwatch migrate into jewelry. In Tobias Alm's hands a tool apron and a feudal form of decoration fuse, an elegant mediation between feminine and masculine features. In combining hard armor and an outfit worn by women chefs or apparel with frills and pleats, Eija Mustonen has undertaken an astonishing reversal of classic stereotypes. Swelling bodies and a sturdy vessel seeming to give way as in the work of Myra Mimlitsch-Gray, Anders Ljungberg, David Clarke, and Luzia Vogt attest to sophisticated juggling with commonplace notions of stable attributes. Erotic references, physical charisma, and the sculptural figure made by the objects suggest they have a life of their own, a personal presence: surrogates for human existence that in their way and in their own language tell of voluptuousness, pleasure, exhaustion, and self-surrender.

Ultimately it is very difficult to draw boundaries because the methods overlap. Nevertheless, certain focal points show up, which we can subsume under temporary headings, one of which is the rubric »Material Illusion«: Anne Fischer lets carded wool or acrylic paint clot into vessel walls; Naama Bergman creates artifacts from solidified salt, which in turn refer to its preservative

das Seiende offenbare, die Welt. Das mache den Unterschied zwischen Künstler und Handwerker aus, dem »Schaffen« und dem »Anfertigen«. Das Kunstwerk führe »einen Stoß mit sich«, erschüttere die »alltägliche Verständnis- und Umgangsweise« [12].

Dergleichen können unsere Exponate wahrhaftig vor Augen führen. An den Schnittstellen philosophischer, ästhetischer, Kulturen überschreitender soziologischer Impulse setzen die Überlegungen unserer Protagonisten und Protagonistinnen ein. Sie siedeln ihre Werke dank der überraschenden »Durchkreuzungen und Unterbrechungen« [13] *des gewohnten Blicks auf ganz selbstverständliche Weise in einem Zwischenraum an, in dem künstlerisches Vorgehen und kunsthandwerkliches Bewusstsein Früchte tragen. Es ist ein Geben und Nehmen. Exemplarisch sei hier die Arbeit Karen Pontoppidans hervorgehoben. Durch die Verzahnung elementarer Merkmale (Farbe und Leinwand auf der einen Seite, Stickerei, ornamentales Zitat auf der anderen Seite) gelingt Pontoppidan auf kleiner Bühne der Dialog zwischen Kunst und Schmuck. Bei* **KNELL II** *– in Feinsilber hohl abgeformte Haushaltsgeräte – überlappen sich erneut »high und low«, das edle Silberschmiedewerk und die prosaische Realität, in der gemeinhin auch geschlechtsspezifische Zuweisungen regieren. Bei Ute Eitzenhöfer kommt es zu einer vergleichbaren Begegnung, wenn sich auf dem Ansteckobjekt aus Plastikmüll das filigrane Netz von fast textiler Qualität abzeichnet und damit groben Abfall und stilvollen Schmuck miteinander versöhnt. Es überschneiden sich folglich mehrere Bedeutungsebenen.*

Überhaupt kommt der Kollision konträrer Substanzen, Requisiten und Destinationen aus divergierenden Kontexten eine ebenso entscheidende Rolle zu wie dem Pendeln zwischen historischen Verweisen. Gedrechselter Zierrat aus der Stilmöbelfabrikation wird von Anna Rikkinen in voluminöse Body-Art überführt. Einen ähnlichen Transfer provoziert Sawa Aso, wenn Fernglas, Kopf- und Telefonhörer oder Stoppuhr in den Schmuck wandern. Bei Tobias Alm fusionieren Werkzeugschürze und feudale Zierform, eine elegante Vermittlung zwischen femininen und maskulinen Zügen. Eija Mustonen nimmt in der Kombination von harter Rüstung und Köchinnen-Outfit oder Rüschen- und Faltengewand eine verblüffende Umkehrung von klassischen Stereotypen vor. Schwellende Körper und das scheinbare Nachgeben des robusten Gefäßes wie bei Myra Mimlitsch-Gray, Anders Ljungberg, David Clarke oder Luzia Vogt zeugen vom raffinierten Jonglieren mit gängigen Vorstellungen fester Attribute. Erotische Verweise, physisches Charisma und plastische Figur der Objekte suggerieren Eigenleben, persönliche Präsenz – Surrogate humaner Existenz, die auf ihre Weise und in ihrer Sprache von Wollust, Genuss, Erschöpfung und Hingabe erzählen.

as well as its destructive properties; this ambivalence is absorbed by the work and symbolized by it. In Kateřina Jirsová it is sugar that imitates the corporeality of utilitarian household objects. Using a natural sponge, Stella Wanisch simulates the familiar lemon squeezer and shifts the result of the application directly into the materiality of her object. By contrast, configurations reminiscent of sculpture come from Tarja Tuupanen. Be they disposable egg cups or scraps of trimming, in any case a monumental typology is created that links trivial trash with the grand gesture of the sculptor. In Markus Pollinger, Hans Stofer, Nils Hint, Karolina Hägg, and Åsa Elmstam a surreal touch is prioritized. Pollinger's parodies of vessels argue at the same time with the sensory polysemy we also see in Mimlitsch-Gray and Ljungberg, to take just two examples. Stofer is reminiscent above all of Duchamp, post-Dadaist agglomerations of heterogeneous elements that seem to reject each other yet are interdependent, gathering in odd arrangements, restructurings, or the beguiling dis-order of his interventions in order to ignite exhilarating sparks in an explosion of imagination and madness, of poetry and mental roaming between the idea of the vessel or that of the object, or neither, simply between the genres. Karolina Hägg and her teapot made of sugar—like a plumed creature from another world—are close to his work. Nils Hint prefers wrought-iron found objects that can easily be transformed into a tool chain or head jewelry. The dominant aspect of Åsa Elmstam's work is criticism of the thoughtless throwaway society, cheap industrial overproduction, and the arbitrary accumulation of its products, as exemplified by **Things 23**, which is neck jewelry inspired by impressions gained at furniture trade fairs and subjected to scathing commentary.

Another heading announces the reference to a distinguished past. Jugs, vases, goblets, cups, jewels, and other treasured items represent the design legacy, a splendid, incriminating, and alluring background, flashes of which come through here and there, only, however, to be demystified by being broken and reduced, defamiliarized and ironized. **Ich bin keine Vase** (I Am Not a Vase), neck jewelry by Jing Yang, might be positioned in this context along with Ai Weiwei's chair installation: antiquitizing vessels, a popular metaphor for the female body, dissected into disc segments, dangle from cotton thread. The movement generated by hanging and wearing them makes them break up into their individual elements, a vividly memorable symbol for the construction and fragility of societal clichés.

Letztlich lassen sich nur schwerlich Grenzen ziehen, denn die Methoden überschneiden einander. Aber es zeichnen sich doch gewisse Schwerpunkte ab, die wir unter provisorischen Stichworten subsumieren können, eines davon die Devise »Materialtäuschung«: Anne Fischer lässt kardierte Wolle oder Acrylfarbe zur Gefäßwand gerinnen, Naama Bergman schöpft aus dem erstarrten Salz Artefakte, die wiederum auf seine bewahrende wie zerstörerische Kraft Bezug nehmen. Diese Ambivalenz wird vom Werk aufgesogen und versinnbildlicht. Bei Kateřina Jirsová ist es der Zucker, welcher den Korpus häuslicher Gebrauchsgegenstände kopiert. Stella Wanisch simuliert mit Hilfe eines Naturschwamms die vertraute Zitronenpresse und verlagert das Ergebnis der Handhabung direkt in die Stofflichkeit ihres Objekts. Von Tarja Tuupanen dagegen stammen skulptural anmutende Gebilde. Ob Eierbecher oder Dekorrelikt – in jedem Fall entsteht eine monumentale Typologie, die trivialen Tand mit der grandiosen Geste des Bildhauers verkoppelt. Eine surreale Note wird bei Markus Pollinger, Hans Stofer, Nils Hint, Karolina Hägg und Åsa Elmstam in den Vordergrund gerückt. Pollingers Gefäßpersiflagen argumentieren gleichzeitig mit der sinnlichen Mehrdeutigkeit, wie wir sie unter anderem bei Mimlitsch-Gray und Ljungberg sehen. Stofer lässt vor allem an Duchamp denken, an post-dadaistische Agglomerationen heterogener, einander quasi verweigernder, aber aufeinander angewiesener Glieder, die sich in seltsamen Anordnungen, Um-Ordnungen oder der betörenden Un-Ordnung seiner Inventionen versammeln, um den zündenden Funken der Explosion von Fantasie und Verrücktheit, von Poesie und gedanklichem Vagabundieren zwischen der Idee von Gefäß, von Objekt oder nichts von dem, nur einfach dem Wandern zwischen den Bereichen zu entfachen. In seine Nähe rücken Karolina Hägg und ihre Teekanne aus Zucker – wie ein gefiedertes Wesen aus einer anderen Welt. Nils Hint bevorzugt das schmiedeeiserne Fundstück, das sich mühelos zur Werkzeugkette oder zum Kopfschmuck wandelt. Bei Åsa Elmstam dominiert die Kritik an der bedenkenlosen Wegwerfgesellschaft, an billiger industrieller Überproduktion und beliebiger Anhäufung ihrer Fabrikate, wie der Halsschmuck **Things 23***, unter dem Eindruck von Möbelmessen entstanden, boshaft kommentiert.*

Eine weitere Devise bekundet die Referenz an prominente Vergangenheit. Kannen, Vasen, Kelche, Pokale, Juwelen und andere Preziosen repräsentieren das gestalterische Erbe, ein prunkvoller, belastender und verführerischer Hintergrund, der hic und da durchblitzt, um dann allerdings

Jing Yang quotes one of numerous variants of the tankard, jug, goblet that spring to mind in connection with myths, cosmologies, and religious rites. We can assume that the vessel stands at the center of every universal history and thus actually performs an essential role of transcultural significance. There is thinking about things through the vessel and thinking about things in vessels.[14]

Astrid Becksteiner-Rasche's contribution adopts a similar line of reasoning. In the wondrous vision of the Holy Grail, the vasa sacra in silver used in the Christian liturgy appears in a chalice made of the finest delicate parchment, translucent and auspicious, set with pearls. The thought of archaic drinking vessels, ritual implements, is also revived in Kanako Ebisawa. Fragile transience, painstaking reconstruction, and poetic elegance, remembrance of a service once perhaps filled with exquisite wine or healing salves, are invoked. Astonishing affinities are thus constantly being elicited, which is to be illustrated by a last example—Luzia Vogt's sugar bowl (Cat.No.113) with a globular shape standing on legs and its presumably unwitting closeness to the pot of the Chinese Qijia culture (late 3rd millennium BC) (Fig.3).[15]

Abstract analytical concepts show up alongside the tendencies outlined above. This holds for the work of Kateřina Jirsová and Kateřina Michálková. Moreover, Michálková transforms a box into a brooch, and Jirsová changes void into mass to overturn dimensions and values and revise them by negating them. Works in jewelry by Junwon Jung carry their containers with them. Be they box brooches or box rings, their home, their case, always accompanies them. **CONVERSATION PIECE**, a cycle of statement works by Beatrice Brovia and Nicolas Cheng, investigates possible scenarios and interactions for jewelry and tableware. Crossing genre boundaries is part of the method. Debate and negotiation constitute the symbolic act of their »performance,« which goes far beyond classic boundary markers. Handles in the form of soaps, or balls of yarn as knops lead to the spheres of privacy and intimacy, explore the themes of transition, disruption, and abnormity. The intention of Brovia and Cheng lies in stimulating fresh associative chains by reflecting on aesthetic conventions and behaviors, to discuss

Fig. 3
Pot with humanized feet,
China, Gansu or Qinghai Province,
Qijia culture (?), late 3rd millennium BC,
Museum Rietberg, Zurich,
on permanent loan from the Meiyintang Stiftung,
inv. no. MYT 2095

durch Bruch und Reduktion, durch Verfremdung und Ironisierung entmystifiziert zu werden. In diesem Zusammenhang könnte man den Halsschmuck von Jing Yang **Ich bin keine Vase** neben Ai Weiweis Stuhlinstallation platzieren: In Scheibensegmente sezierte antikisierende Gefäße, eine beliebte Metapher des weiblichen Körpers, baumeln am baumwollenen Faden. In der Bewegung des Hängens und Tragens zerfallen sie in ihre Einzelteile – ein anschauliches Sinnbild von Konstruktion und Fragilität gesellschaftlicher Klischees. Jing Yang zitiert eine der zahlreichen Variationen, wie sie in der Imagination von Krug, Kanne, Kelch die Mythen, Kosmologien und religiösen Riten seit Menschengedenken durchziehen. Wir können davon ausgehen, dass das Gefäß im Zentrum einer jeden Universalgeschichte steht und damit eigentlich eine wesentliche Rolle transkultureller Bedeutung erfüllt. Es gibt ein Nachdenken durch das Gefäß und ein Nachdenken in Gefäßen.[14]

Astrid Becksteiner-Rasches Beitrag greift eine ähnliche Argumentation auf. Im Kelch aus feinstem, zartem Pergament, durchscheinend und verheißungsvoll, von Perlen besetzt, erscheint die wundersame Vision von Gral oder »Vasa Sacra«. Auch bei Kanako Ebisawa wird das Gedenken an altertümliche Trinkschalen, an rituelles Gerät wiederbelebt. Zerbrechliche Vergänglichkeit, mühevolle Rekonstruktion und poetische Eleganz, Erinnerung an ehemals vielleicht mit kostbarem Wein oder heilsamen Salben gefüllte Service werden beschworen. So kommt es immer wieder zu verblüffenden Affinitäten, die mit einem letzten Beispiel – Luzia Vogts Zuckerdose *(Kat. Nr. 113)* mit bauchigem Körper und Standbeinen und ihrer vermutlich unbewussten Nähe zum Topf der chinesischen Qijia-Kultur des späten 3. Jahrtausends v. Chr.[15] *(Abb. 3)* – illustriert werden soll.

Neben diesen Tendenzen zeichnen sich abstraktanalytische Konzepte ab. Das gilt für die Arbeiten von Kateřina Jirsová und Kateřina Michálková. Darüber hinaus verwandelt Michálková die Schachtel in eine Brosche und Jirsová die Leere in Masse, um Dimensionen und Wertigkeiten zu kippen und in ihrer Negation zu revidieren. Schmuckarbeiten von Junwon Jung tragen ihre Behälter mit sich. Ob Box-Broschen oder Box-Ringe – immer ist ihre Beheimatung, ihr Gehäuse mit dabei. Beatrice Brovias

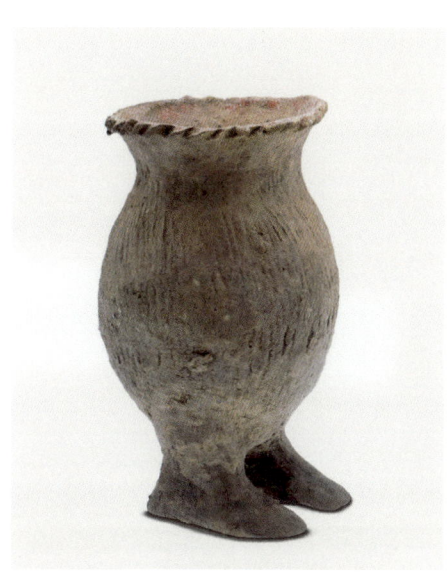

Abb. 3
Topf mit menschlichen Füßen,
*China, Provinz Gansu oder Qinghai,
Qijia-Kultur (?), spätes 3. Jtd. v. Chr.,
Museum Rietberg, Zürich,
Dauerleihgabe Meiyintang Stiftung,
Inv.-Nr. MYT 2095*

things, their use, and their environment, starting from their inner logic, and thus to develop a language of forms that confounds traditional notions of what constitutes a work. Extension, expansion, constant infringement of boundaries lead to the erosion of customary aesthetic experience and culminate in a »threshold experience« that arbitrarily accompanies performative appearances.[16] Brovia/Cheng especially weave a complex web of thought that exploits cross references—textile work, carrying out repairs, hygiene, and consumer goods, as well as their sociopolitical predicates—in artistic-intellectual appropriation.

The exhibiting artists systematically explore the history and the status quo of their respective fields. Whether historical confession or a tendency to posit the »abject«—the mechanisms of which revolve paradigmatically around »inclusions and exclusions«[17] and are a reaction to gender-specific adversities—or softening up and abandoning familiar territory by reduplicating work materials and implements, art jewelry and ceramics are currently moving in a similar direction, which is true of the arts in general.

At the beginning of this trend, when it became evident that expressions through art could no longer be clearly assigned, Rosalind Krauss spoke of an »expanded field«[18] and of a »categorical no-man's land« because—and at the time she meant the sculptural stagings that are subsumed under the term »Land Art«—other, previous classifications no longer seemed appropriate: »Thus the field provides both for an expanded but finite set of related positions for a given artist to occupy and explore, and for an organization of work that is not dictated by the conditions of a particular medium.«[19] If we apply these thoughts on postmodernism to our field, it is possible not only to ascertain that a lot has been going on since then. Expansion is not the only factor that counts but also the increasing interpretation of art as commentary, research, and sociopolitical statement, in brief as »a place for constructing reality«[20] and above all anchored in currently prevailing situations.

und Nicolas Chengs programmatischer Werkzyklus **CONVERSATION PIECE** untersucht mögliche Szenarien und Interaktionen für Schmuck und Gerät. Der medienüberschreitende Sprung gehört zur Methode. Debatte und Verhandeln konstituieren den symbolischen Akt ihrer »Performance«, die weit über die klassischen Eckpfeiler hinausreicht. Handgriffe in Seifenform oder Garnwickel als Knauf leiten über in die Sphären des Privaten, Intimen, thematisieren Übergang, Bruch und Abnormität. Die Absicht von Brovia und Cheng liegt darin, über ästhetische Konventionen und Verhaltensweisen reflektierend, neue Assoziationsketten zu stimulieren, die Dinge, ihren Gebrauch und ihr Umfeld aus deren innerer Logik heraus zu diskutieren und dafür eine Formensprache zu entwickeln, welche das traditionelle Werkverständnis ins Schleudern bringt. Ausdehnung, Erweiterung, permanente Überschreitung von Grenzen führen zu einer Erosion des gewohnten ästhetischen Erlebens und münden in eine »Schwellenerfahrung«, die unwillkürlich mit dem performativen In-Erscheinung-Treten einhergehen.[16] Gerade Brovia | Cheng spinnen ein komplexes Gedankengewebe, das Querverweise – textile Arbeit, Reparieren, Hygiene, Konsumgut sowie deren sozialpolitische Prädikate – in künstlerisch-intellektueller Vereinnahmung ausbeutet.

In einer großen Bandbreite problematisieren die ausgestellten Künstler und Künstlerinnen Geschichte und Status quo ihres Arbeitsfeldes. Ob nun historisches Bekenntnis oder Neigung zum »abjekten« Postulat, dessen Mechanismen sich paradigmatisch um »Ein- und Ausschlüsse« drehen[17] und auf geschlechtsspezifische Widrigkeiten reagieren, oder das Aufweichen und Verlassen vertrauten Terrains durch Vervielfältigung der Werkstoffe und -instrumente – Schmuck- und Gefäßkunst bewegt sich gegenwärtig in eine ähnliche Richtung, wie dies generell für die Künste gilt.

Am Anfang, als sich Kunstäußerungen offensichtlich nicht mehr klar zuweisen ließen, sprach Rosalind Krauss vom »expanded field«[19] und

They include bidding farewell to »beauty,« beyond »measure, proportion, and harmony,« because »only knowledge also of political context and implications […] in the sensory and intellectual attention to what is ›differently beautiful‹« secures the quality of an artwork."[21] It focuses on »revealing the complexity of societal conditions, political structures, and ideological power as well as the fine threads that interweave individuals with those systems, in a way that […] leads to an attitude of sensory and intellectual attentiveness.«[22]

Our artists are on the way there. Embedded in old rules yet underway with innovative tools, seemingly iron laws are being overcome. »Intergeneric« and »transgeneric« infringements of boundaries[23] end in the finding of hybrid forms, perhaps less from a need for a radical refusal of ideological content than as a necessary, legitimate, and dynamic enhancement of capacities that always aims at reconciling art and life. Hence also the performative impact and presentation of numerous works resembling happenings.

Following the exhibitions Open Space—Mind Maps in 2016 (Nationalmuseum, Kulturhuset Stockholm) and Schmuckismus in 2019 (Die Neue Sammlung – The Design Museum, Pinakothek der Moderne, Munich), this presentation once again strongly supports the eye-opening effect and change in perspective that is here demanded of viewers responding to it. Not everything is clear yet, and some things are confusing, but do we always have to be given unambiguous answers? Or wouldn't we rather also leave some things in the in-between?

vom »categorical no-man's land«, weil – und sie meinte damals jene skulpturalen Inszenierungen, die unter dem Begriff Land Art firmieren – keine bisherige Zuordnung mehr zu greifen schien. »Thus the field provides both for an expanded but finite set of related positions for a given artist to occupy and explore, and for an organization of work that is not dictated by the conditions of a particular medium.«[19] Wenn wir diese Überlegungen zum Postmodernismus als Anregung auf unseren Bereich übertragen, lässt sich nicht nur feststellen, dass sich seitdem eine Menge getan hat. Nicht allein Erweiterung zählt, sondern das zunehmende Verständnis von Kunst als Kommentar, Forschung und soziopolitische Stellungnahme, kurz als »Ort der Konstruktion von Wirklichkeit«[20] und vor allem in den gegenwärtigen Situationen verankert.

Dazu gehört der Abschied von der »Schönheit«, jenseits von »Maß, Proportion und Harmonie«, denn »erst das Wissen auch um die politischen Kontexte und Implikationen (…) in der sinnlichen und denkenden Aufmerksamkeit des ›anders schön‹« sichert die Qualität des Kunstwerks.[21] Sie richtet sich darauf, »Komplexität gesellschaftlicher Zustände, politischer Strukturen und ideologischer Gewalt sowie die feinen Fäden, welche die Individuen mit diesen Systemen verweben, in einer Weise zu zeigen, die (…) in eine Haltung sinnlicher und denkender Aufmerksamkeit führt«[22].

Auf diesem Wege befinden sich unsere Künstler und Künstlerinnen. Eingebettet in alte Regeln und doch mit innovativem Werkzeug unterwegs, werden scheinbar eherne Gesetze überwunden. »Intergenerische« und »transgenerische« Entgrenzungen[23] münden in hybriden Formfindungen, weniger vielleicht aus einem Bedürfnis nach radikaler Absage an

1
Kerstin Stakemeier, Entgrenzter Formalismus: Verfahren einer antimodernen Ästhetik, Berlin 2017, p. 21.

2
Max Fröhlich (1908–1997), quoted in Christianne Weber-Stöber, »From the Nimbus of the Luxurious to Sustainability—Contemporary Silver Design Mirrored by the Silver Triennial,« in Sabine Runde and Matthias Wagner K., eds., Arts and Crafts is Cactus: The Collection from 1945 to Today, exh. cat. Museum für angewandte Kunst, Frankfurt/M., Stuttgart 2022, pp. 456–459, here p. 458.

3
See Heinz Friedrich, »Ende der Kunst—Zukunft der Kunst«: Einleitung in das Thema,« in Ende der Kunst—Zukunft der Kunst, published by the Bayerischen Akademie der Schönen Künste, Munich 1985, pp. 7–15, esp. p. 13.

4
See Werner Haftmann, »Das Ding und seine Verwandlung« (1972), in Werner Haftmann, Das antwortende Gegenbild: Ausgewählte Texte 1947–1990, ed. Evelyn Haftmann and Wouter Wirth, Munich 2012, pp. 172–214.

5
See Christianne Weber-Stöber, ed., Silvertriennial International: 20th Worldwide Competition, exh. cat. Goldschmiedekunst e.V., Deutsches Goldschmiedehaus Hanau, Stuttgart 2022, p. 7 f.

6
Eva Linhart, »Arts and Crafts as Adventure,« in Runde and Wagner K., Arts and Crafts is Cactus, pp. 42–52, here pp. 43, 50, and 51.

7
See exhibition Mona Hatoum, at the Georg Kolbe Museum Berlin, September 15, 2022–January 8, 2023; also see the 2022 installation **Electrified (variable V)**, in which kitchen utensils are strung together, linked by electric current.

8
Valentina Ornaghi and Claudio Prestinari, Sbilenco, exhibition at Galleria Continua, San Gimignano, January 21–May 7, 2023.

9
Press release, www.galleriacontinua.com.

10
Annabelle Hirsch, Die Dinge: Eine Geschichte der Frauen in 100 Objekten, Zurich/Berlin 2022, p. 10.

11
Konrad Paul Liessmann, Das Universum der Dinge: Zur Ästhetik des Alltäglichen, Vienna 2010, p. 30.

12
See Martin Heidegger, GA (Gesamtausgabe) [Collected Works], vol. 5, ed. Friedrich-Wilhelm von Herrmann, Frankfurt/M. 1977, pp. 32 and 52; quoted in Francisco de Lara, »Kunstwerke und Gebrauchsgegenstände: Ding, Zeug und Werk in ihrer Widerspiegelung,« in David Espinet and Tobias Keiling, eds., Heideggers Ursprung des Kunstwerks: Ein kooperativer Kommentar, vol. 5 from the series Heidegger Forum, ed. Günter Figal, Frankfurt/M. 2011, pp. 19–32, here p. 27 ff.

13
See Liessmann, Das Universum der Dinge, p. 34.

14
See Gerhard Wolf, Die Vase und der Schemel: Ding, Bild oder eine Kunstgeschichte der Gefäße, vol. 4 from the series Connecting Art Histories in the Museum, published by Kunsthistorisches Institut Florenz [Florence]/Max-Planck-Institut, and Staatliche Museen zu Berlin—Preußischer Kulturbesitz, Dortmund 2019, pp. 21 and 166.

15
Museum Rietberg, Zurich, here quoted in ibid., p. 11.

16
See Erika Fischer-Lichte, »Ästhetische Erfahrung als Schwellenerfahrung,« in Joachim Küpper and Christoph Menke, Dimensionen ästhetischer Erfahrung, Frankfurt/M. 2003, pp. 138–161.

17
Anja Zimmermann, »Sicherung der Außengrenzen: Transgressive Weiblichkeit, abject art und andere Strategien am Rand der Kunst,« in Christiane Kruse and Annika Frye, eds., Kunst an den Rändern: Wie aus Bildern und Objekten Kunst werden kann, Berlin 2021, pp. 163–182, here p. 163.

18
Rosalind E. Krauss, »Sculpture in the Expanded Field« (New York 1978), in R. E. Krauss The Originality of the Avant-Garde and Other Modernist Myths, 5th edn., Cambridge, MA/London 1988, pp. 277–290.

19
Ibid., p. 284 ff., here p. 288 f.

20
Monika Leisch-Kiesl and Susanne Winder, »Die ›Entgrenzung des Ästhetischen‹ und die Kunstwissenschaft,« in Monika Leisch-Kiesl, Susanne Winder, and Max Gottschlich, eds., Ästhetische Kategorien: Perspektiven der Kunstwissenschaft und der Philosophie, vol. 7 from the series Linzer Beiträge zur Kunstwissenschaft und Philosophie, Bielefeld 2017, pp. 47–52, here p. 50.

21
Monika Leisch-Kiesl, »Wenn Gegenwartskunst und die Kategorie des Schönen aufeinandertreffen,« in: ibid., pp. 53–73, here p. 69.

22
Ibid., p. 70.

23
See Ruth Reiche, Iris Romanos, and Bernika Szymanski, »Transformationen, Grenze und Entgrenzung,« in Ruth Reiche, Iris Romanos, Bernika Szymanski, and Saskia Jogler, eds., Transformationen in den Künsten: Grenzen und Entgrenzung in bildender Kunst, Film, Theater und Musik, Bielefeld 2011, pp. 13–30, here p. 17 ff.

1
Kerstin Stakemeier, Entgrenzter Formalismus. Verfahren einer antimodernen Ästhetik. *Berlin 2017, S. 21.*

2
Max Fröhlich (1908–1997), zit. n. Christianne Weber-Stöber, Vom Nimbus des Luxuriösen zur Nachhaltigkeit – Zeitgenössische Silbergestaltung im Spiegel der Silbertriennale. *In: Ausstellungskatalog* Kunsthandwerk ist Kaktus. Die Sammlung von 1945 bis heute. *Hg. von Sabine Runde & Matthias Wagner K., Museum für angewandte Kunst. Frankfurt/M. 2022, S. 456–459; hier S. 458.*

3
Vgl. Heinz Friedrich, ›Ende der Kunst – Zukunft der Kunst‹. Einleitung in das Thema. *In:* Ende der Kunst – Zukunft der Kunst. *Hg. von der Bayerischen Akademie der Schönen Künste. München 1985, S. 7–15, insbes. S. 13.*

4
Vgl. Werner Haftmann, Das Ding und seine Verwandlung *(1972). In: Ders.*, Das antwortende Gegenbild. Ausgewählte Texte 1947–1990. *Hg. von Evelyn Haftmann & Wouter Wirth. München 2012, S. 172–214.*

5
Vgl. Ausstellungskatalog Silbertriennale. 20. Weltweiter Wettbewerb. *Hg. von Christianne Weber-Stöber für Goldschmiedekunst e.V., Deutsches Goldschmiedehaus Hanau. Stuttgart 2022, S. 7 f.*

6
Eva Linhart, Abenteuer Kunsthandwerk. *In: Ausstellungskatalog* Kunsthandwerk ist Kaktus, *a.a.O., S. 42–52; hier S. 43, 50 und 52.*

7
Vgl. Ausstellung Mona Hatoum, *Georg Kolbe Museum Berlin 15.9.2022 bis 8.1.2023; dabei auch Installation* **Electrified (variable V)** *von 2022, in der sich Küchenutensilien aneinanderreihen, von elektrischem Strom verknüpft.*

8
Valentina Ornaghi & Claudio Prestinari, Ausstellung Sbilenco, *Galleria Continua, San Gimignano 21.1–7.5.2023.*

9
Pressetext, www.galleriacontinua.com.

10
Annabelle Hirsch, Die Dinge. Eine Geschichte der Frauen in 100 Objekten. *Zürich/Berlin 2022, S. 10.*

11
Konrad Paul Liessmann, Das Universum der Dinge. Zur Ästhetik des Alltäglichen. *Wien 2010, S. 30.*

12
Vgl. GA (Gesamtausgabe), Bd. 5. Hg. von Friedrich-Wilhelm von Herrmann. Frankfurt/M. 1977, S. 32, 52; zit. n. Francisco de Lara, Kunstwerke und Gebrauchsgegenstände. Ding, Zeug und Werk in ihrer Widerspiegelung. *In:* Heideggers Ursprung des Kunstwerks. Ein kooperativer Kommentar. *Hg. von David Espinet & Tobias Keiling. Reihe Heidegger Forum. Hg. von Günter Figal. Frankfurt/M. 2011, S. 19–32; hier S. 27 ff.*

13
Siehe Liessmann, a.a.O., S. 34.

14
Vgl. Gerhard Wolf, Die Vase und der Schemel. Ding, Bild oder eine Kunstgeschichte der Gefäße. *Reihe Connecting Art Histories in the Museum, Bd. 4. Hg. vom Kunsthistorischen Institut Florenz/Max-Planck-Institut und den Staatlichen Museen zu Berlin – Preußischer Kulturbesitz. Dortmund 2019, S. 21 und S. 166.*

15
Museum Rietberg, Zürich, hier n. Wolf, a.a.O., S. 11.

16
Vgl. Erika Fischer-Lichte, Ästhetische Erfahrung als Schwellenerfahrung. *In: Joachim Küpper & Christoph Menke*, Dimensionen ästhetischer Erfahrung. *Frankfurt/M. 2003, S. 138–161.*

17
Anja Zimmermann, Sicherung der Außengrenzen. Transgressive Weiblichkeit, abject art und andere Strategien am Rand der Kunst. *In:* Kunst an den Rändern. Wie aus Bildern und Objekten Kunst werden kann. *Hg. von Christiane Kruse & Annika Frye. Berlin 2021, S. 163–182; hier S. 163.*

18
Rosalind E. Krauss, Sculpture in the Expanded Field *(New York 1978). In: Dies.*, The Originality of the Avant-Garde and Other Modernist Myths. *Cambridge, Mass./London 1988 (5. Ausg.), S. 277–290.*

19
Ebd., S. 284 ff., hier S. 288 f.

20
Monika Leisch-Kiesl & Susanne Winder, Die »Entgrenzung des Ästhetischen« und die Kunstwissenschaft. *In: Dies. & Max Gottschlich (Hg.)*, Ästhetische Kategorien. Perspektiven der Kunstwissenschaft und der Philosophie. *Linzer Beiträge zur Kunstwissenschaft und Philosophie, Bd. 7. Bielefeld 2017, S. 47–52; hier S. 50.*

21
Monika Leisch-Kiesl, Wenn Gegenwartskunst und die Kategorie des Schönen aufeinandertreffen. *In: a.a.O., S. 53–73; hier S. 69.*

22
Ebd., S. 70.

23
Vgl. Ruth Reiche, Iris Romanos & Bernika Szymanski, Transformationen, Grenze und Entgrenzung. *In:* Transformationen in den Künsten. Grenzen und Entgrenzung in bildender Kunst, Film, Theater und Musik. *Hg. von Dens. & Saskia Jogler. Bielefeld 2011, S. 13–30; hier S. 17 ff.*

bisherige Lehrinhalte als vielmehr als notwendige, legitime und dynamische Steigerung der Kapazitäten, welche stets auf eine Verständigung von Kunst und Leben abzielt. Daher auch die performative Wirkung und der happening-artige Auftritt zahlreicher Werke.

Nach den Ausstellungen Open Space – Mind Maps *2016 (Nationalmuseum, Kulturhuset Stockholm) und* Schmuckismus *2019 (Die Neue Sammlung – The Design Museum München, Pinakothek der Moderne) ergreift diese Präsentation einmal mehr Partei für das Öffnen der Augen und den Perspektivwechsel, der hier vom rezipierenden Beobachter verlangt wird. Es ist noch nicht alles klar und manches verwirrend, aber müssen wir immer eindeutige Antworten erhalten? Oder lassen wir nicht lieber auch einiges im Dazwischen?*

Niche

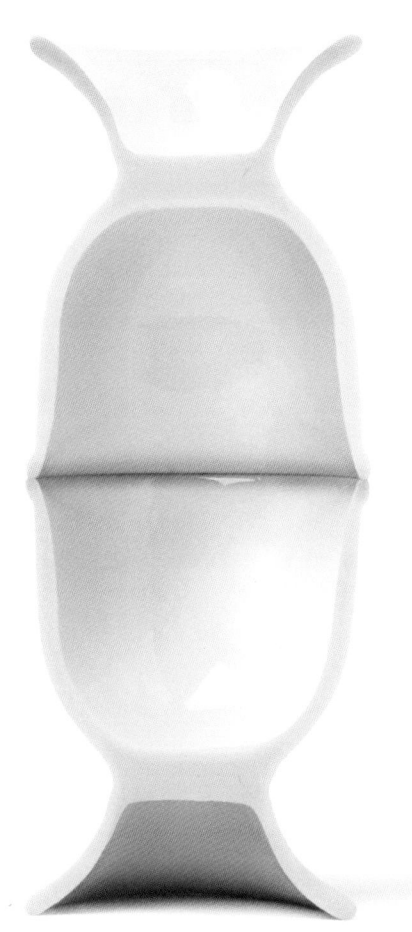

32
Brosche | Brooch
2021 | 2022

Kanako Ebisawa

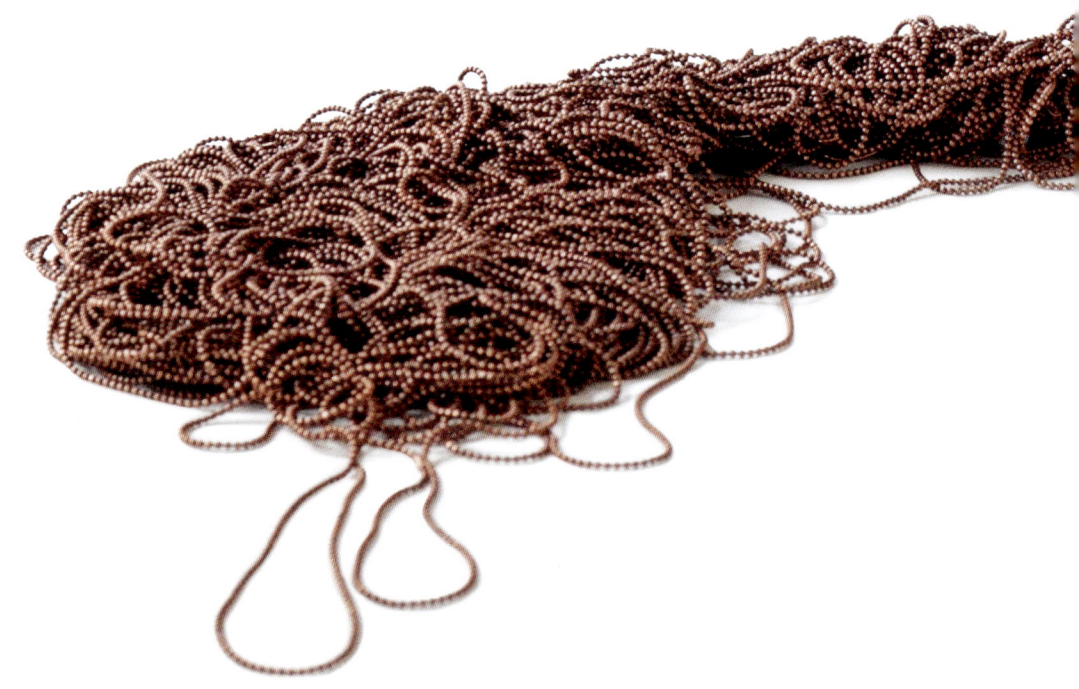

Hot Mess

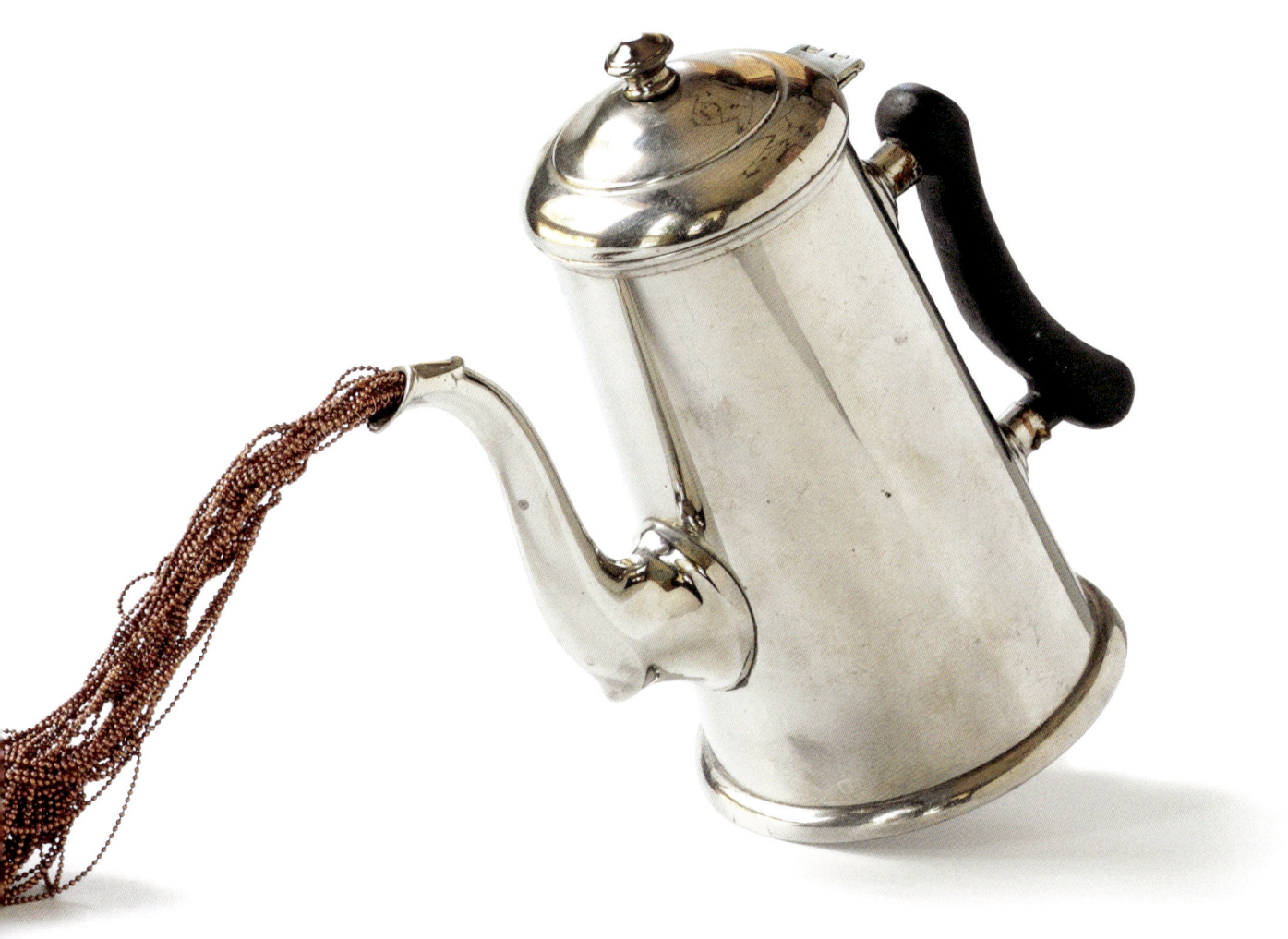

101
Objekt / Object
2023

Anna Rikkinen

Everyday utensils like bowls, handles, cups, plates, and trays have a connection to the body. They are so ordinary that in some ways they are invisible. For me the used artifacts present lost memories and lost time but also man's will over nature.

I want to make the body uneasy, to wake the body from its stupor. The body needs to feel the beauty and the weight of the beauty. Wearing jewelry is uncomfortable, but the façade is essential.

Alltagsgerät wie Schalen, Griffe, Tassen, Teller und Tabletts haben eine Verbindung zum Körper. Sie sind so gewöhnlich, dass sie in mancherlei Hinsicht unsichtbar werden. Für mich stellen die benutzten Artefakte verlorene Erinnerungen und verlorene Zeit dar, aber auch die Macht des Menschen über die Natur.

Ich möchte dem Körper Unbehagen bereiten, ihn aus seiner Benommenheit befreien. Der Körper muss die Schönheit und das Gewicht der Schönheit spüren. Schmuck zu tragen, ist unbequem, doch die Fassade ist unverzichtbar.

Woods Baroque 2

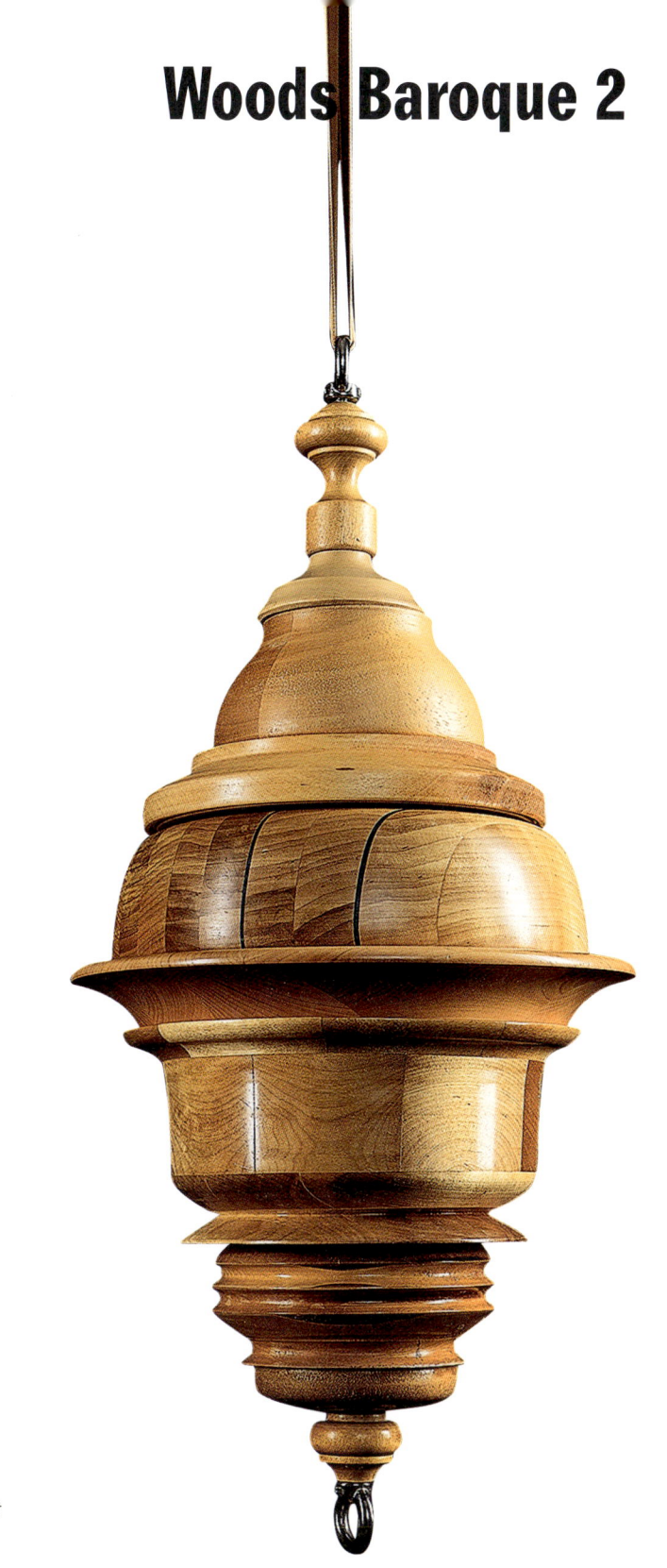

102
Objekt / Object
2022

Anna Rikkinen

A Dutch Encounter VII

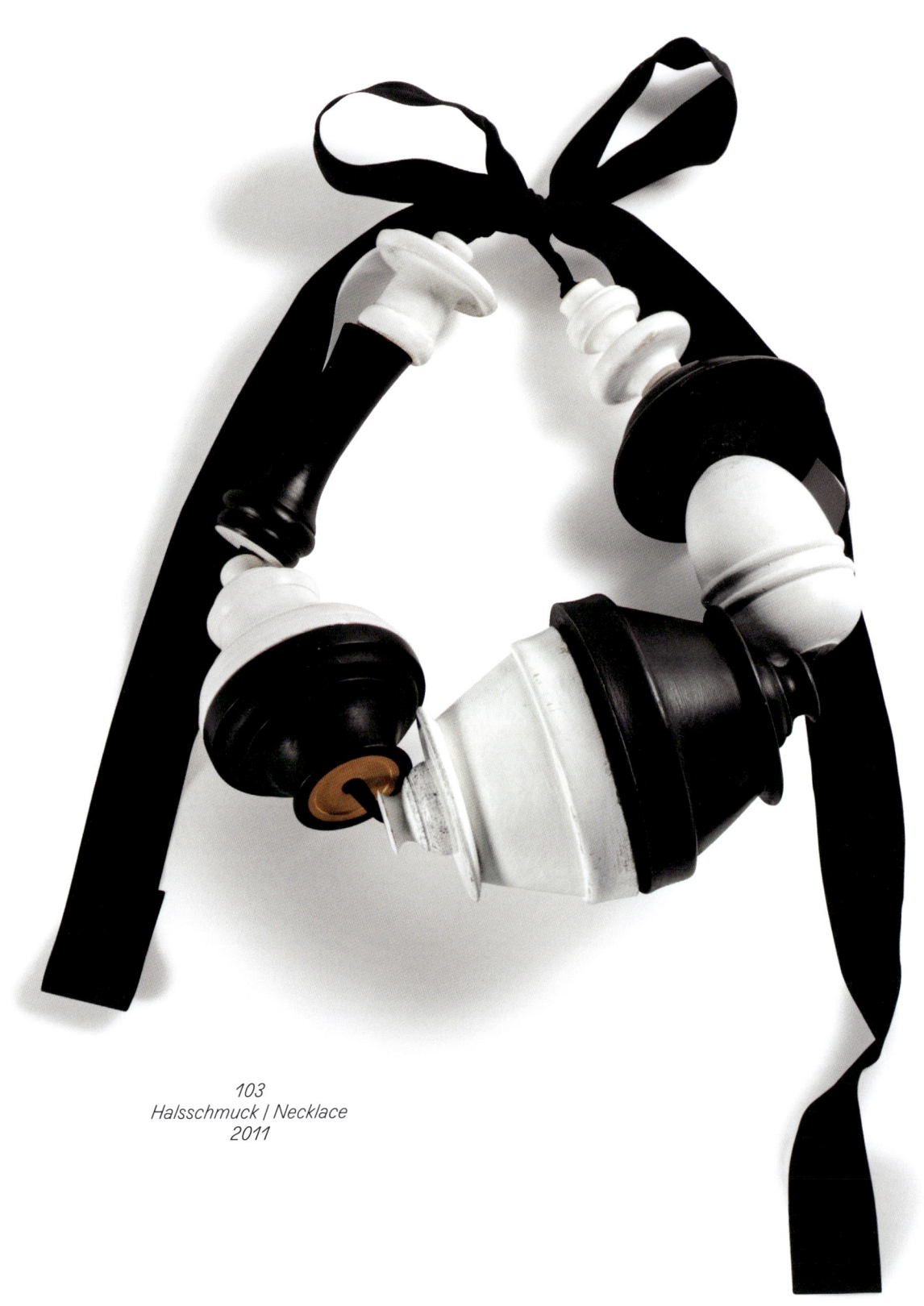

103
Halsschmuck | Necklace
2011

Anna Rikkinen

Teapot

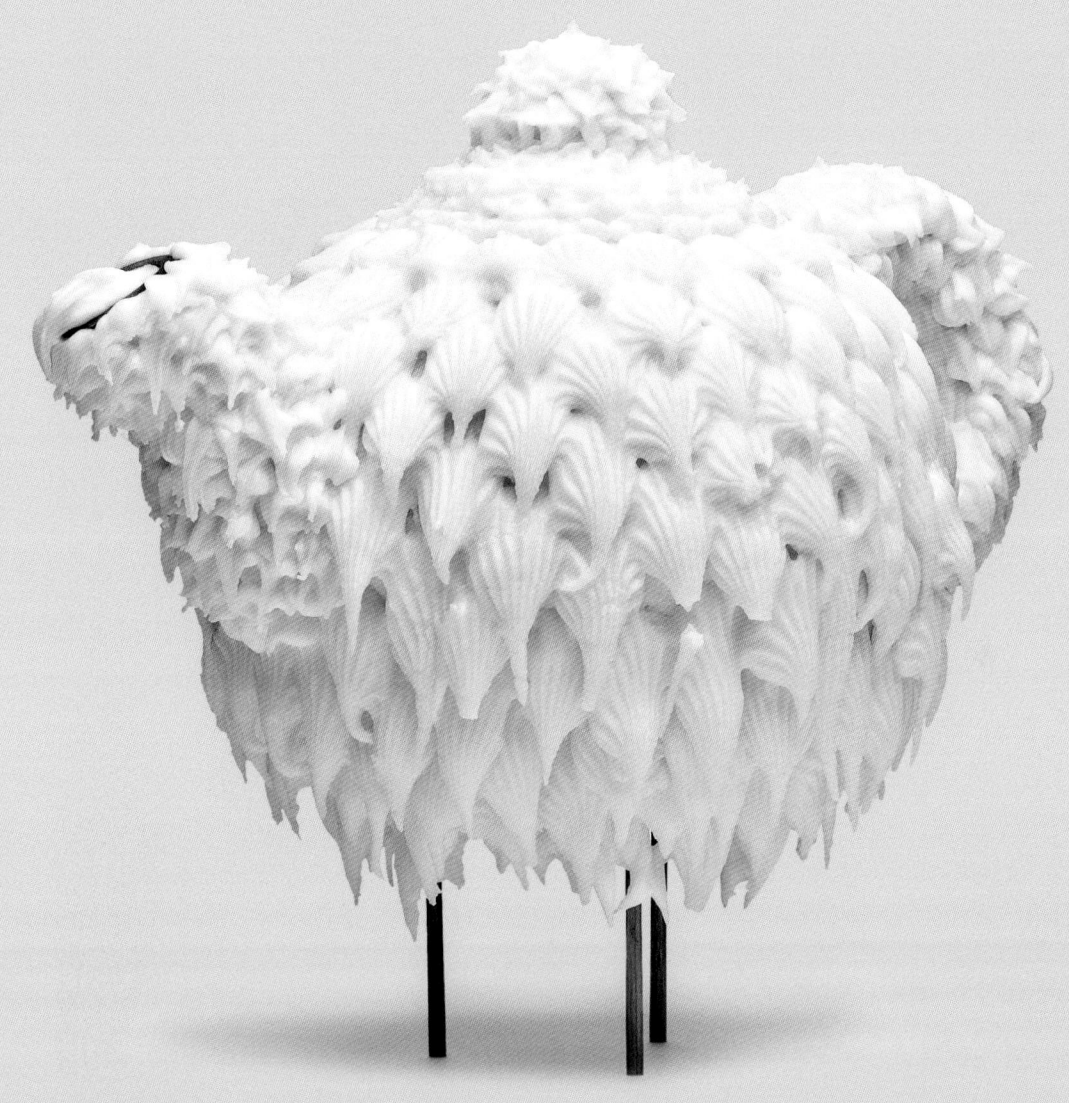

48
Objekt / Object
Aus der Reihe / From the series
The Cocktail Effect
2013

Karolina Hägg

Spectacle Bread and Mother-of-Pearl

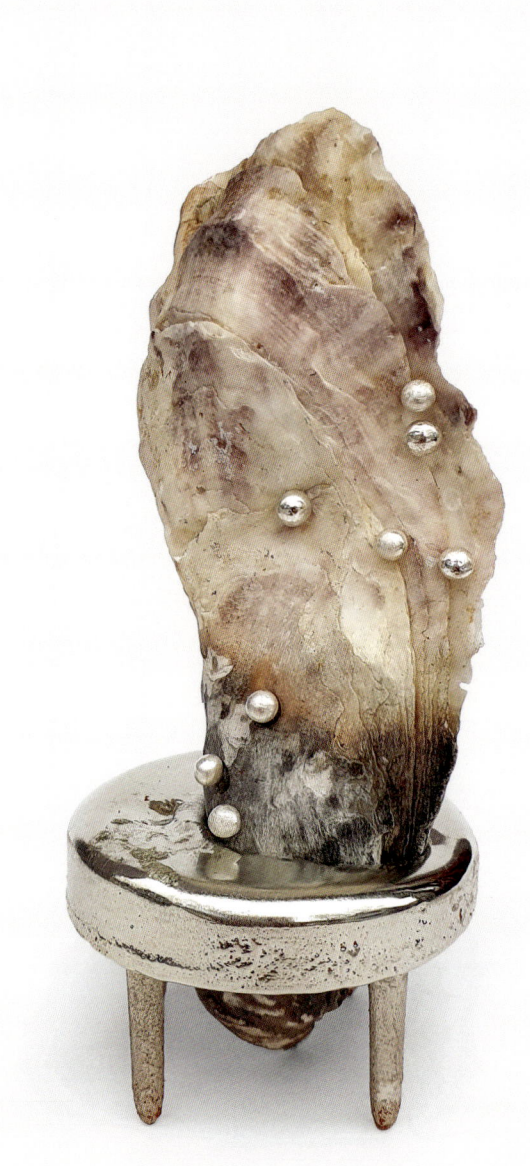

Karolina Hägg

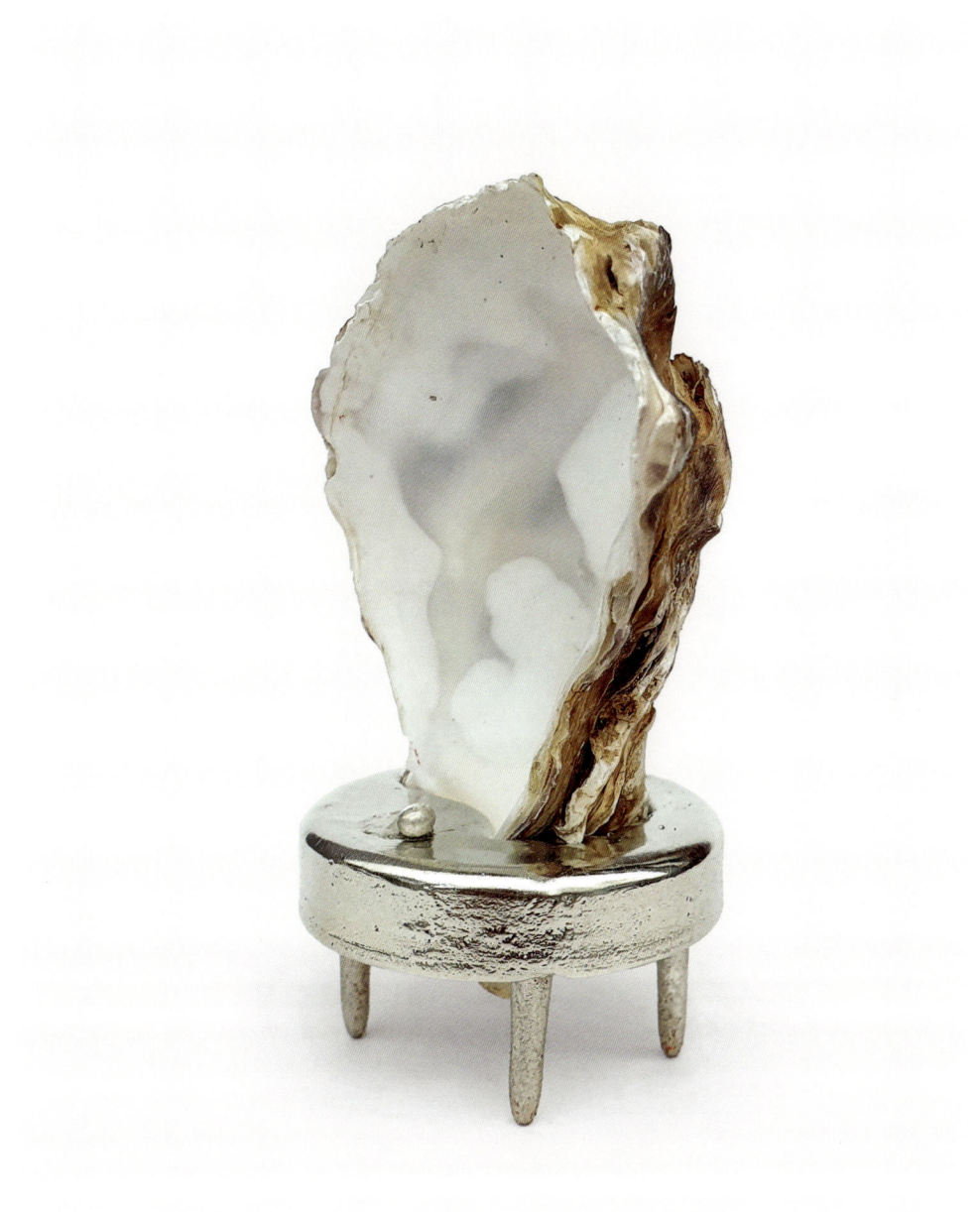

*46
Objekte | Objects
2023*

Karolina Hägg

The objects I make often comment on function and decoration and the balance or imbalance between them. They can, for example, express the exaggerated and absurdly overdecorated in relation to a rather small and insignificant function. An important aspect and driving force in my work is my curiosity for how materials are made and which techniques enable these materials to become something else.

Meine Objekte sind oft als Kommentare zu Funktion und Dekoration angelegt – und zu dem Gleichgewicht oder Ungleichgewicht, das zwischen beiden besteht. Sie können zum Beispiel das Übertriebene und absurd Überdekorierte im Verhältnis zu einer eher bescheidenen und unbedeutenden Funktion ausdrücken. Ein wichtiger Aspekt und zugleich Triebfeder meiner Arbeit ist meine Neugier. Ich will wissen, wie Materialien entstehen und welche Techniken es diesen Materialien ermöglichen, zu etwas anderem zu werden.

Vine Glass

49
Objekt / Object
Aus der Reihe / From the series
The Cocktail Effect
2013

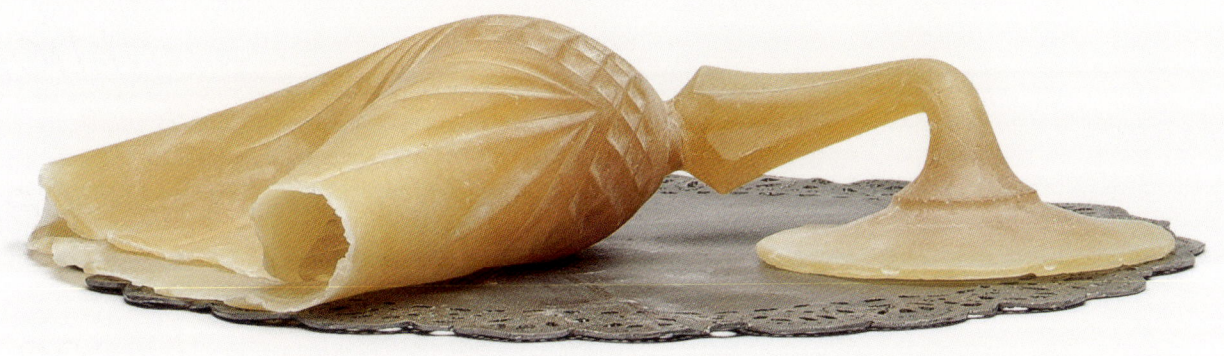

Karolina Hägg

Ohne Titel / Untitled
(Vessel / Hanging container)

42
Objekt / Object
2016–2017

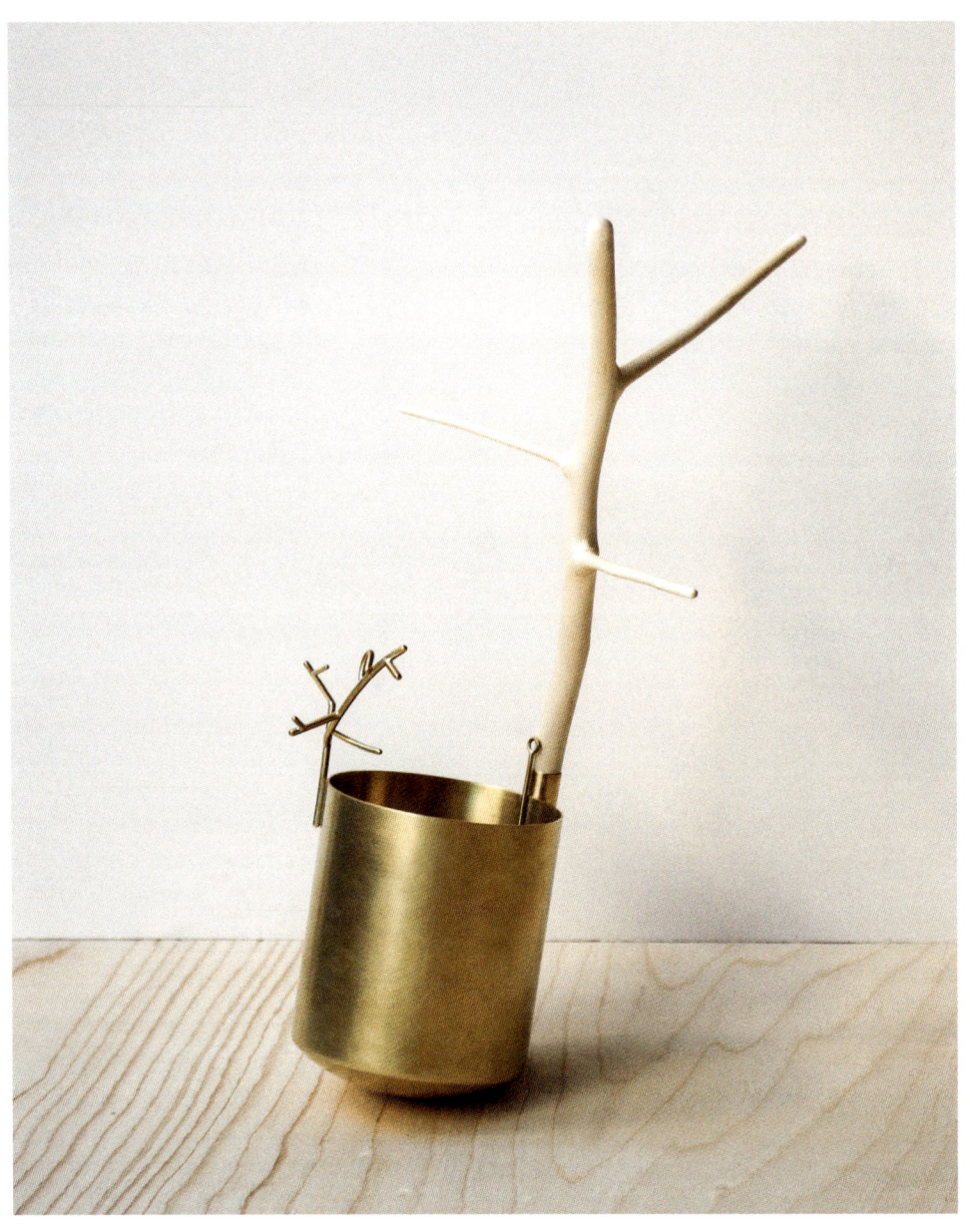

Åsa Elmstam

Things 2

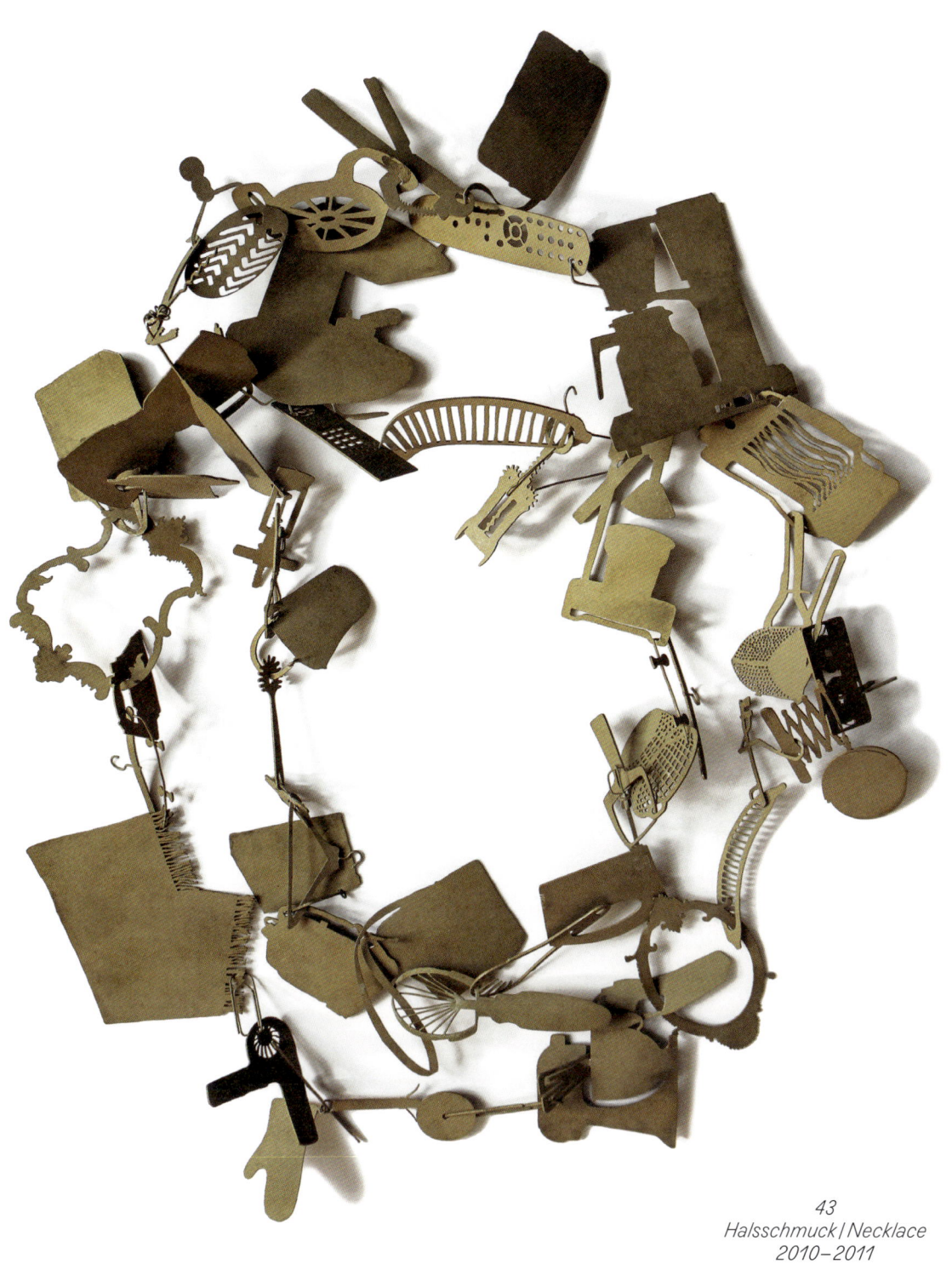

43
Halsschmuck / Necklace
2010–2011

Åsa Elmstam

Lure of Space Collection—
space sketches

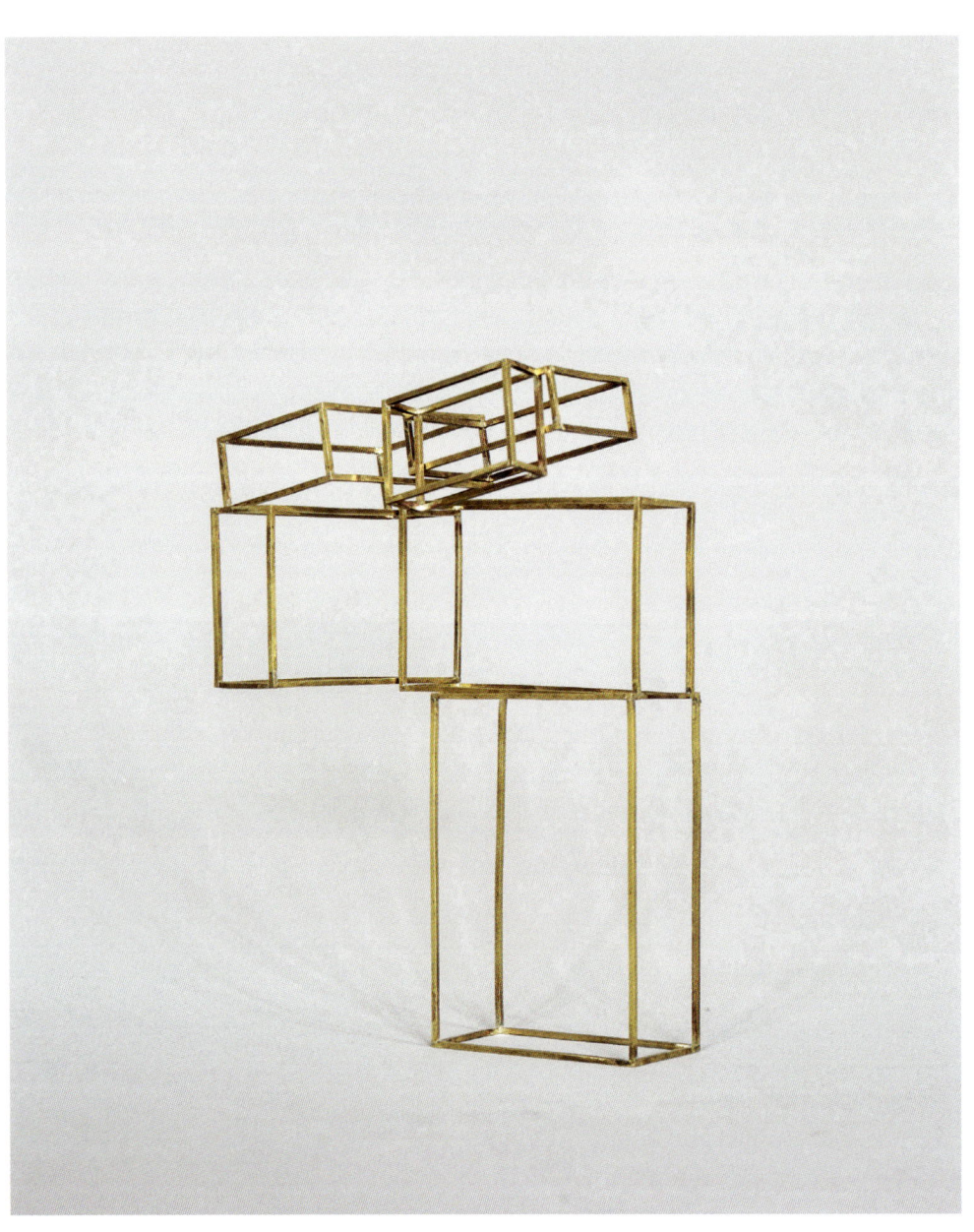

Kateřina Michálková

72
Objekte | Objects
2018

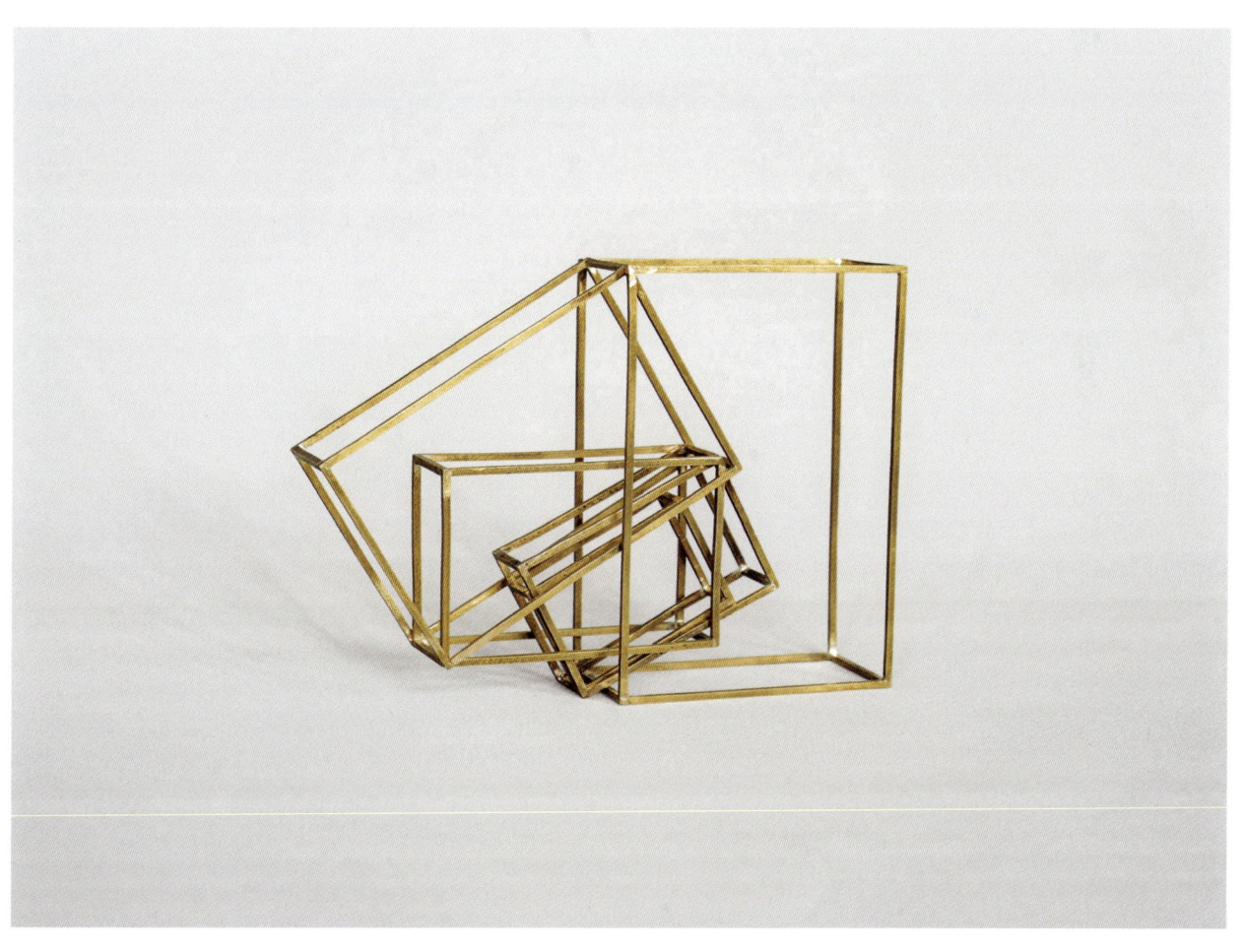

Kateřina Michálková

Gefäß / Container

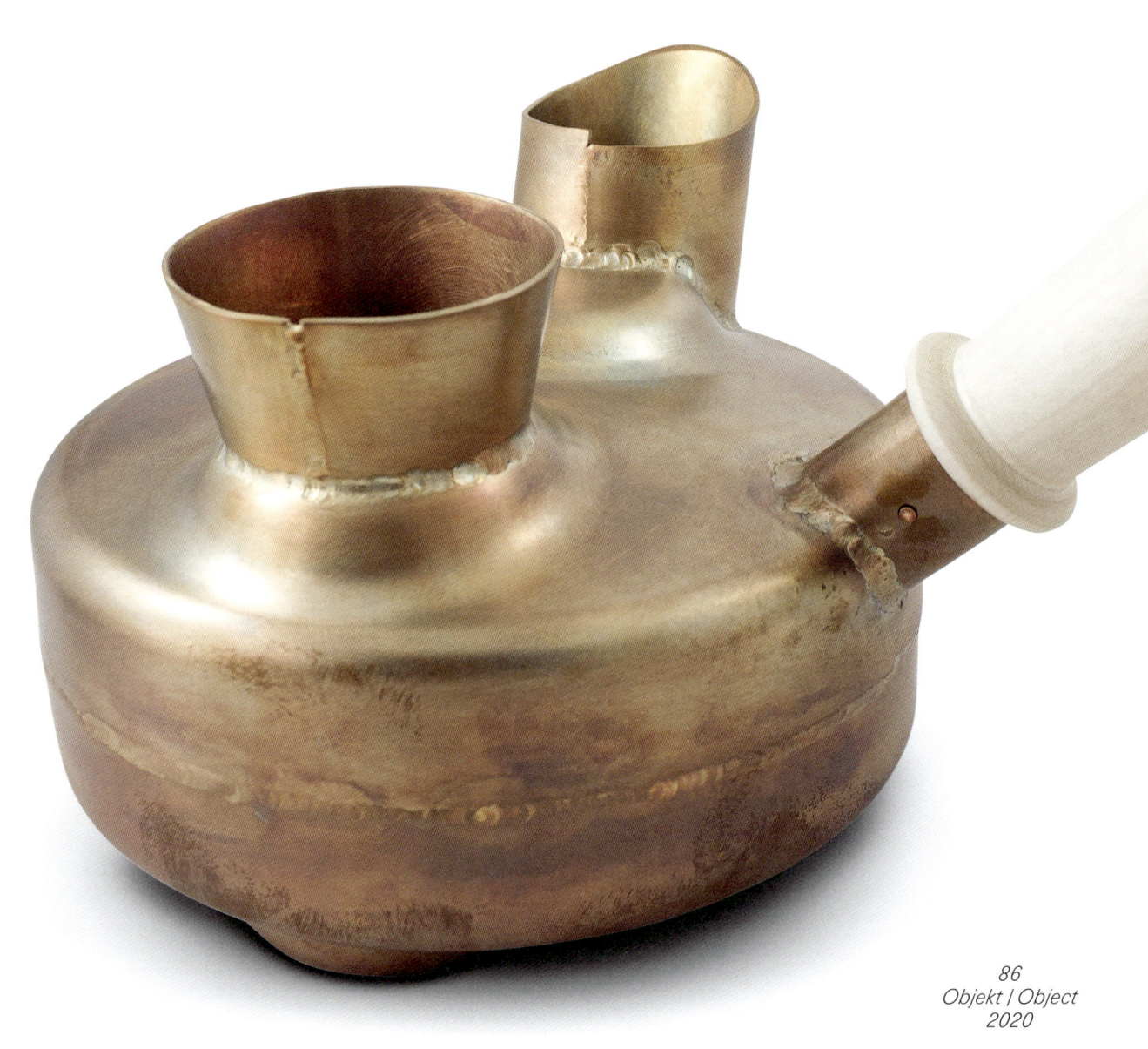

86
Objekt / Object
2020

Markus Pollinger

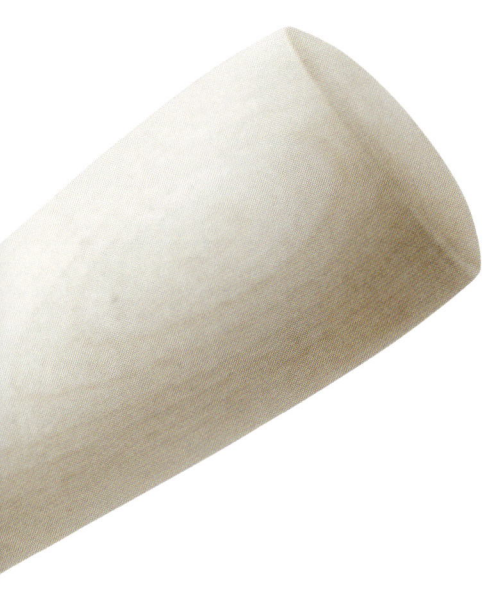

Gefäß / Container

84
Objekt / Object
2020

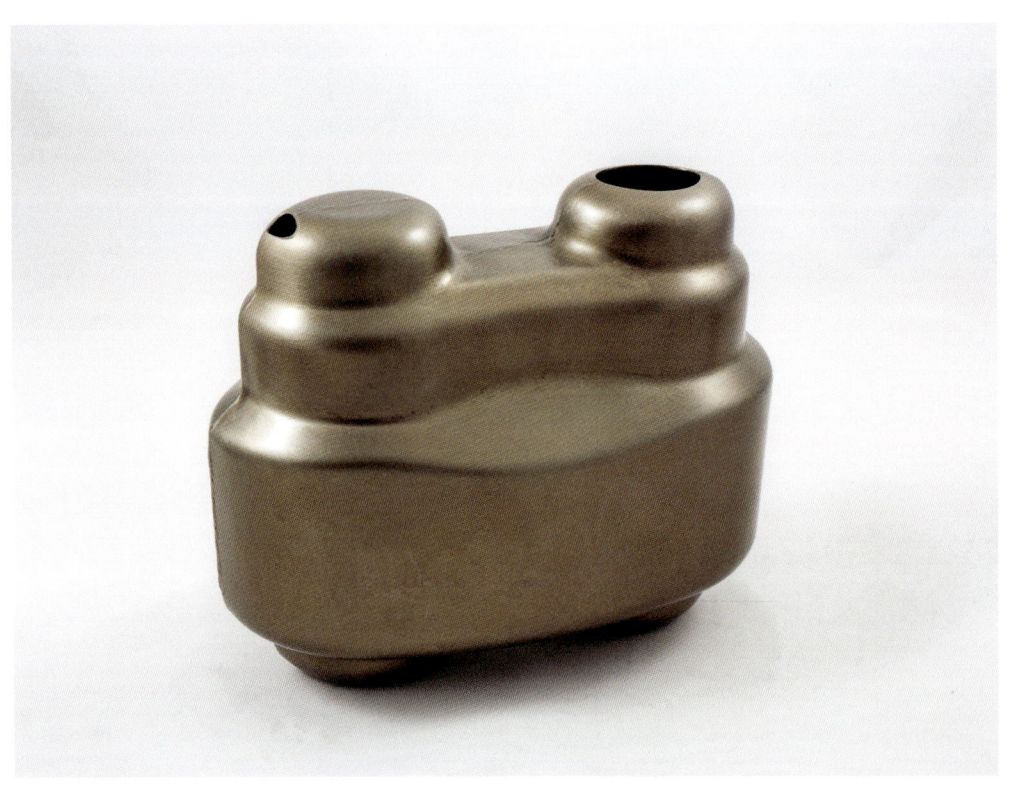

Markus Pollinger

Gefäß / Container

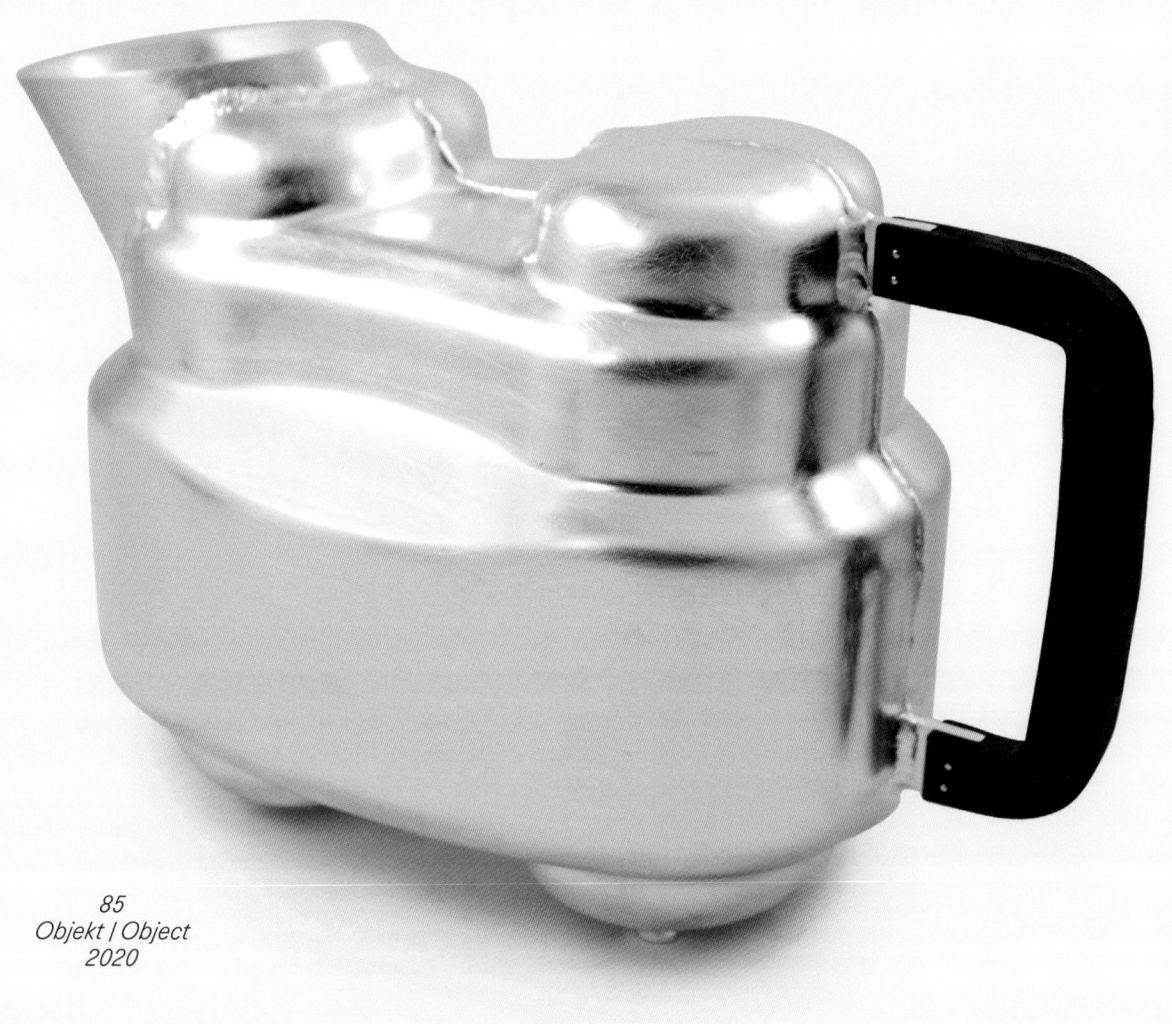

85
Objekt / Object
2020

Markus Pollinger

Shalo boli duge

33
Ansteckobjekt | Pin-on Jewelry
2022

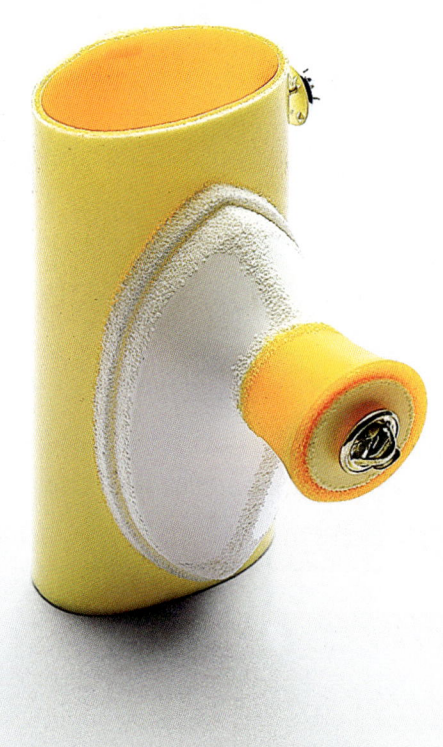

Ute Eitzenhöfer

Plastic: contemporary driftwood. It is manufactured thousandfold in identical forms, yet I am reluctant to throw away a piece of plastic packaging.
Work with packaging waste began in 2002 and featured such concepts as the affluent society, environmental pollution, recycling, but, most importantly, this material seemed to me ideally suited to being the vehicle for visualizing the value of time and the work process.

Plastik – Treibholz der Gegenwart. Es wird tausendfach in gleichen Formen hergestellt, und doch widerstrebt es mir, eine Plastikverpackung wegzuwerfen. Am Beginn der Arbeit mit Verpackungsmüll im Jahr 2002 standen Begriffe wie Überfluss, Umweltverschmutzung, Recycling – aber vor allem erschien mir das Material perfekt geeignet, als Träger den Wert der Zeit und des Arbeitsprozesses sichtbar zu machen.

Ute Eitzenhöfer

Ensha
circle 02

38
Ansteckobjekt | Pin-on Jewelry
2002

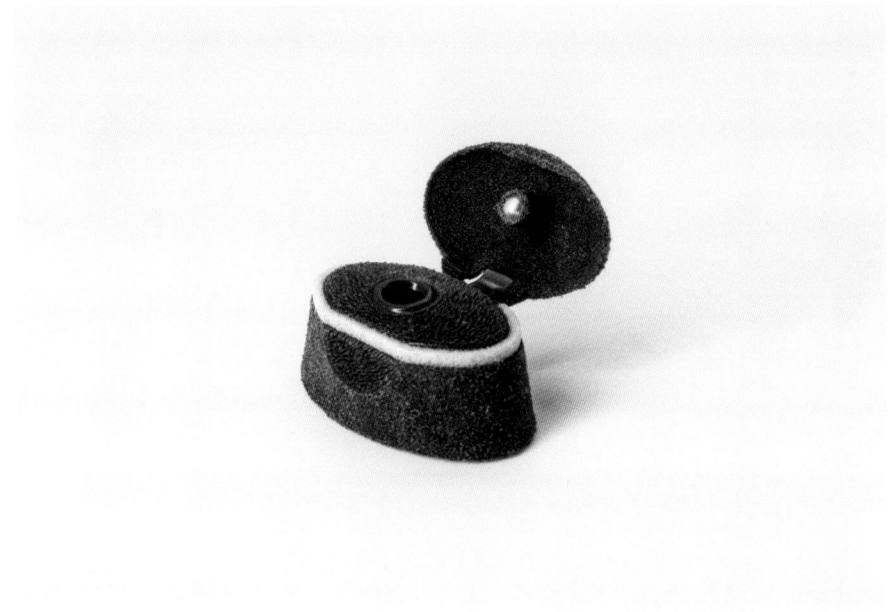

34
Brosche | Brooch
2019

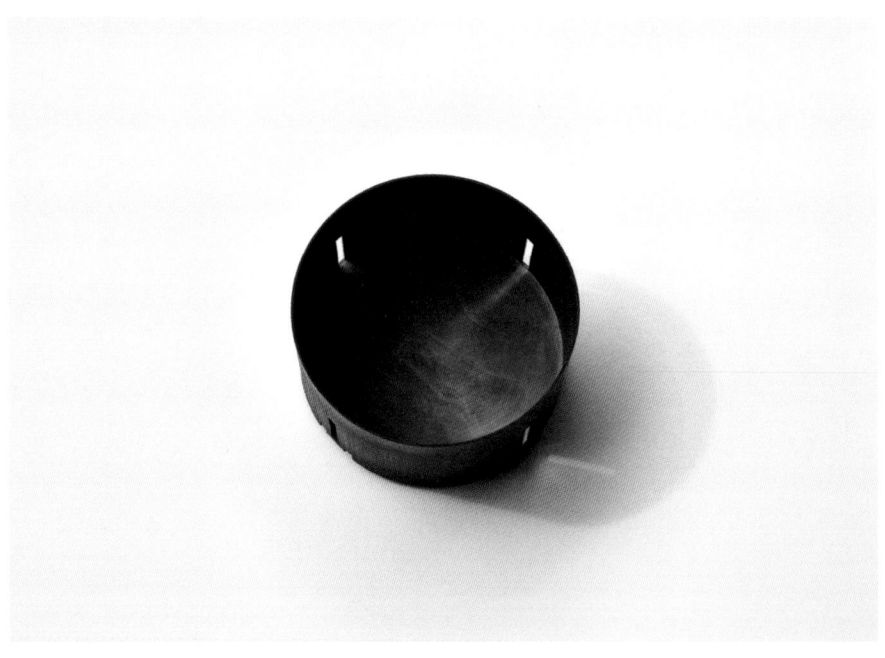

Ute Eitzenhöfer

Deckel mit Pins 1–3

37
Ansteckobjekte | Pin-on Jewelry
2002

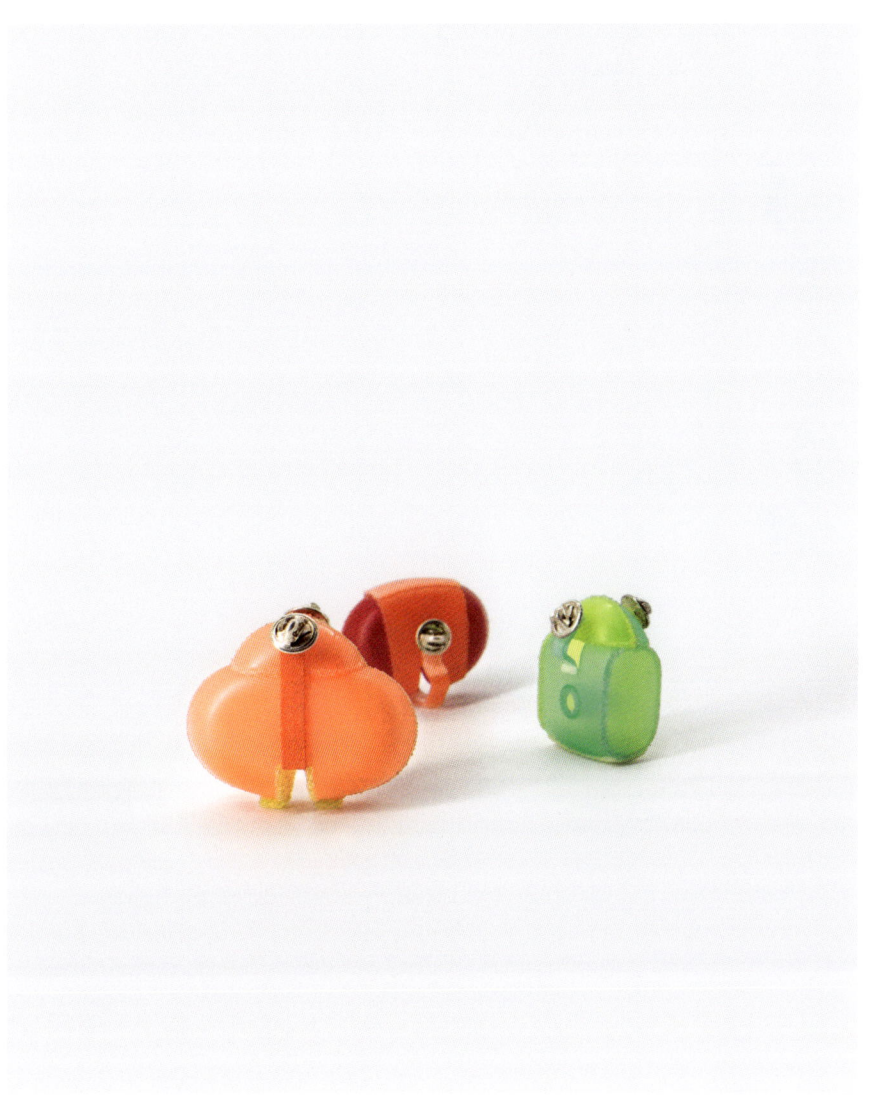

Ute Eitzenhöfer

Craft is for something. In my work, its purpose is to provoke questions. Examining craft's social function and identity prompts new interpretations. A familiar object is rendered abstractly—exaggerated and surreal. It is conceptually revised while physically present and connected to domestic utility. The craft process is integral to the work's content. Sketch, action, and image are frozen together in the constructed metal outcome. Meaning is contained within the making and the moment; the object is a document of this realization.

Kunsthandwerk wird für etwas gemacht. In meiner Arbeit soll es Fragen provozieren. Die soziale Funktion und Identität des Kunsthandwerks zu untersuchen, löst neue Interpretationen aus. Ein vertrautes Objekt wird abstrakt wiedergegeben – übertrieben und surreal. Es ist konzeptionell überarbeitet, aber körperlich präsent und mit der Hauswirtschaft verknüpft. Der handwerkliche Prozess ist wesentlich für den Inhalt des Werks. Skizze, Handlung und Bild erstarren gemeinsam zum konstruierten metallenen Ergebnis. Die Bedeutung steckt in der Herstellung und im Moment; das Objekt ist ein Dokument dieser Erkenntnis.

Penguin
Double Cylinder Slide

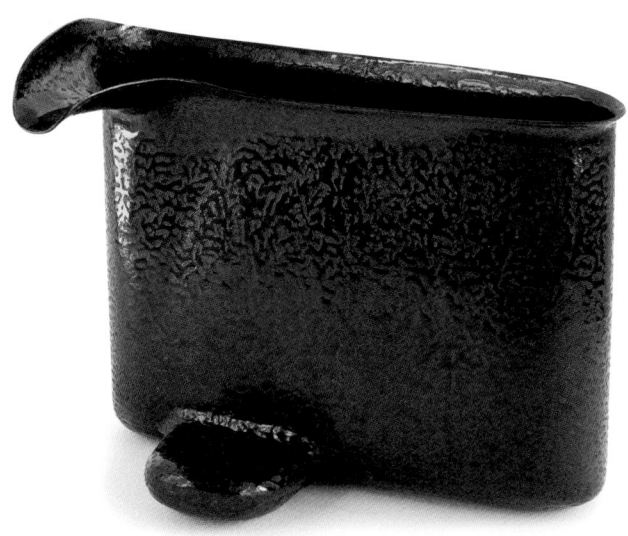

76
Objekt | Object
2017

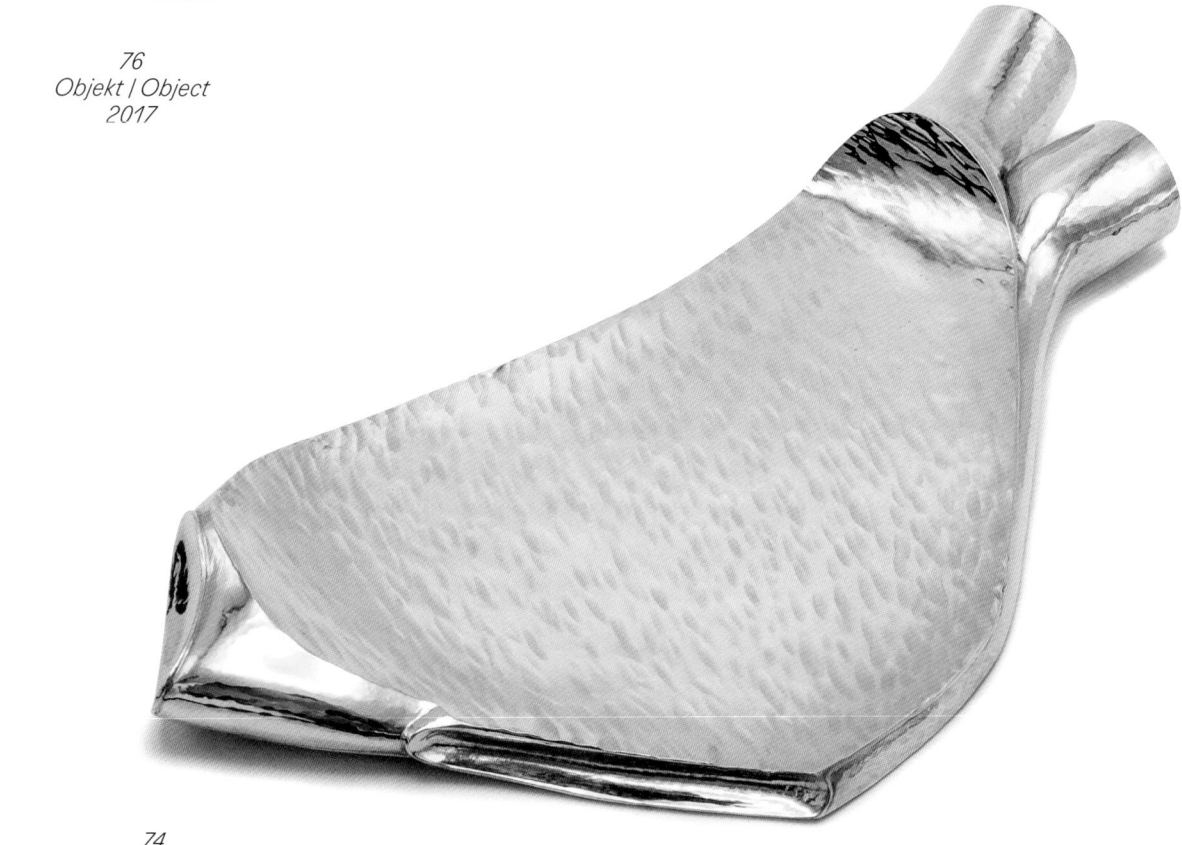

74
Tischobjekt | Table Object
2021

Myra Mimlitsch-Gray

Freistehende Bratpfanne / Freestanding skillet

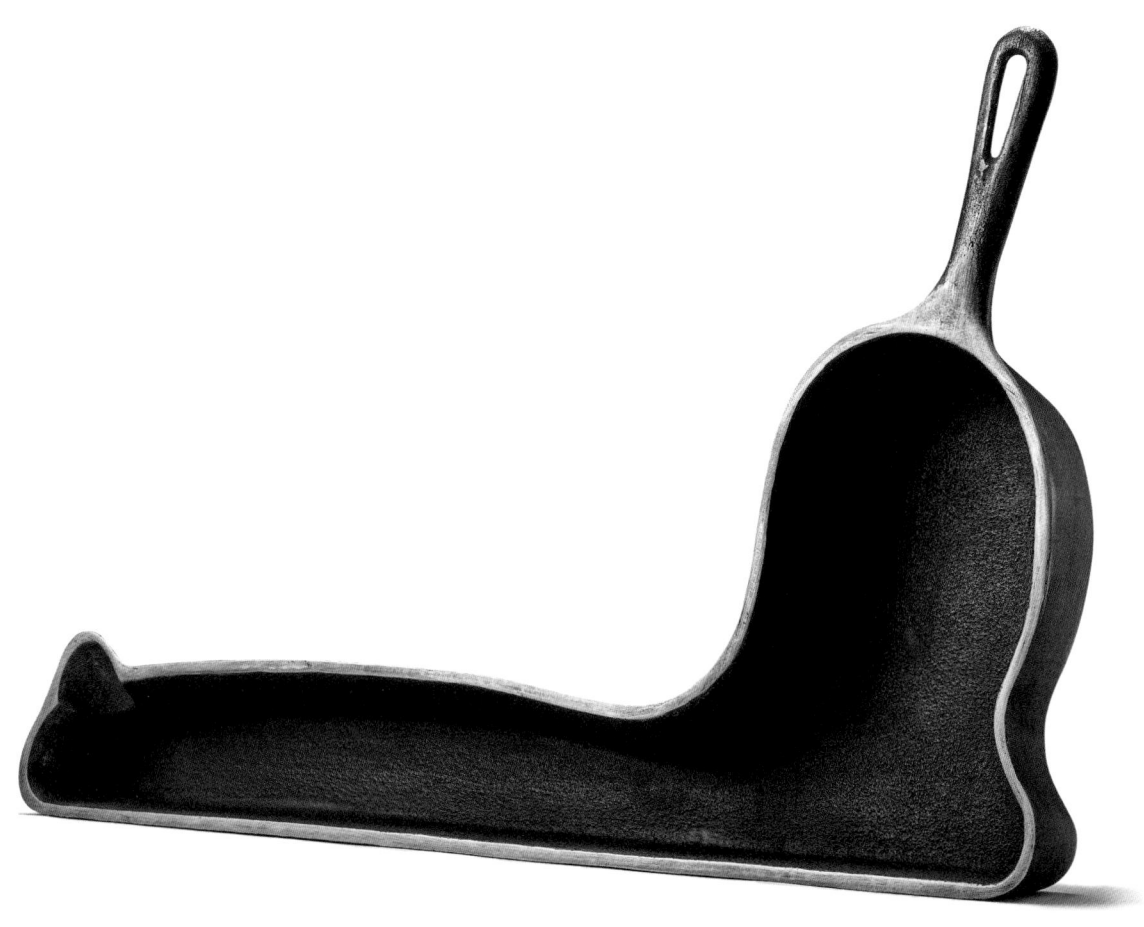

78
Objekt / Object
2007

Myra Mimlitsch-Gray

Gefäße / Vessels

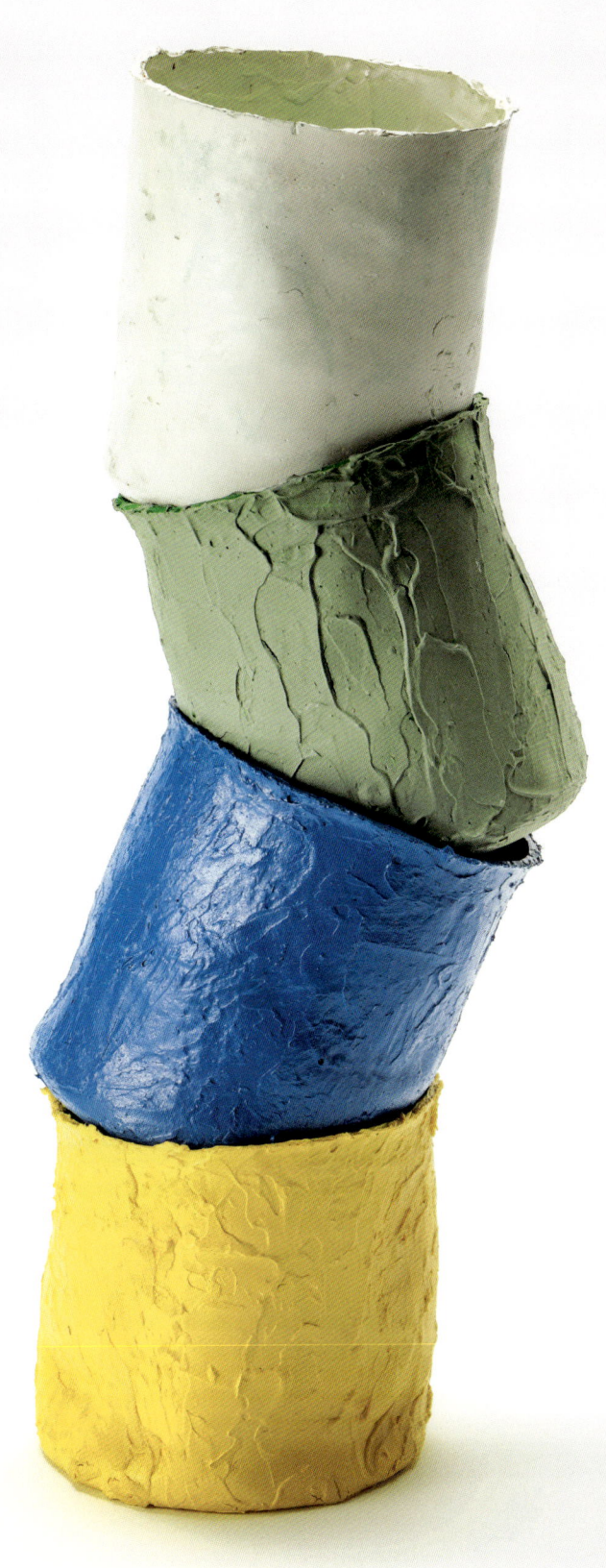

45
Objekte / Objects
2010

Anne Fischer

Gefäß / Vessel

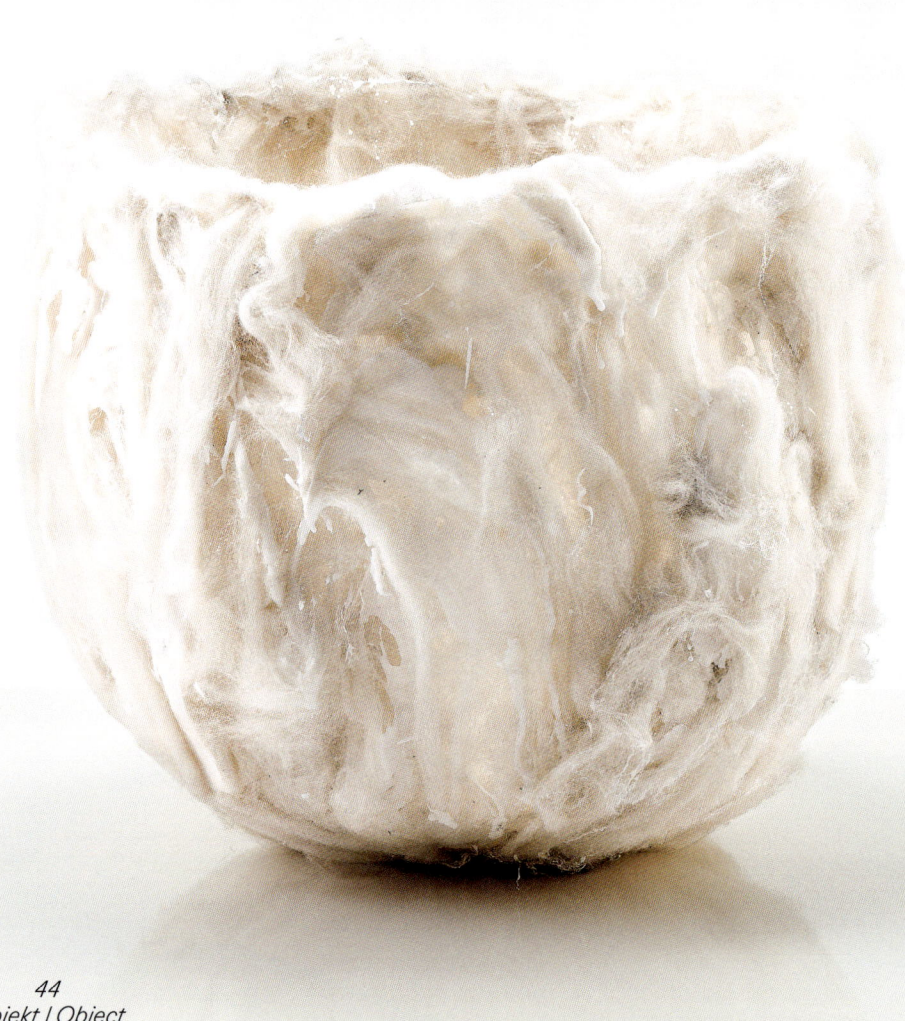

44
Objekt / Object
2013

Anne Fischer

Extraordinary Piece No.2

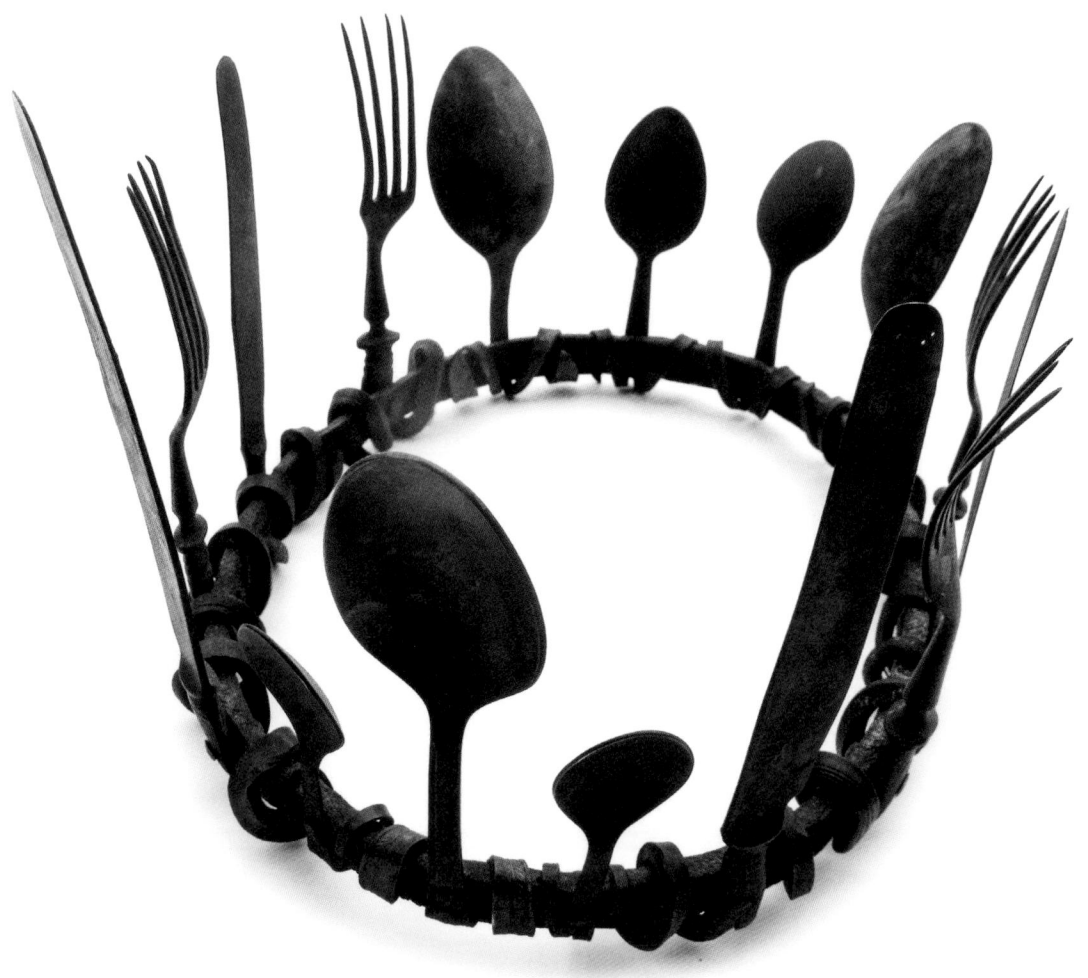

54
Kopfschmuck | Headdress
2011

Nils Hint

Shadow

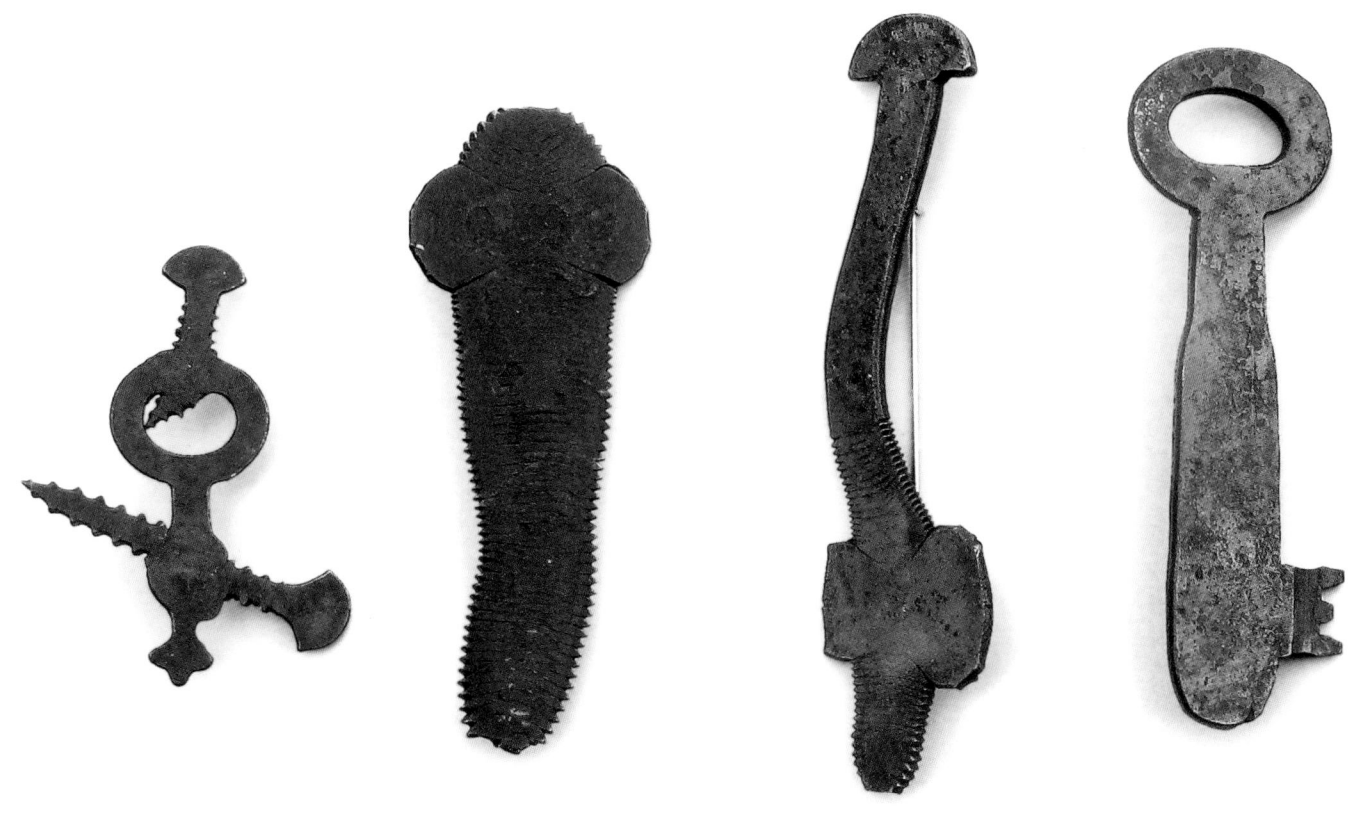

Nils Hint

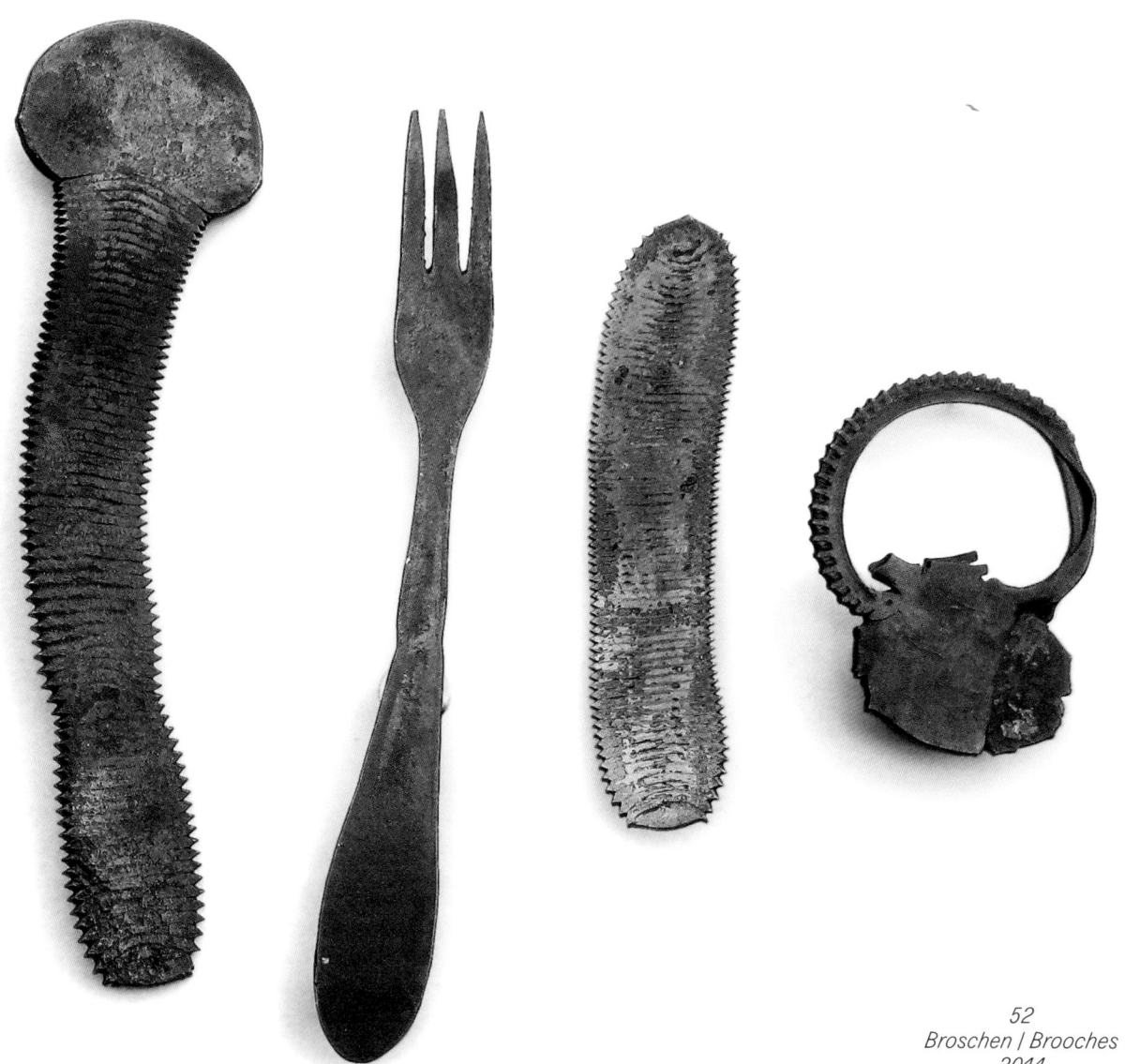

52
Broschen | Brooches
2014

BEYOND REPAIR / LILIES VASE

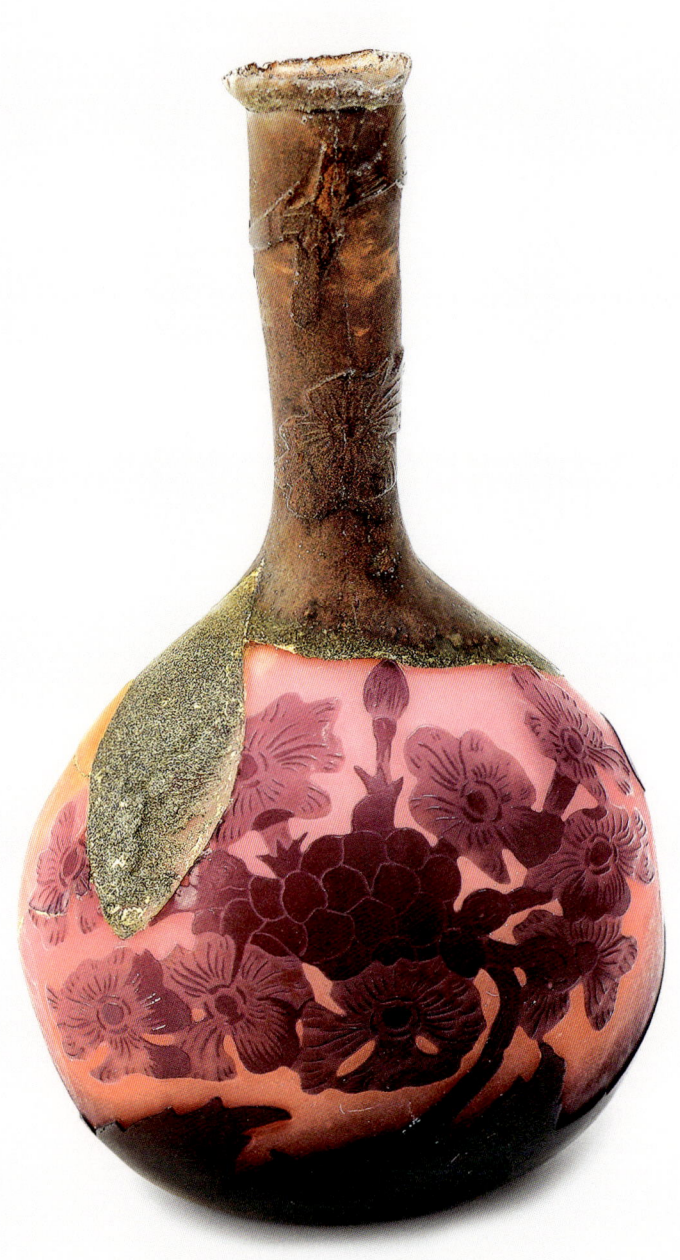

24
Objekt / Object
2017

Beatrice Brovia / Nicolas Cheng

SOAP HANDLE
TEXTILE HANDLE

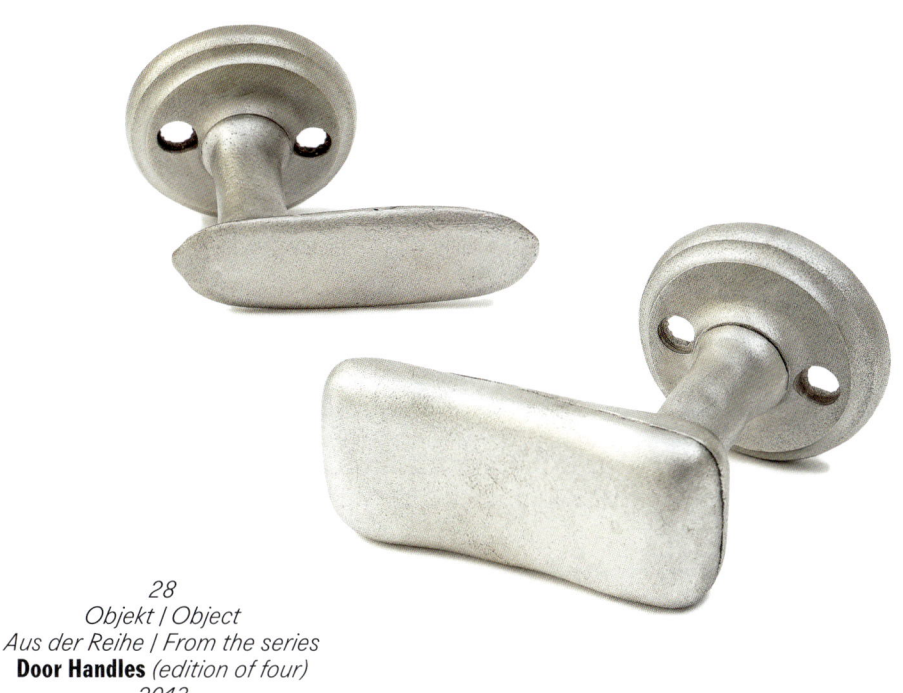

28
Objekt | Object
Aus der Reihe | From the series
Door Handles (edition of four)
2013

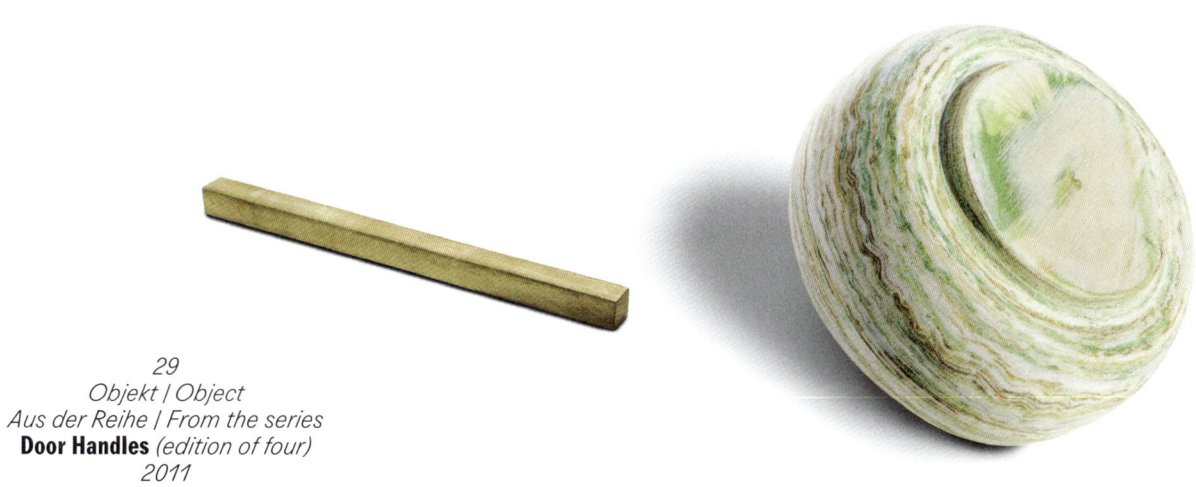

29
Objekt | Object
Aus der Reihe | From the series
Door Handles (edition of four)
2011

Beatrice Brovia | Nicolas Cheng

A little more than one,
certainly less than two

Through our ongoing, shared practice, we have come to experience collaboration as a method to engage with tricky questions emergent from the field we work in, in connection with larger political, social, and economic phenomena. To stay with these questions and the complexity they entail, it has been necessary to go beyond ideals of self-reliance, independency, and even autarchy implied in the single author or maker vision and to embrace the sense of interdependency implied in »collaboration.«

*Etwas mehr als eins,
mit Sicherheit weniger als zwei*

Durch unsere fortlaufende gemeinsame Tätigkeit haben wir Kooperation als einen Weg erlebt, uns mit schwierigen Fragen auseinanderzusetzen, die in Verbindung mit größeren politischen, sozialen und wirtschaftlichen Phänomenen aus unserem Arbeitsbereich erwachsen. Um an diesen Fragen und der Komplexität, die sie mit sich bringen, dranzubleiben, war es notwendig, über die Ideale von Eigenständigkeit, Unabhängigkeit und sogar Autarkie, die der Blick eines einzelnen Urhebers oder Produzenten impliziert, hinauszugehen und die im Begriff »Kooperation« mitgedachte gegenseitige Abhängigkeit schätzen zu lernen.

Ohne Titel / Untitled (Kino 11)

26
Brosche | Brooch
2014–2016

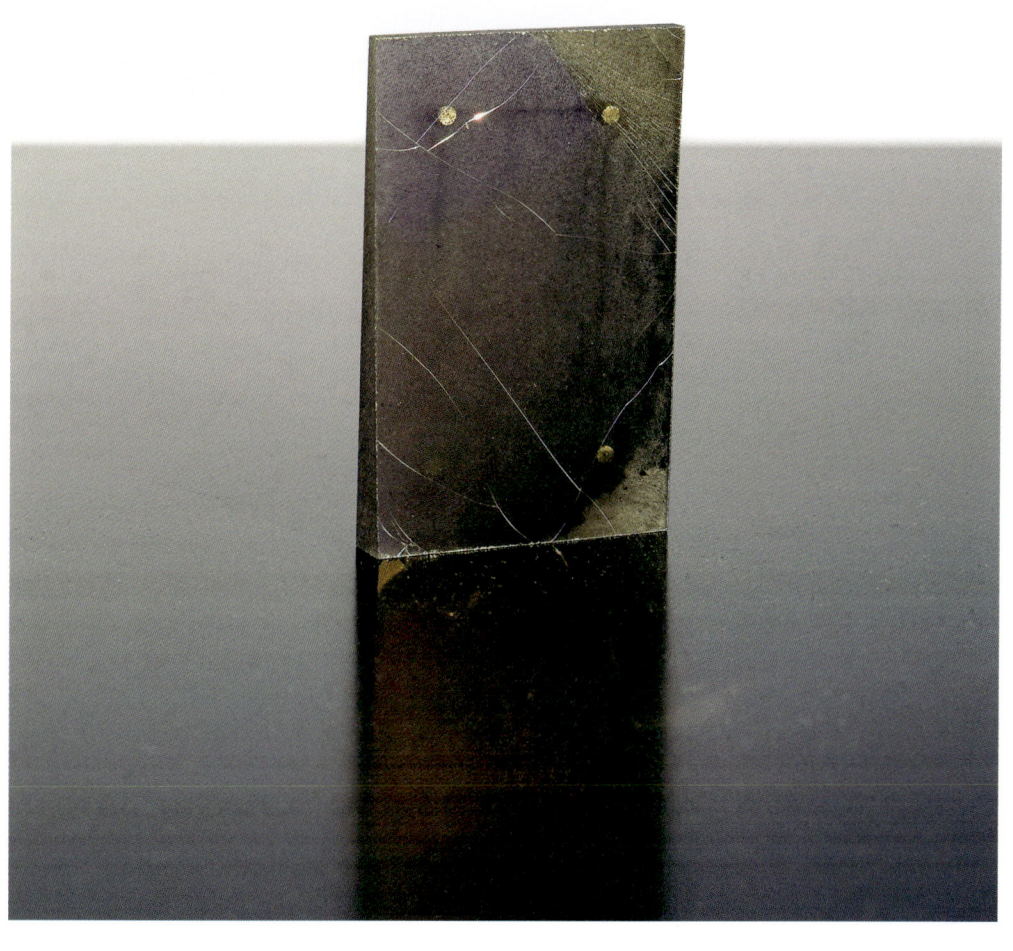

Beatrice Brovia / Nicolas Cheng

box

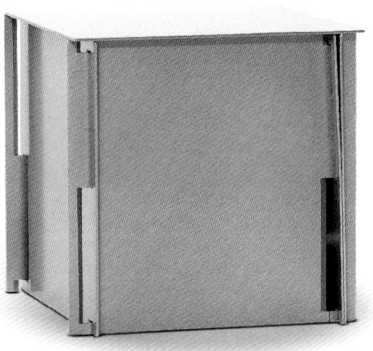

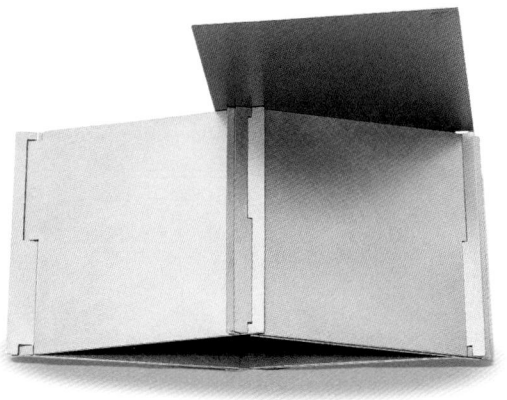

59
Brosche | Brooch
2022

empty
Nadel und Box / Pin and box

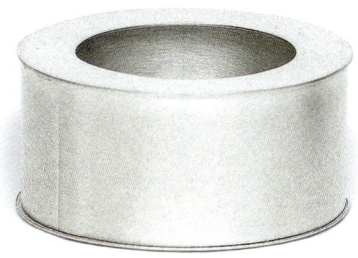

60
Ring-Box | Ring box
2022

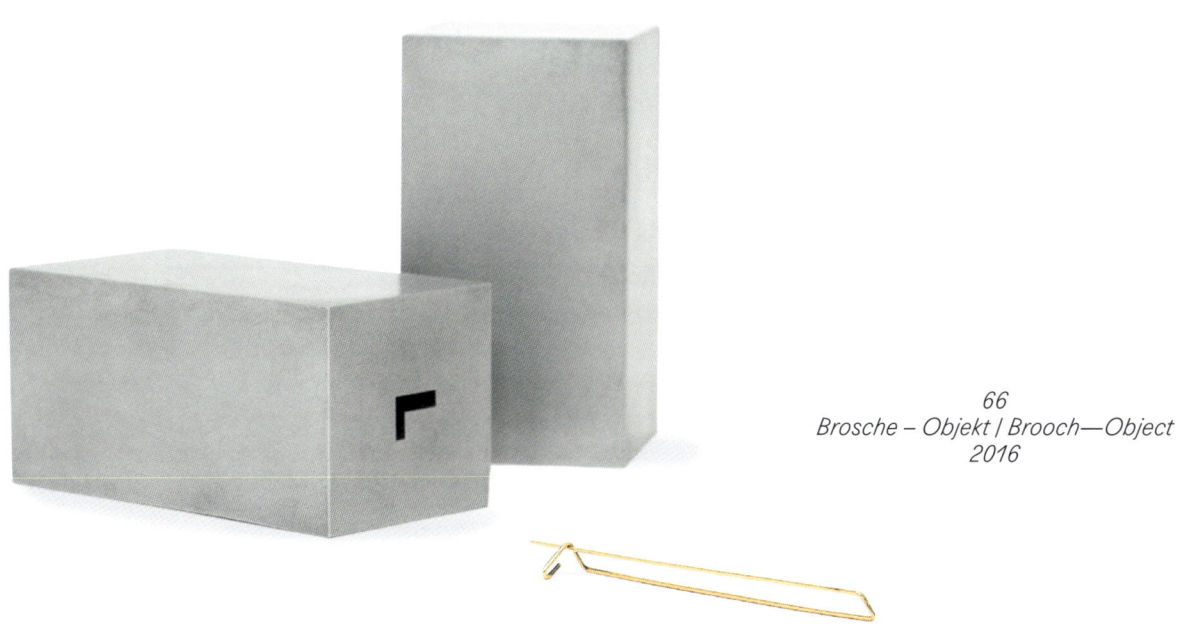

66
Brosche – Objekt | Brooch—Object
2016

Junwon Jung

pawn

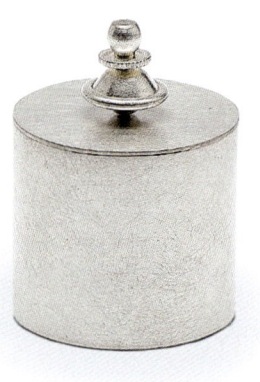

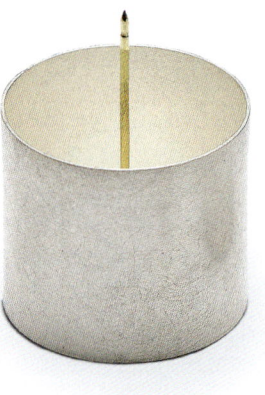
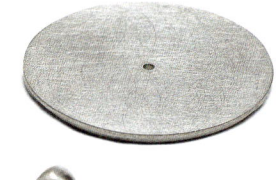

65
Brosche | Brooch
2018

Junwon Jung

Zuckerdose / Sugar bowl

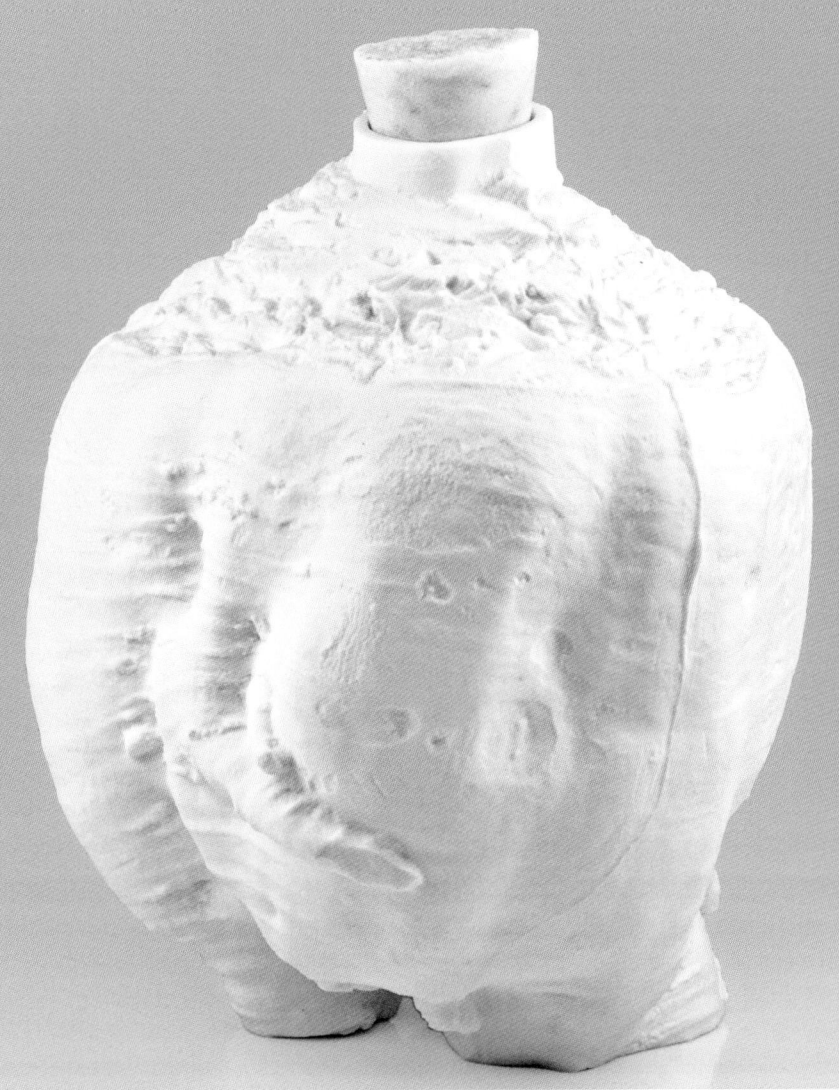

113
Objekt / Object
2013

Luzia / Vogt

I Am Hungry Nr. V

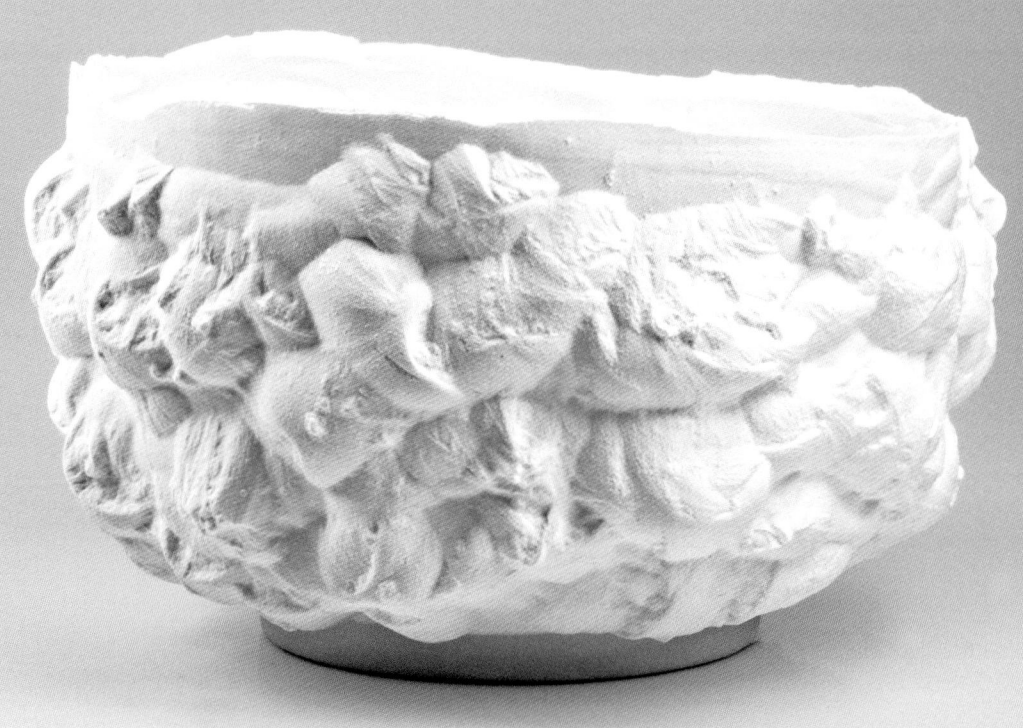

115
Schale | Bowl
2008

Luzia Vogt

Rhythmus

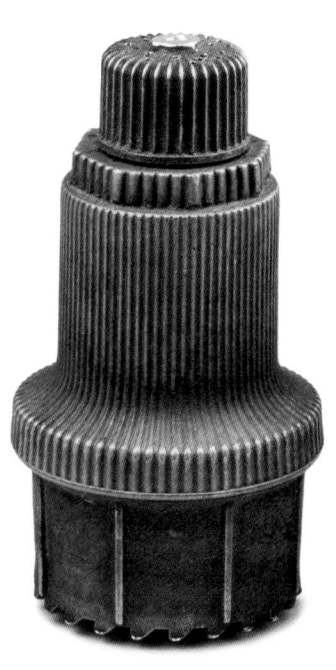 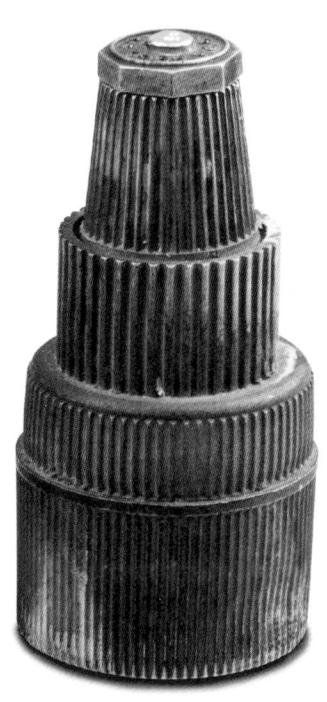

114
Salz- und Zuckerstreuer /
Salt and sugar shakers
2008–2011

Luzia Vogt

Salt has constructive and destructive forces within it. It is a preservative but also causes decay in materials often perceived as strong, such as iron or steel. At the same time, it is itself a fragile material—brittle and water soluble. The transformative power of salt, both physically and conceptually, presents this vital mineral as a carrier for private and social narratives. It enables me to create objects in a state of transit, reminding us that upon usage or wear each of the precious creations is at risk of being affected by time and user alike.

Salz birgt konstruktive und destruktive Kräfte in sich. Es ist Konservierungsmittel, aber auch Ursache für den Zerfall von Materialien, die oft als stabil wahrgenommen werden, wie Eisen oder Stahl. Gleichzeitig ist es ein fragiles Material – spröde und wasserlöslich. Die verändernde Kraft von Salz, sowohl physisch als auch konzeptuell, lässt dieses lebenswichtige Mineral zum Träger von persönlichen und gesellschaftlichen Erzählungen werden. Es erlaubt mir, Objekte im Übergangszustand zu erschaffen, und erinnert uns daran, dass jede dieser kostbaren Kreationen gefährdet ist, von der Zeit und der Trägerin gleichermaßen in Mitleidenschaft gezogen zu werden, sobald sie genutzt oder angelegt wird.

Salt Necklace 09

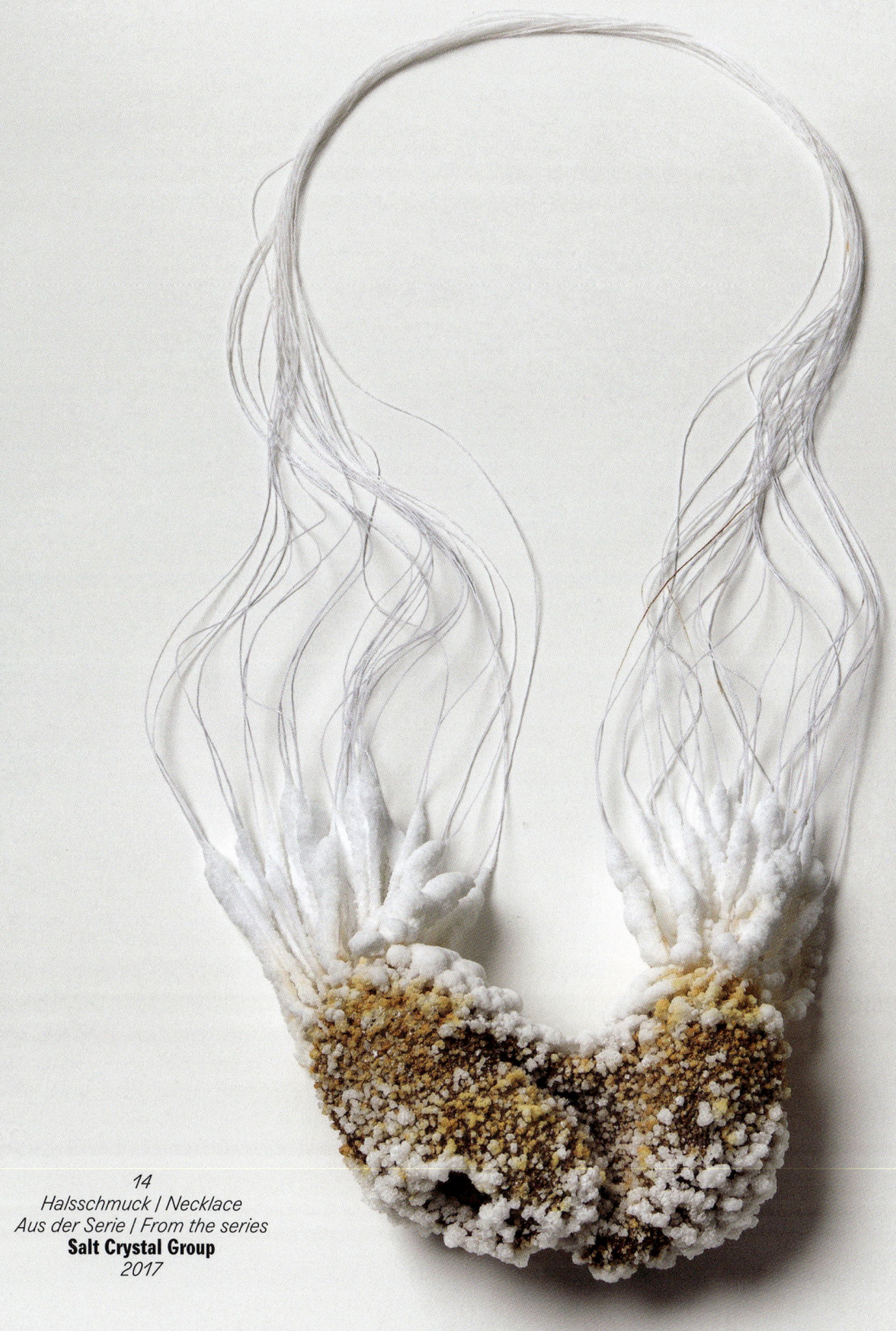

14
Halsschmuck / Necklace
Aus der Serie / From the series
Salt Crystal Group
2017

Naama Bergman

Salt Shakers

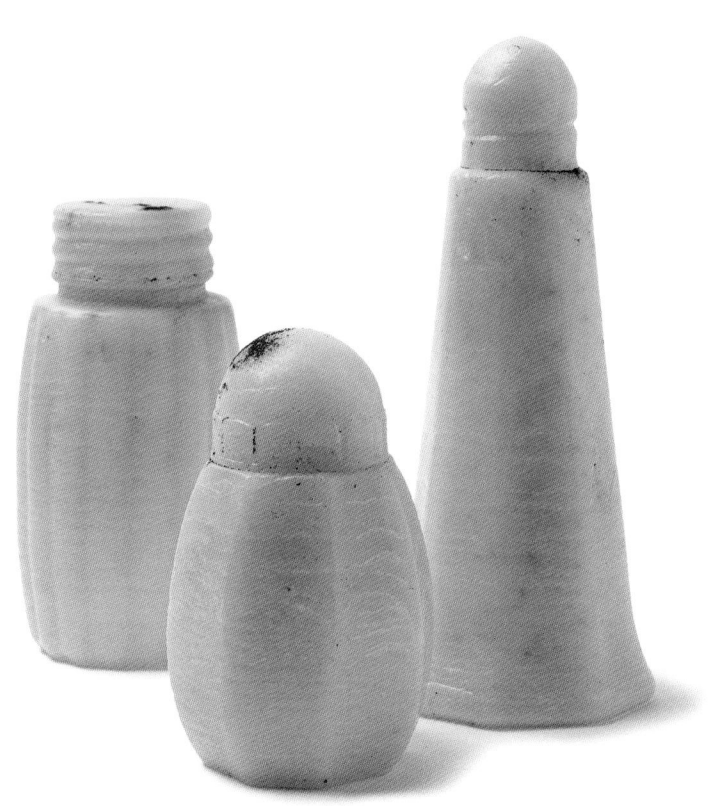

16
Objekte / Objects
2002

Naama Bergman

Salt Vessel

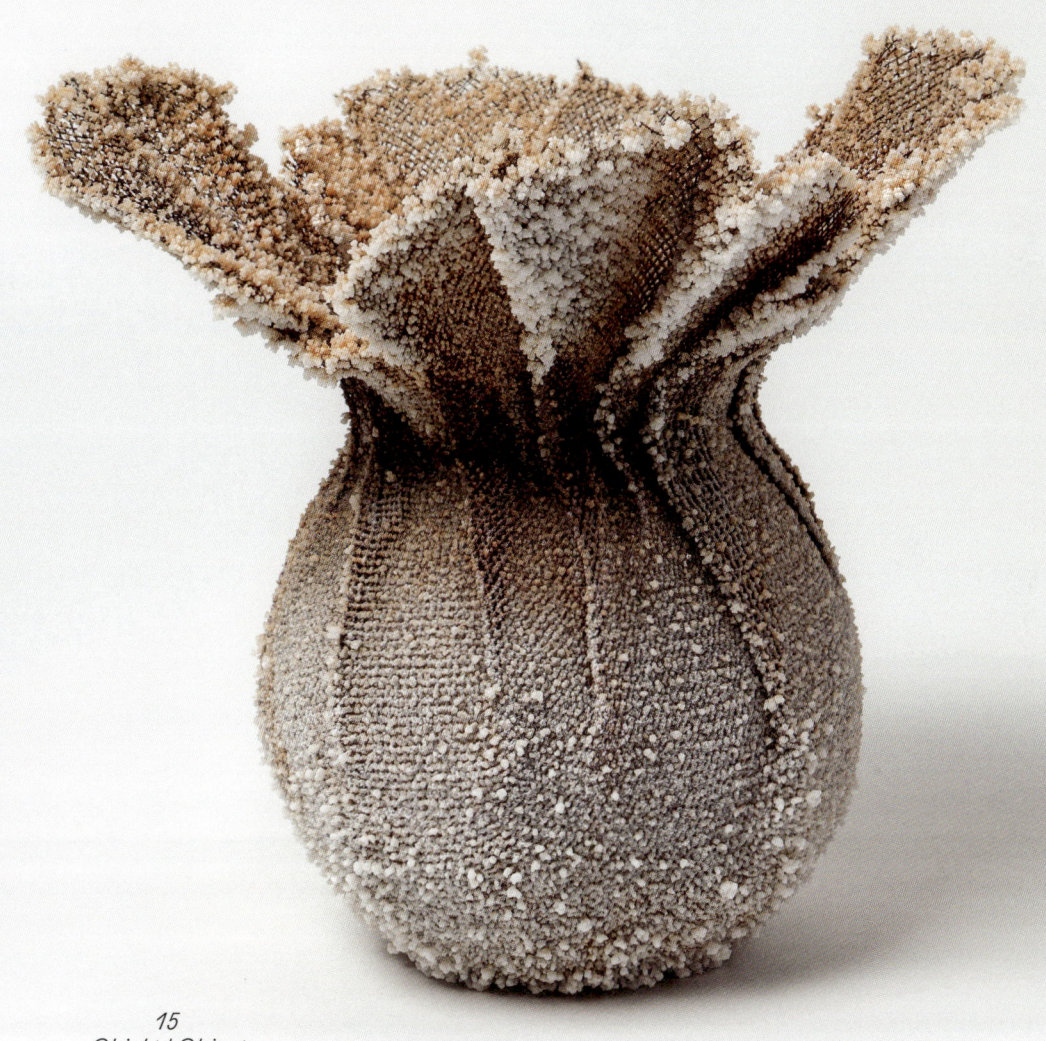

15
Objekt / Object
Aus der Serie / From the series
Salt Crystal Group
2016

Naama Bergman

The Châtelaine

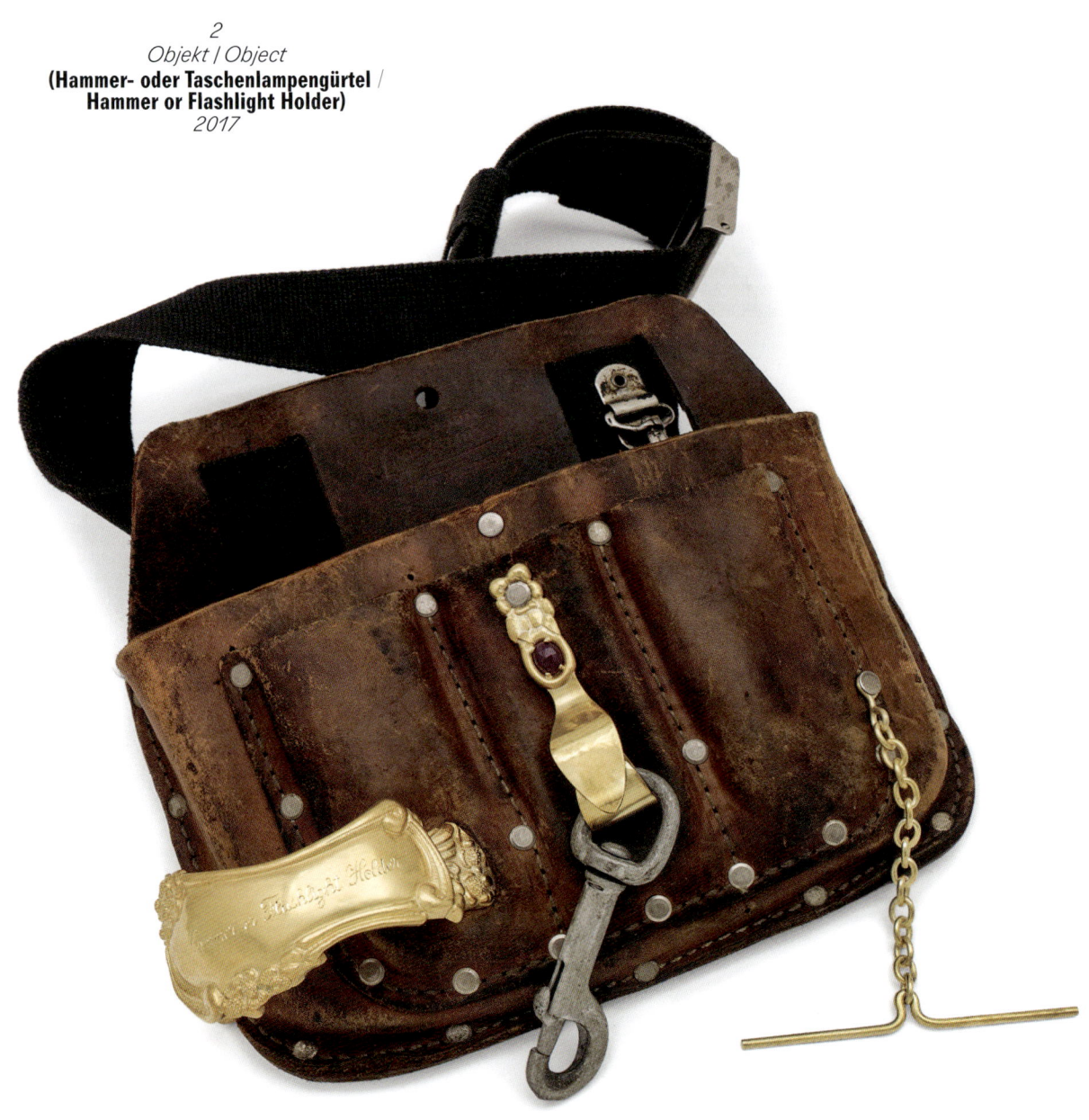

2
Objekt / Object
**(Hammer- oder Taschenlampengürtel /
Hammer or Flashlight Holder)**
2017

Tobias Alm

The Châtelaine

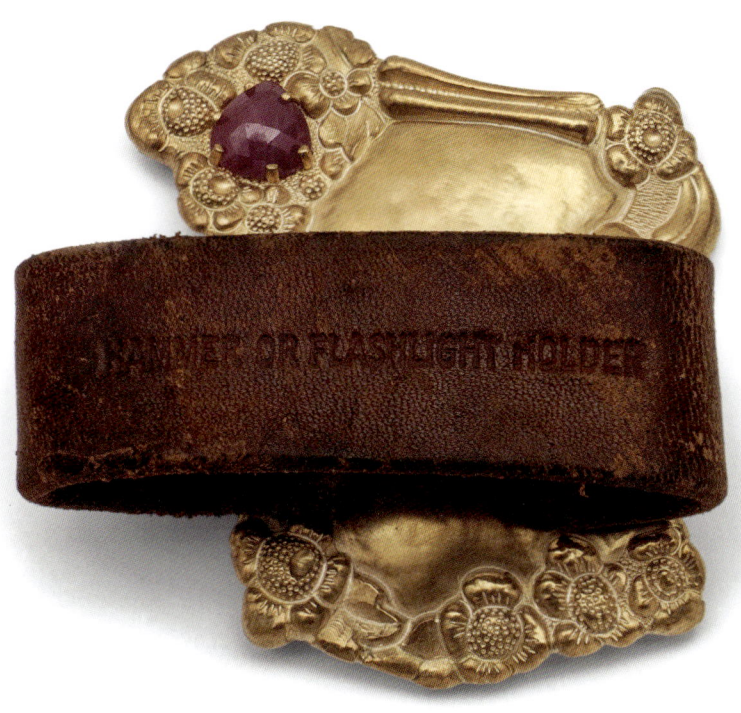

3
Objekt / Object
**(Hammer- oder Taschenlampengürtel /
Hammer or Flashlight Holder)**
2017

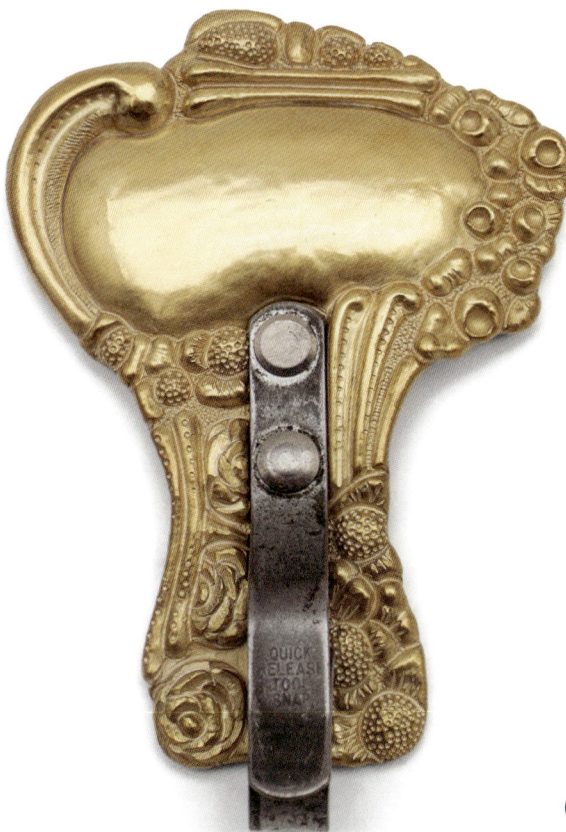

4
Objekt / Object
(Quick Release Tool Snap)
2017

Tobias Alm

An old-fashioned gray plastic telephone receiver from a junk shop—that is how my exploration of the subject »Transformation of mundane objects« began. I translate mundane objects into metal and represent them as jewelry. Through being thus transferred to another world, such simple utilitarian things are significantly upgraded; they become one-offs, something special. When worn, the objects look like awarded distinctions, make the wearer look their best, convey meaning, add a touch of witty irony.

Ein altmodischer grauer Telefonhörer aus Plastik vom Trödel – so begann meine Recherche zum Thema »Umwandlung der Alltagsobjekte«. Ich setze Alltagsgegenstände in Metall um und stelle sie als Schmuck dar. Die einfachen, nützlichen Dinge erfahren durch diesen Transfer in eine andere Welt eine signifikante Aufwertung, sie werden zum Unikat, etwas Besonderem. Getragen erscheinen die Objekte wie eine Auszeichnung, bringen die Erscheinung zur Geltung, vermitteln Bedeutung, setzen einen ironisch-witzigen Akzent.

Telefonhörer

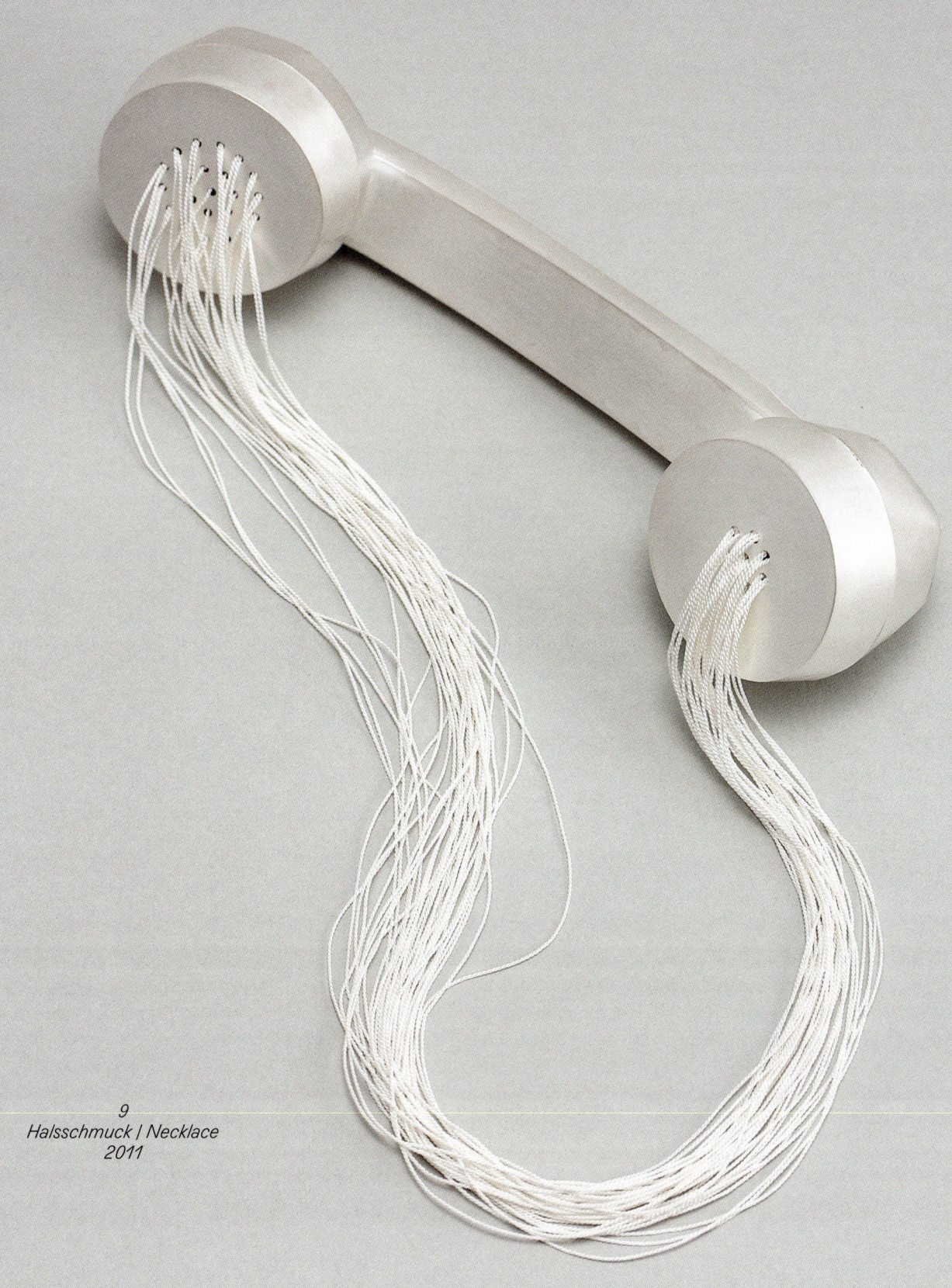

9
Halsschmuck | Necklace
2011

Sawa Aso

Ohrschützer

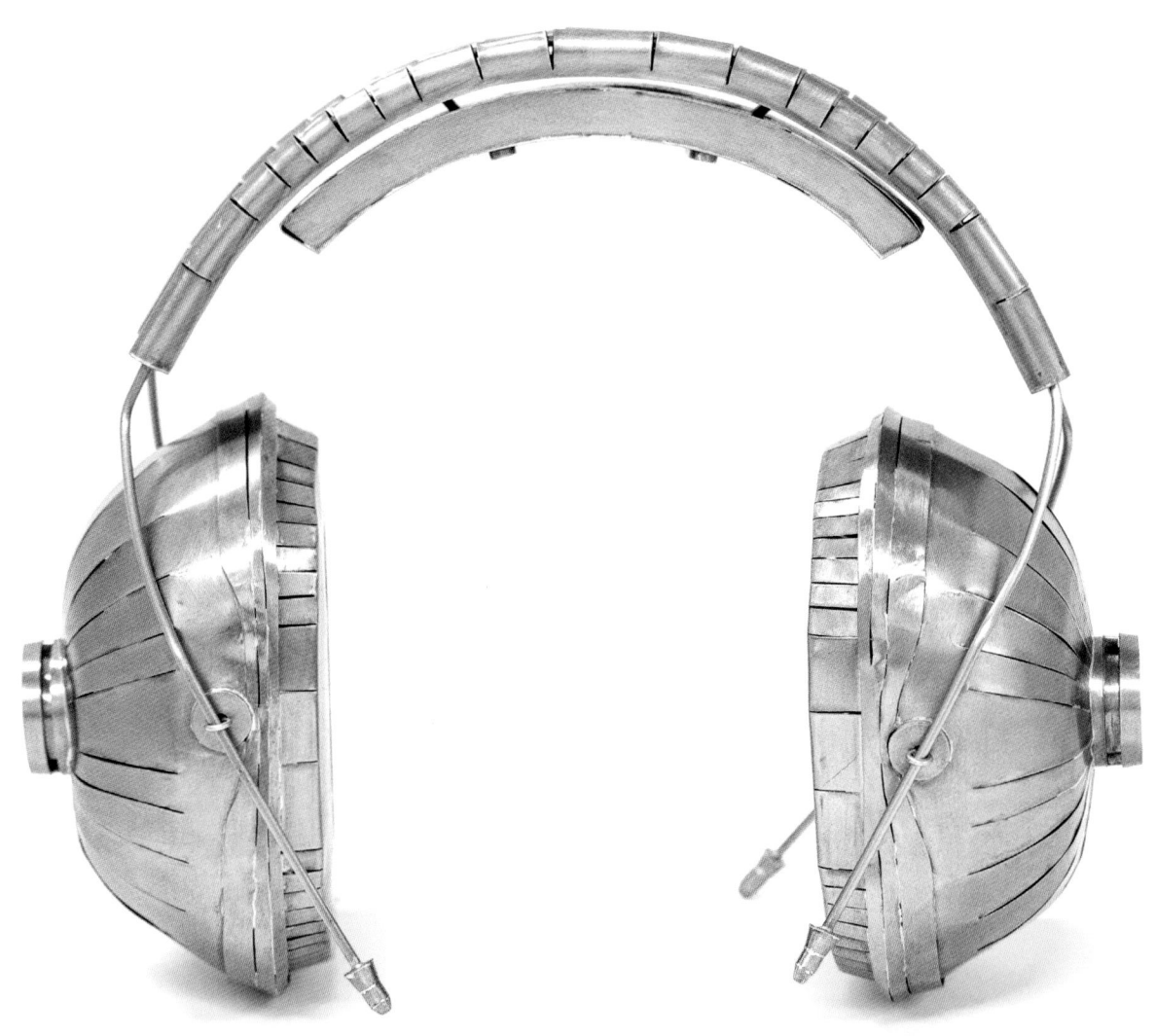

8
Kopfschmuck | Headdress
2012

Sawa Aso

Alltagslöcher 1

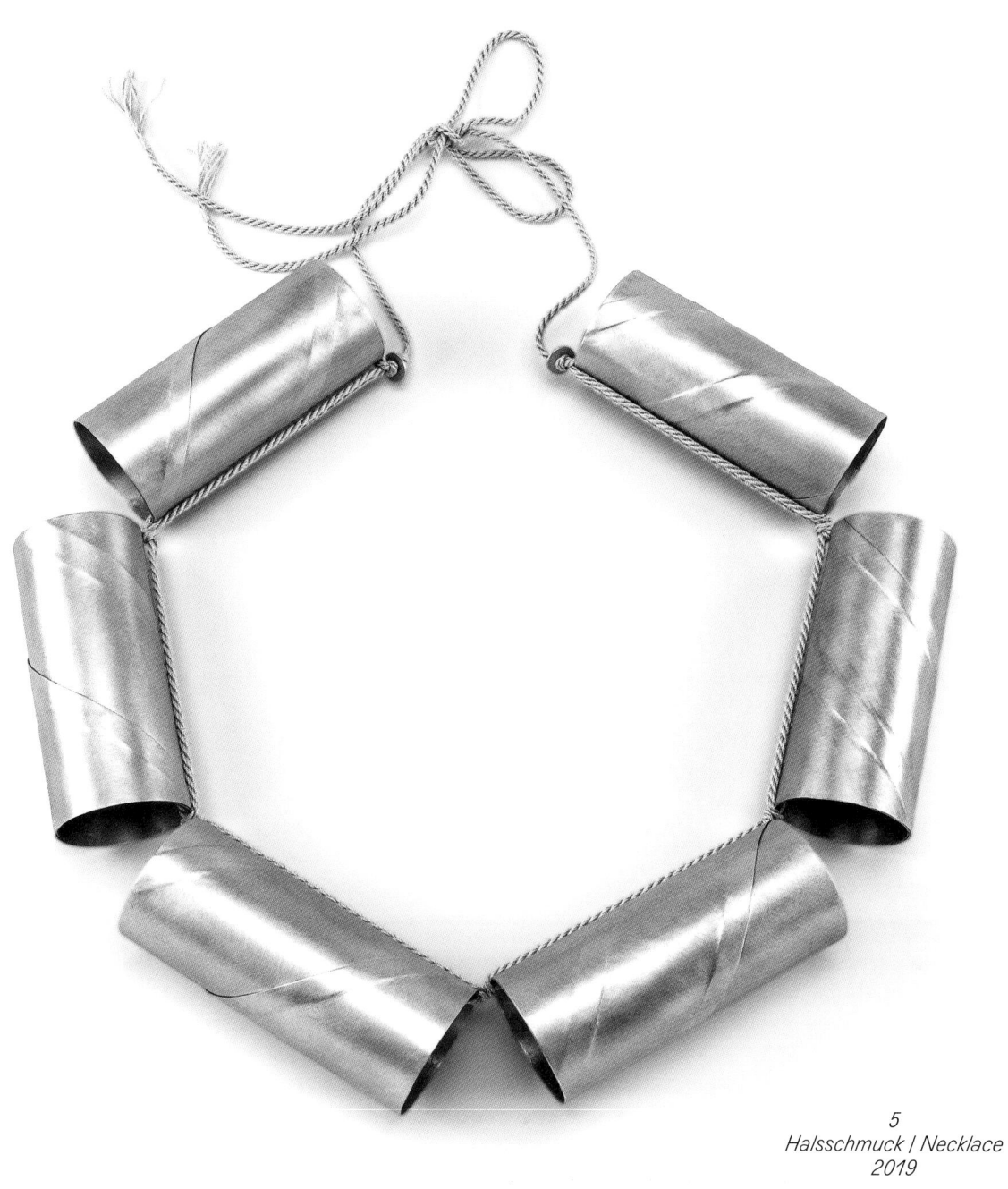

5
Halsschmuck | Necklace
2019

I studied to be a silversmith. I forgot my skills for a long time, until I rediscovered the method of working metal while working on a shelter theme. We need protection from heat, from cold, from dirt, from shocks, from eyes. We need protection when working in the garden, thinning the forest, harvesting crops, working on a building site, cooking in the kitchen, fighting, being in the sun or in the rain, meeting others. Hammered and folded metalwork can be seen as part of body clothing. The mood of the works mixes the historical and the contemporary.

Ich habe Silberschmieden studiert. Über lange Zeit vergaß ich, was ich konnte, bis ich bei einer Arbeit zum Thema Schutz die Metallbearbeitung wiederentdeckte. Wir brauchen Schutz vor Hitze, vor Kälte, vor Schmutz, vor Schocks, vor Blicken. Wir brauchen Schutz, wenn wir Gartenarbeit machen, den Wald lichten, Feldfrüchte ernten, auf dem Bau arbeiten, am Herd stehen und kochen, kämpfen, uns in der Sonne oder im Regen aufhalten, andere Menschen treffen. Gehämmerte und gefaltete Metallarbeiten sind als Teil der Körperbekleidung zu verstehen. Die Stimmung der Arbeiten vermengt das Historische mit der Gegenwart.

Eija Mustonen

Apron, Mittens and Mask

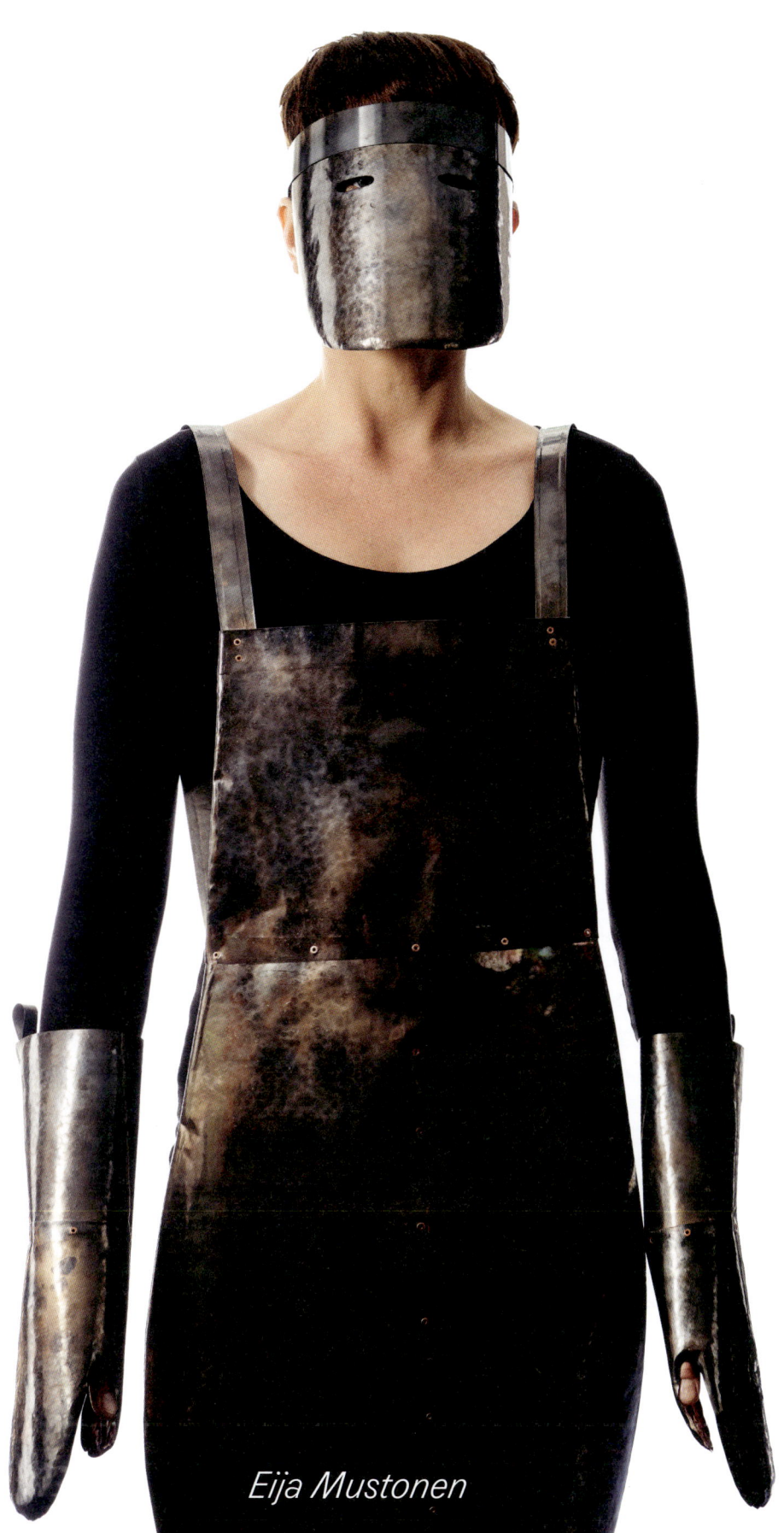

79
Ensemble
2022

Eija Mustonen

Ohne Titel / Untitled

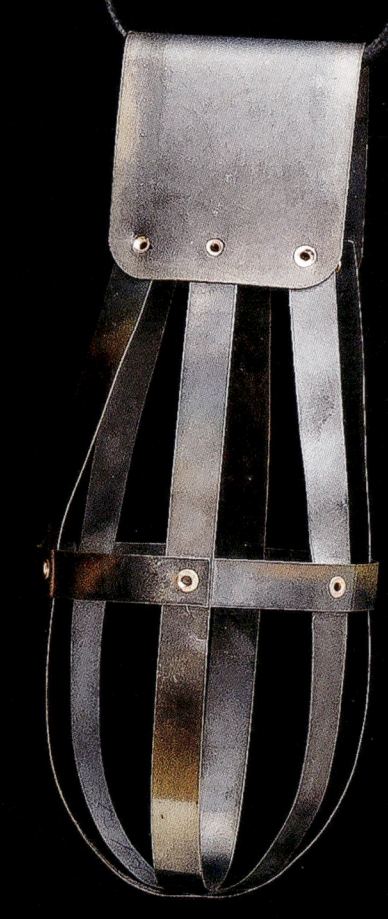

83
Halsschmuck | Necklace
2016

Eija Mustonen

Sleeves and Skirt

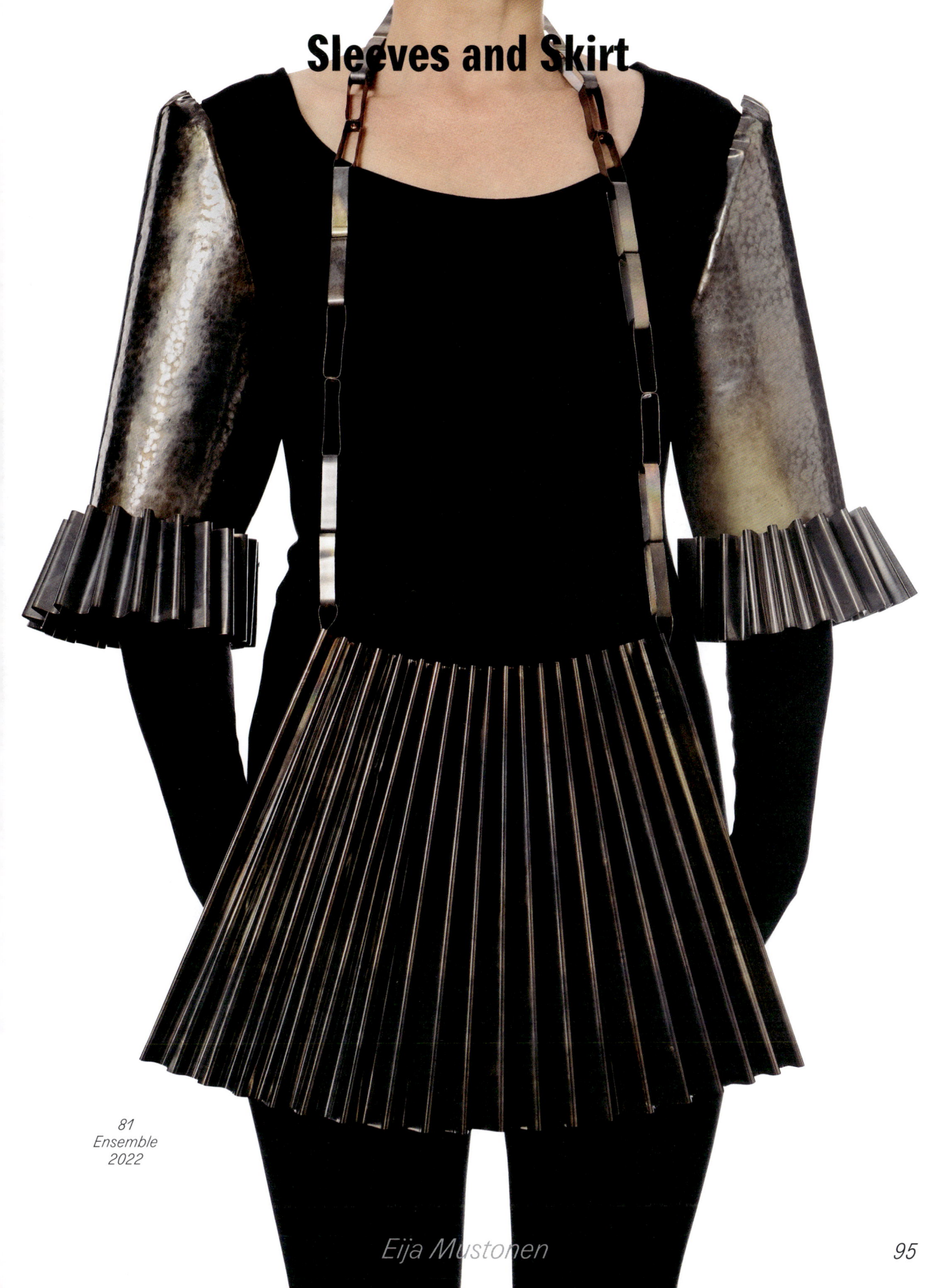

81
Ensemble
2022

Off Balance

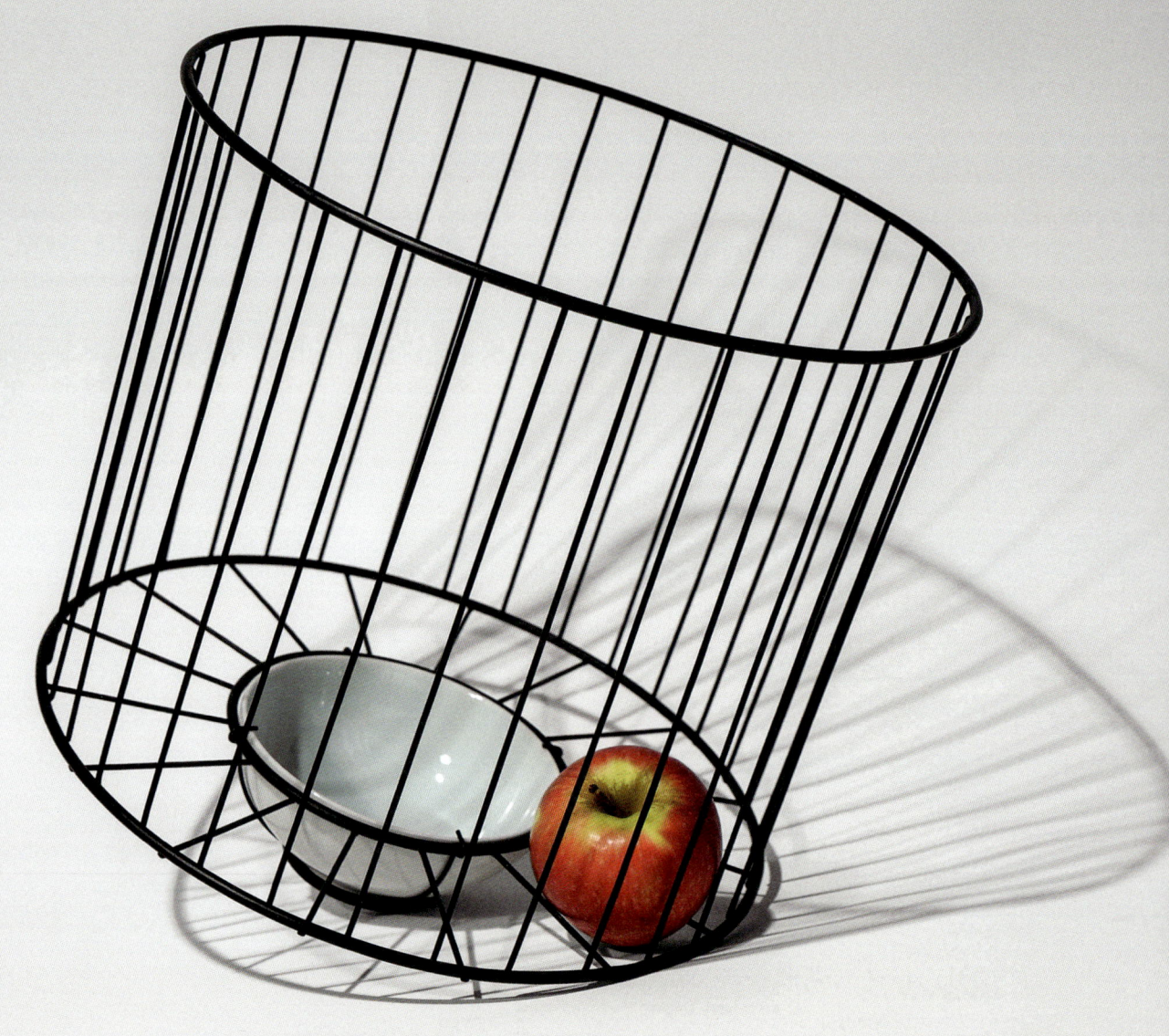

106
Objekt / Object
2010

Hans Stofer

Creation

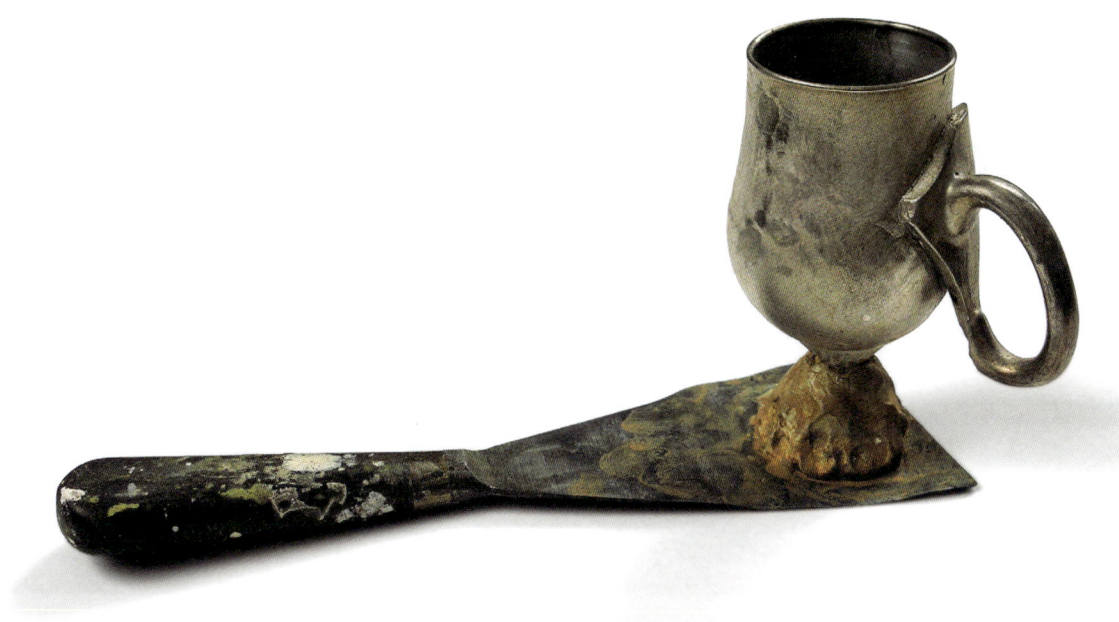

105
Objekt / Object
2010

Hans Stofer

String Theory – ST2

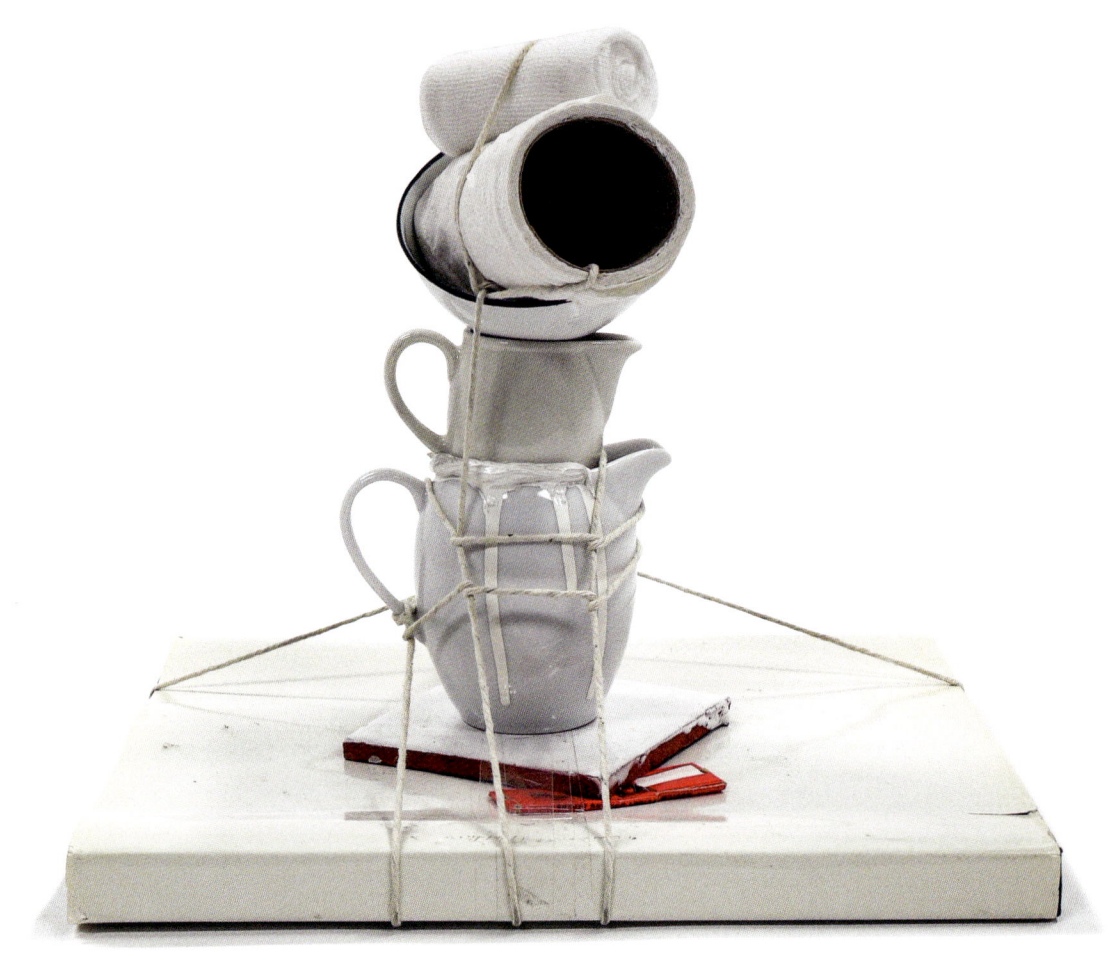

104
Objekt | Object
2014

Presse

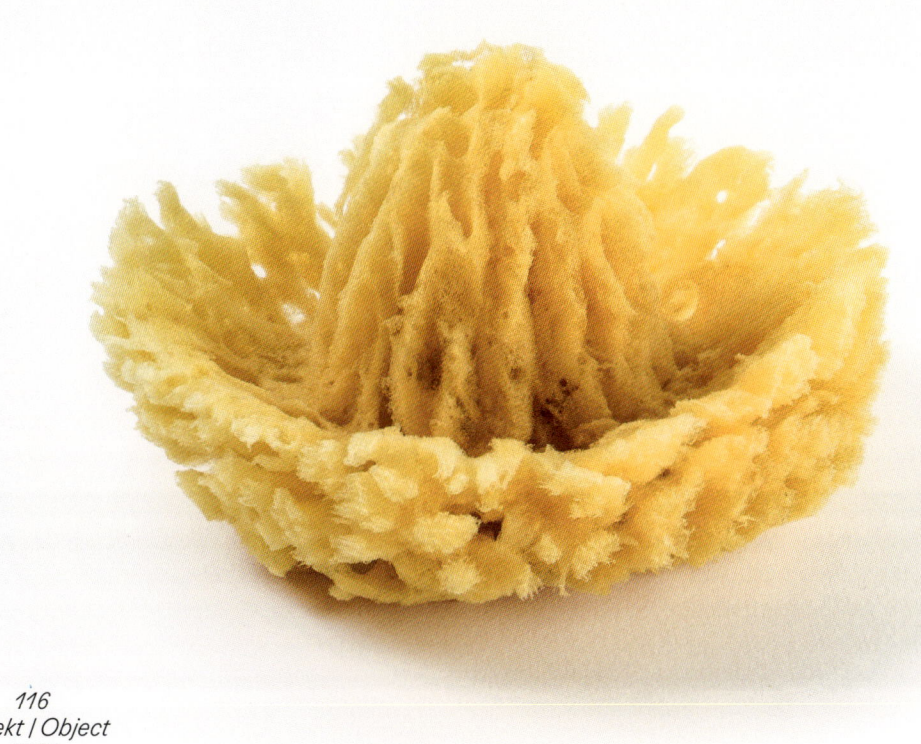

116
Objekt | Object
2021

Stella Wanisch

Nudelholz / Rolling pin

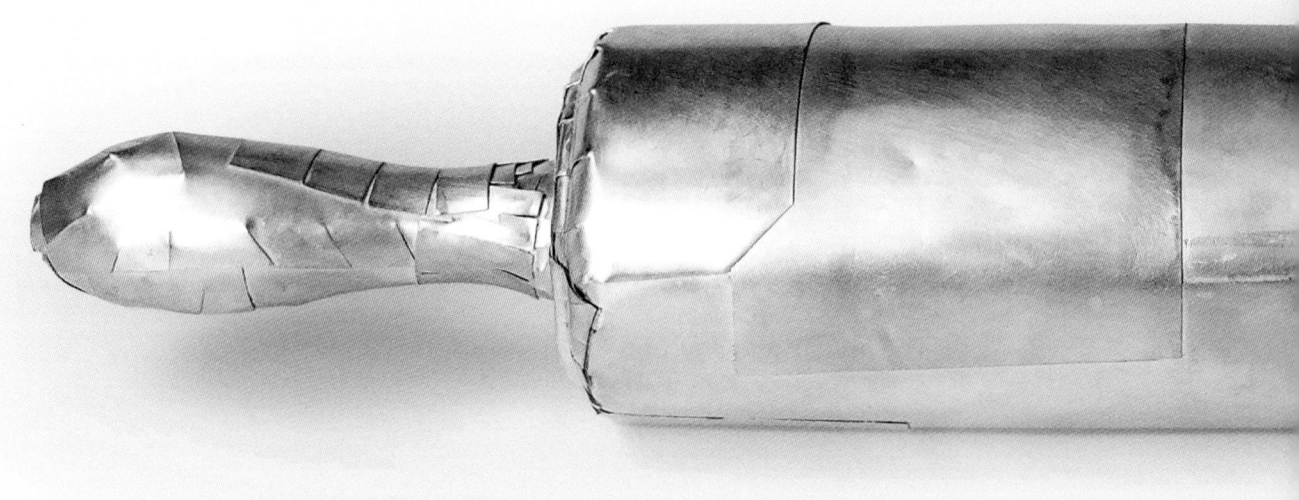

Karen Pontoppidan

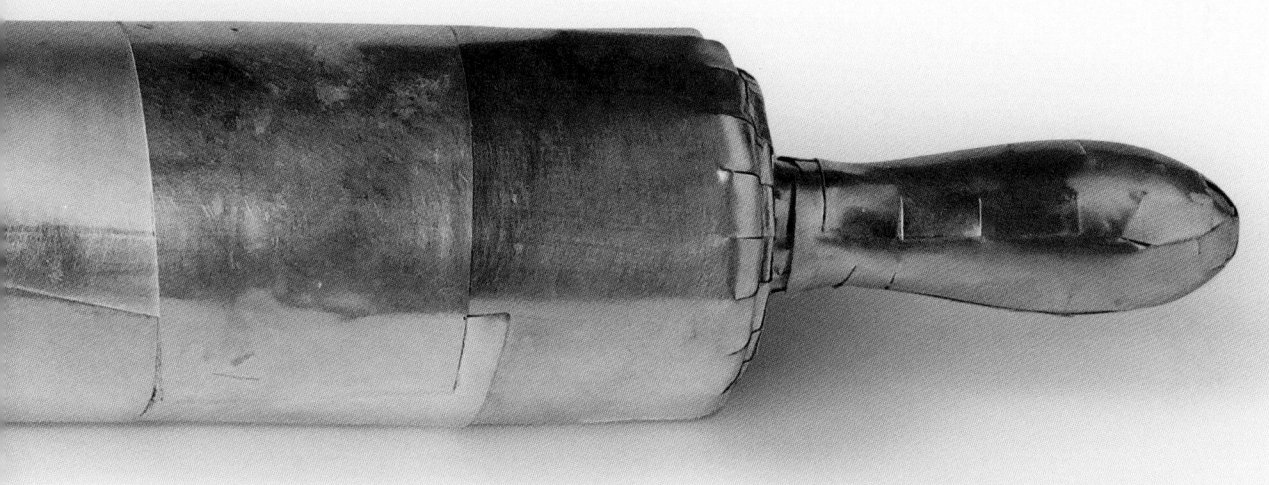

91
Objekt | Object
Aus der Reihe | From the series
KNELL II
2019

Objects are witnesses to cultural developments; they reflect the values prevailing in a given society and can, therefore, attest to both historical and contemporary trends. That is why the everyday objects we surround ourselves with disclose so much about us. They make sociopolitical statements about the social structures in which we live.

Objekte sind Zeugen kultureller Entwicklungen, sie spiegeln die vorherrschenden Wertevorstellungen der jeweiligen Gesellschaften wider und können somit von historischen als auch zeitgenössischen Tendenzen zeugen. Daher geben die alltäglichen Dinge, mit denen wir uns umgeben, viel preis über uns. Sie machen soziopolitische Aussagen über die Gesellschaftsstrukturen, in denen wir leben.

Bügeleisen / Flat iron

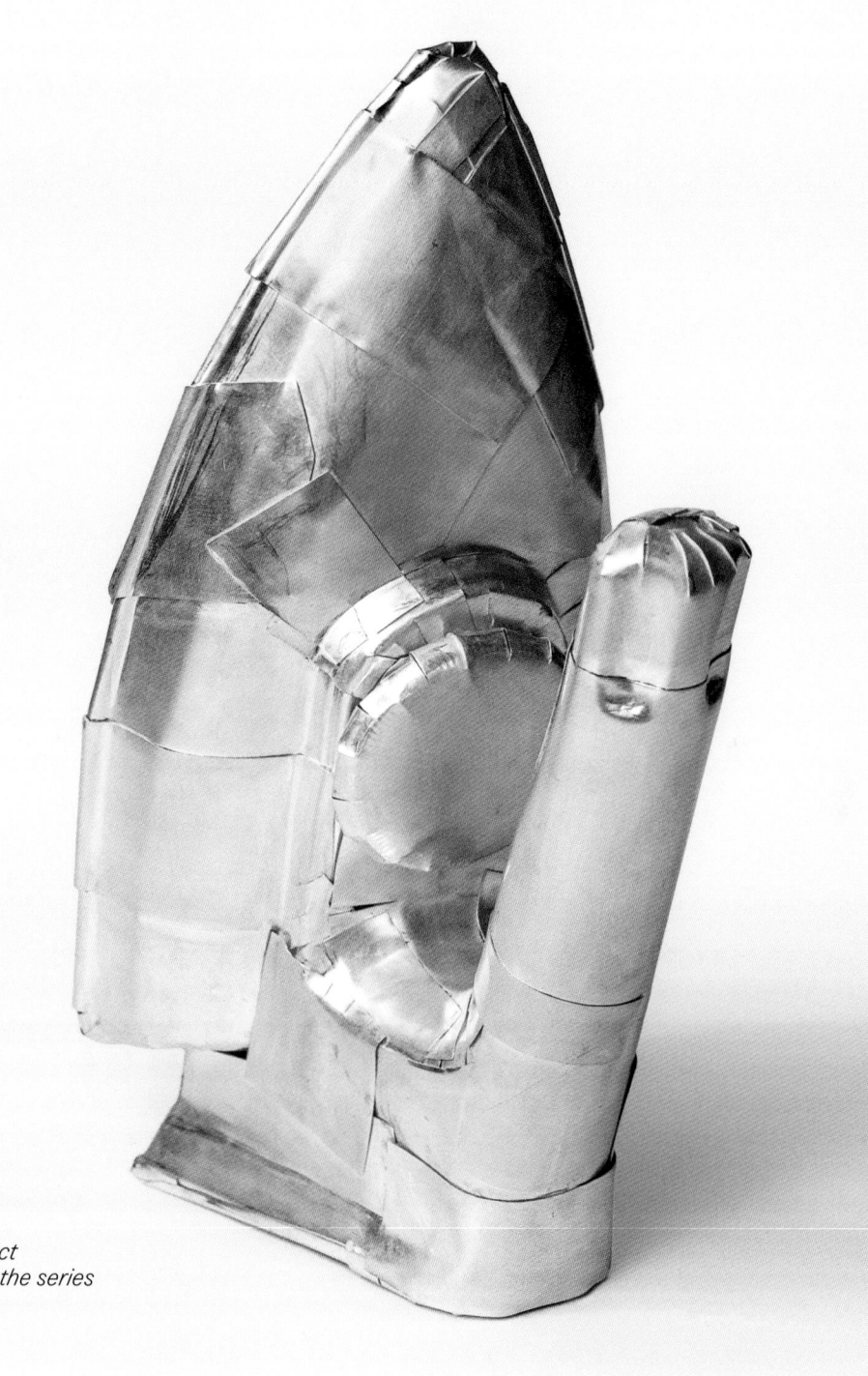

95
Objekt / Object
Aus der Reihe / From the series
KNELL II
2017

Karen Pontoppidan

KNELL – The Gender Bell#2

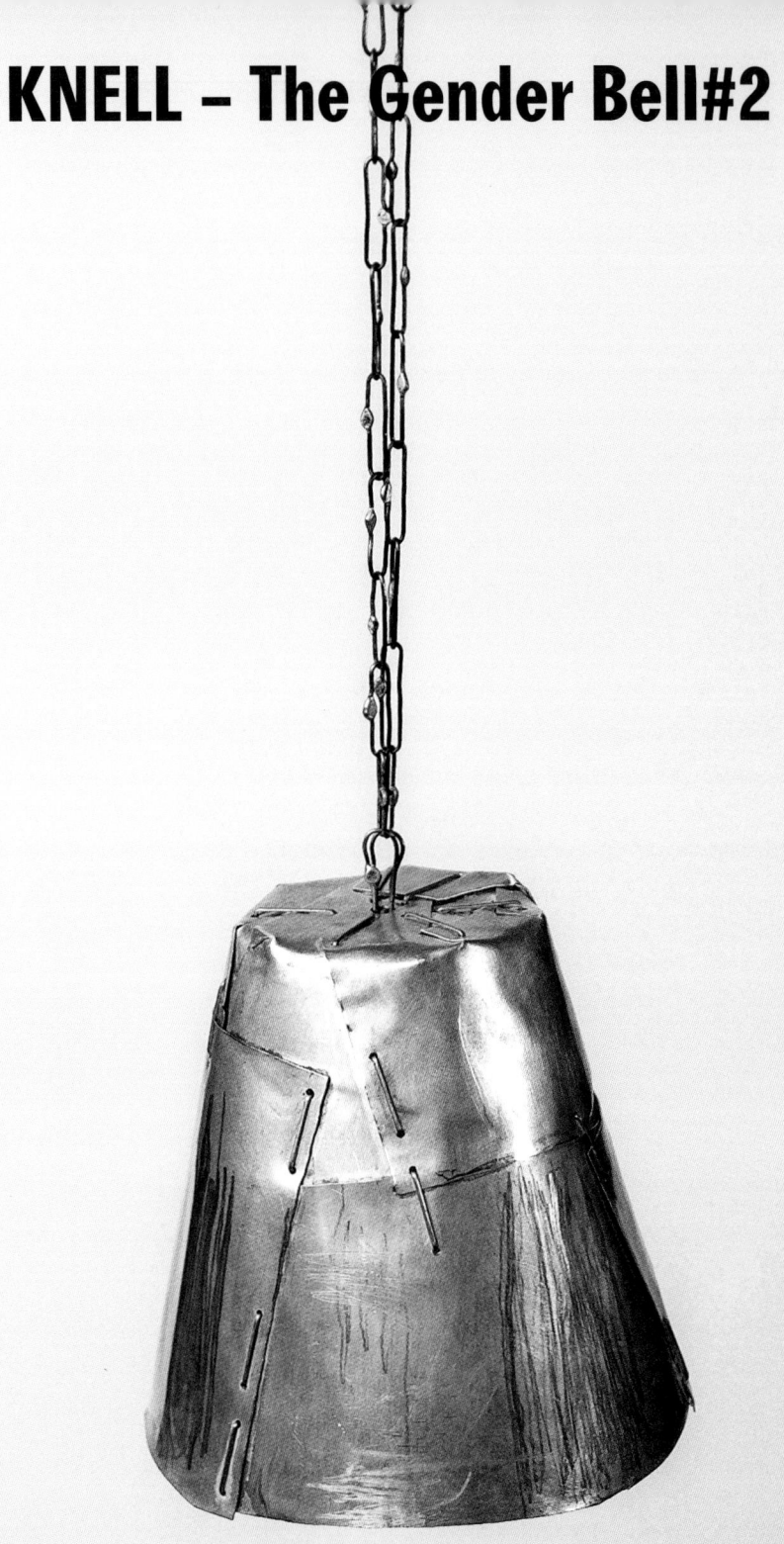

98
Halsschmuck | Necklace
Aus der Reihe | From the series
KNELL – The Gender Bell
2016

Karen Pontoppidan

innen#2

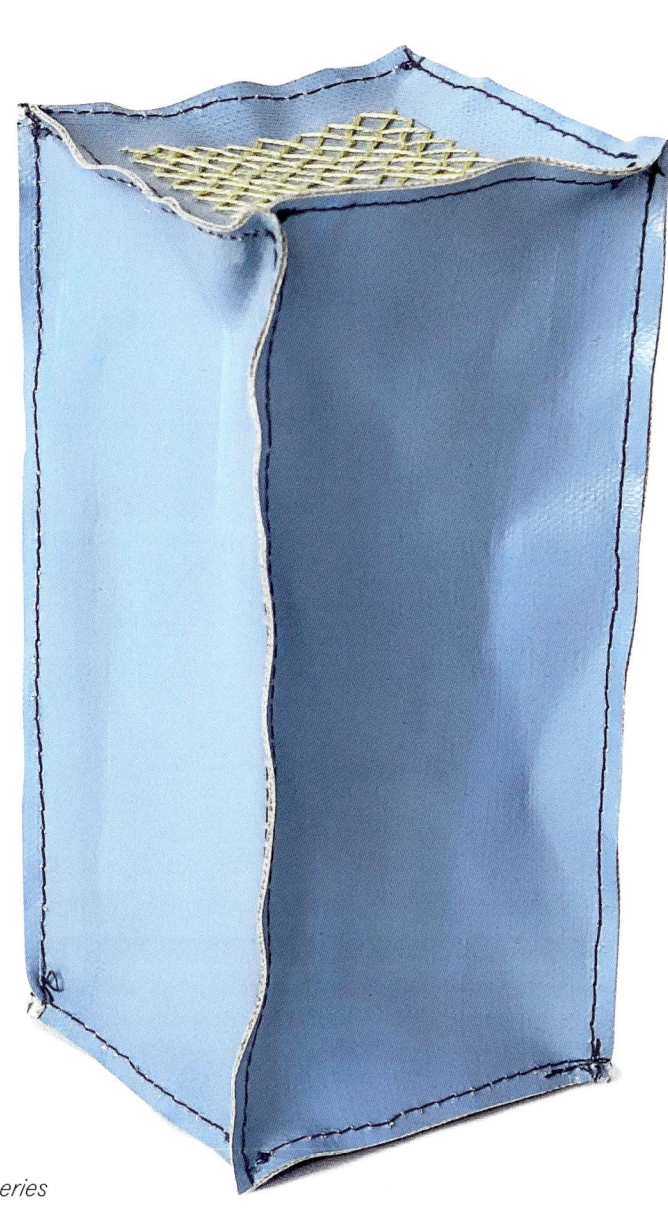

89
Brosche | Brooch
Aus der Reihe | From the series
innen
2023

Karen Pontoppidan

Ich bin keine Vase

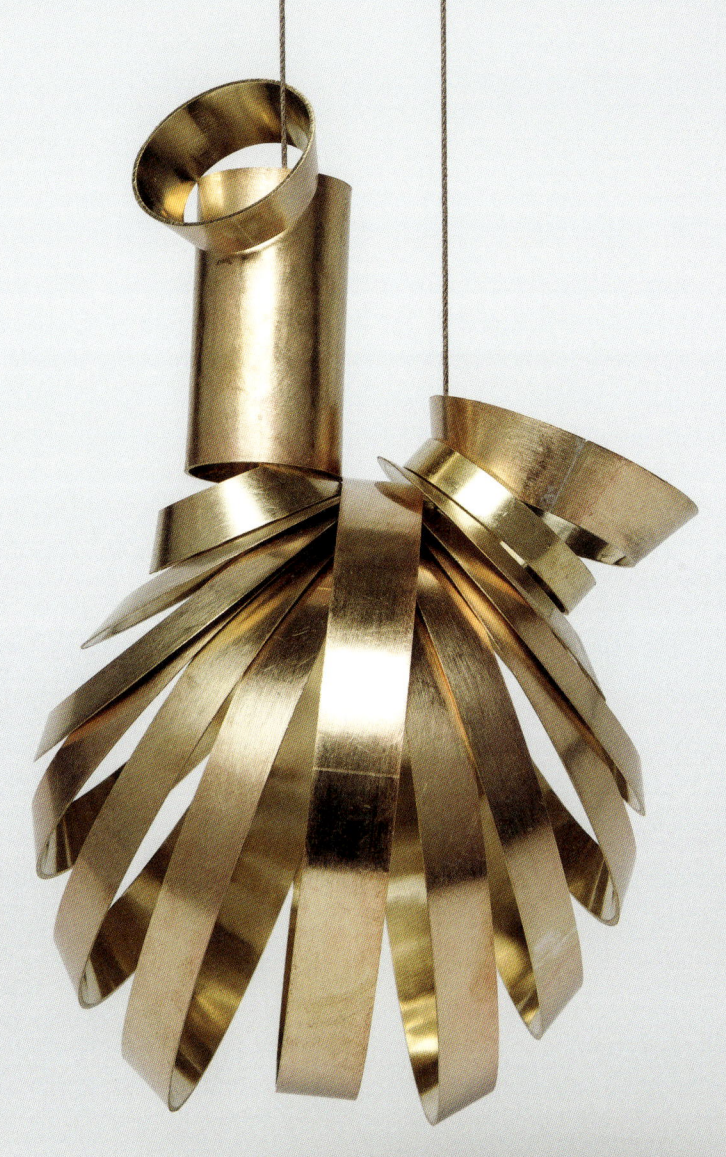

119
Halsschmuck | Necklace
2016

Jing Yang

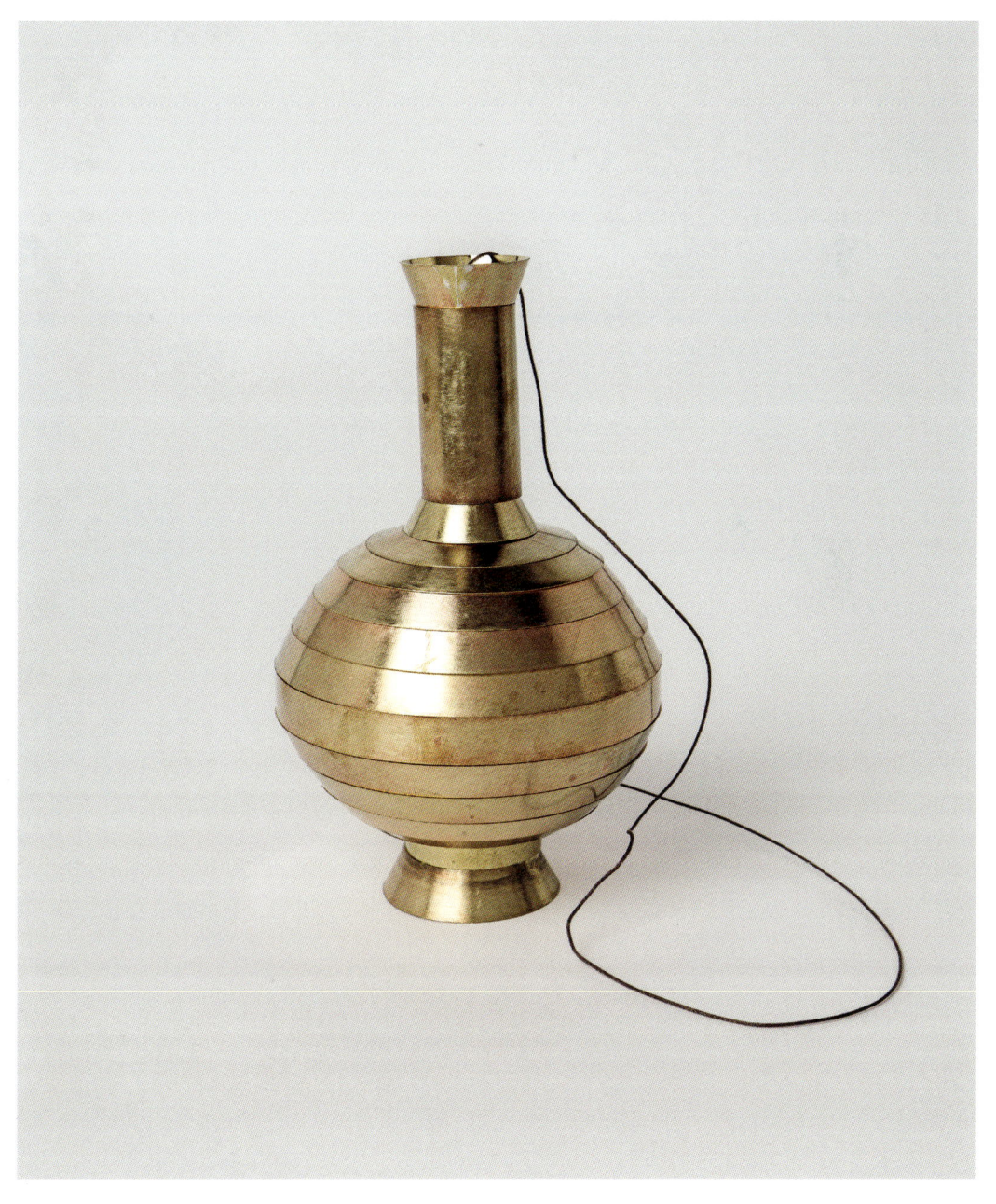

Ich bin keine Vase

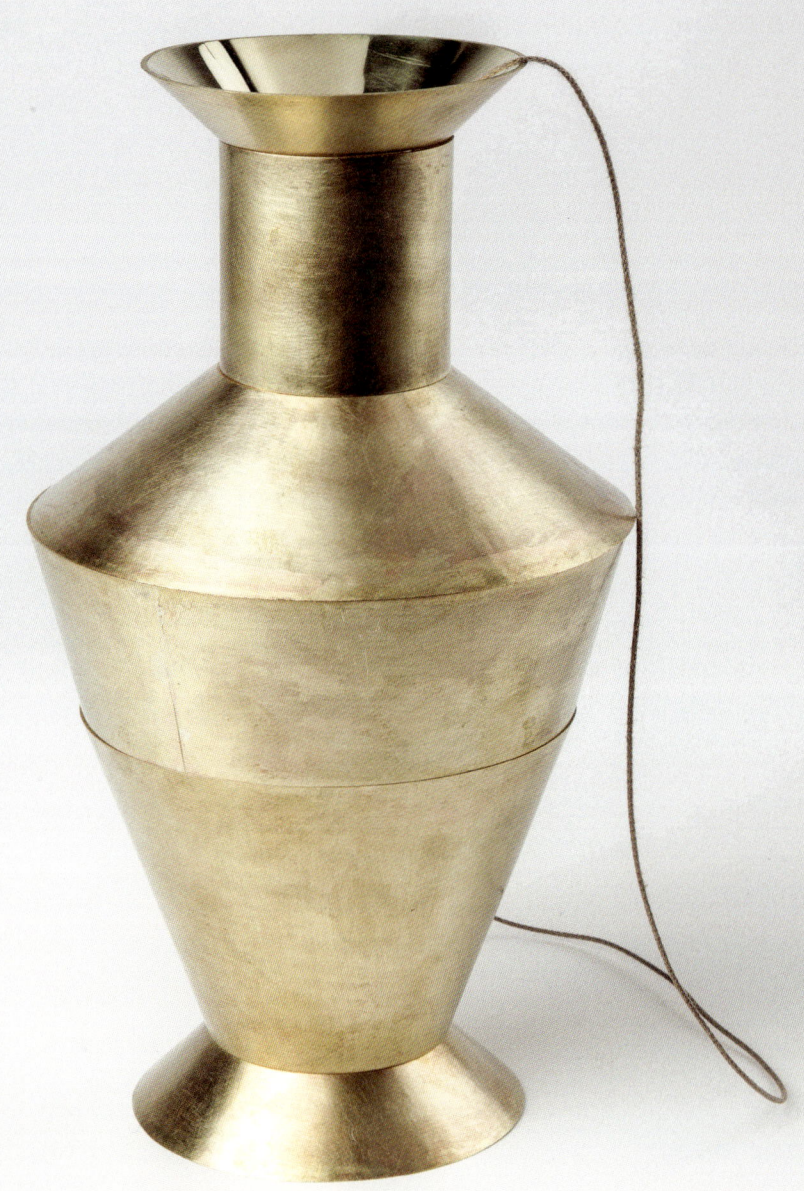

118
Halsschmuck | Necklace
2016

Jing Yang

Hommage to Hannah Höch

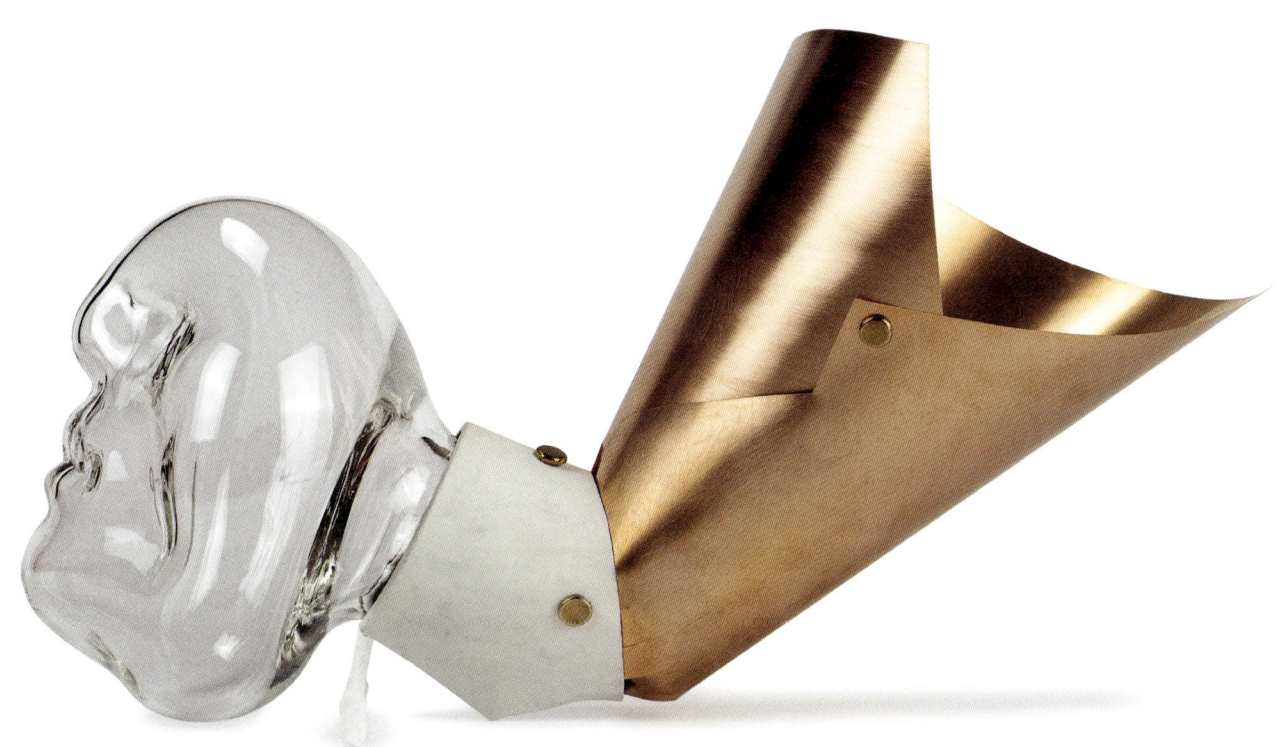

108
Objekt | Object
2023

Vivi Touloumidi

Expeditions

Nuances run through expanses of sky to find
bewildering depths \
and then in the sea-distance—reeling \
Yttrium iron garnet circulates in the redness of veins \
A person, light-footed, lustful in wine,
enclosed in a flower calyx, \
from milky white to French gray is only a pearl's throw \
Holy Water breaks through form, dissolves it \
Honey yellow confers weight, in the depths of space, \
overwhelming the power of Transubstantiation— \
dragged into the tale of a beautiful world

Expeditionen

*Nuancen durchlaufen die Weite des Himmels,
um verwirrende Tiefen zu finden /
und dann in der Ferne des Meeres – taumelnd /
Eisengranat zirkuliert im Rot der Vene /
Der Mensch leichtfüßig, voll Lust im Wein,
eingeschlossen im Blütenkelch, /
vom Milchweiß zum Französischgrau ist es nur
ein Perlensprung /
Das Weihwasser durchbricht die Form, löst sie auf /
Das Honiggelb schenkt Gewichtigkeit,
in der Tiefe des Weltenraumes, /
überwältigend die Kraft der Transsubstantiation – /
hineingezogen in die Erzählung von der schönen Welt /*

Astrid Becksteiner-Rasche

Kelch

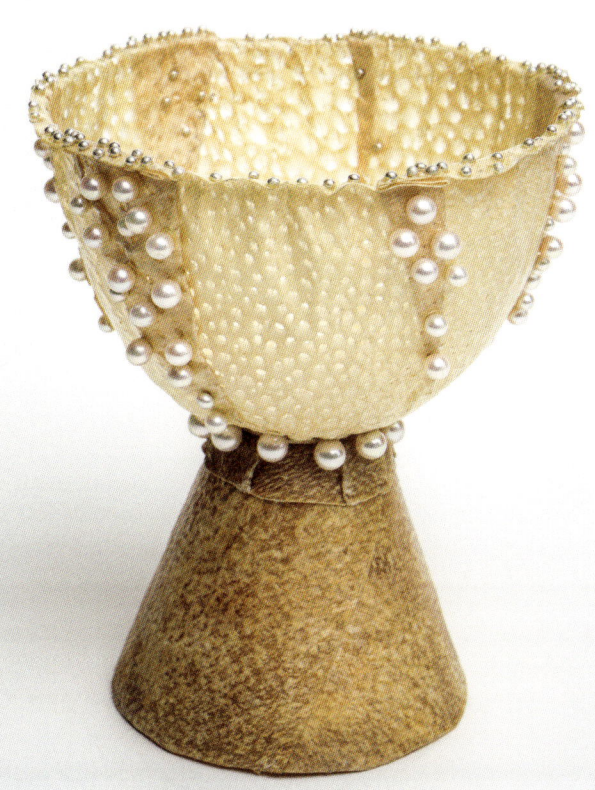

12
Objekt / Object
2023

Astrid Becksteiner-Rasche

Für die kleine Messe

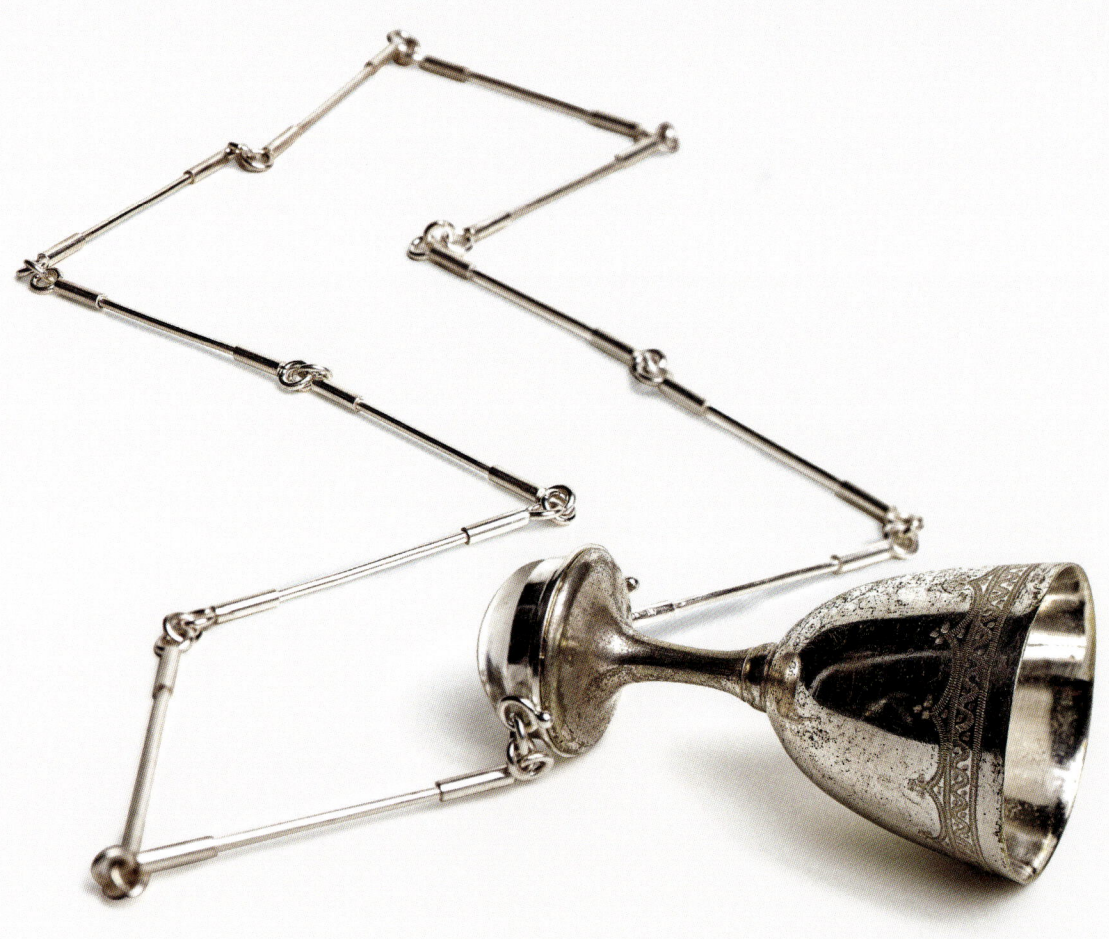

11
Halsschmuck | Necklace
2023

About Ornament II

109
Halsschmuck | Necklace
2020

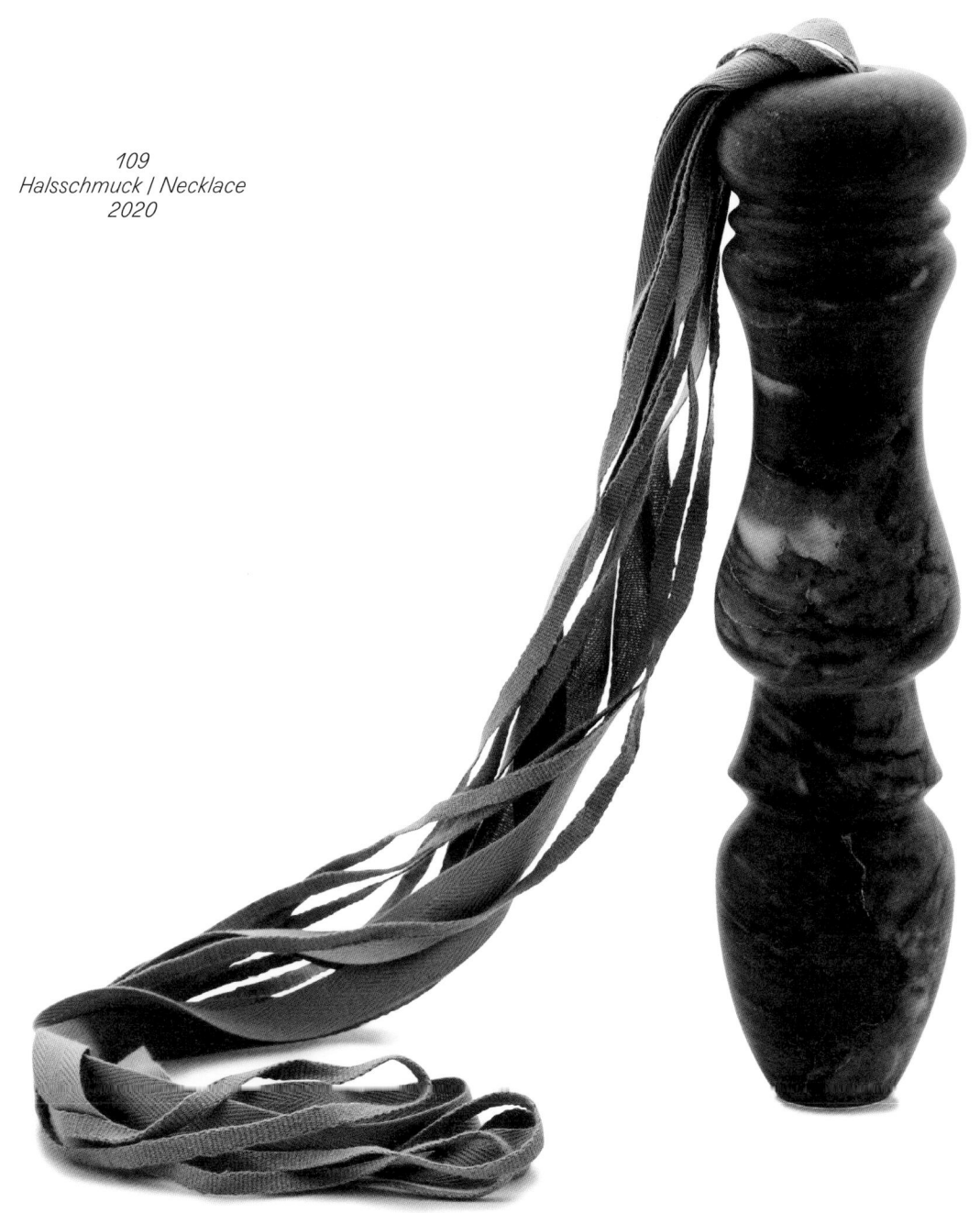

Tarja Tuupanen

Baking Pin

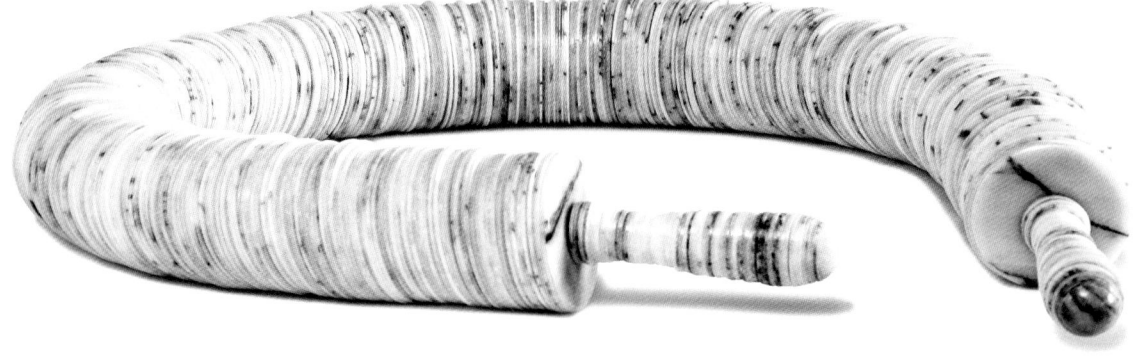

111
Objekt | Object
2017

Table

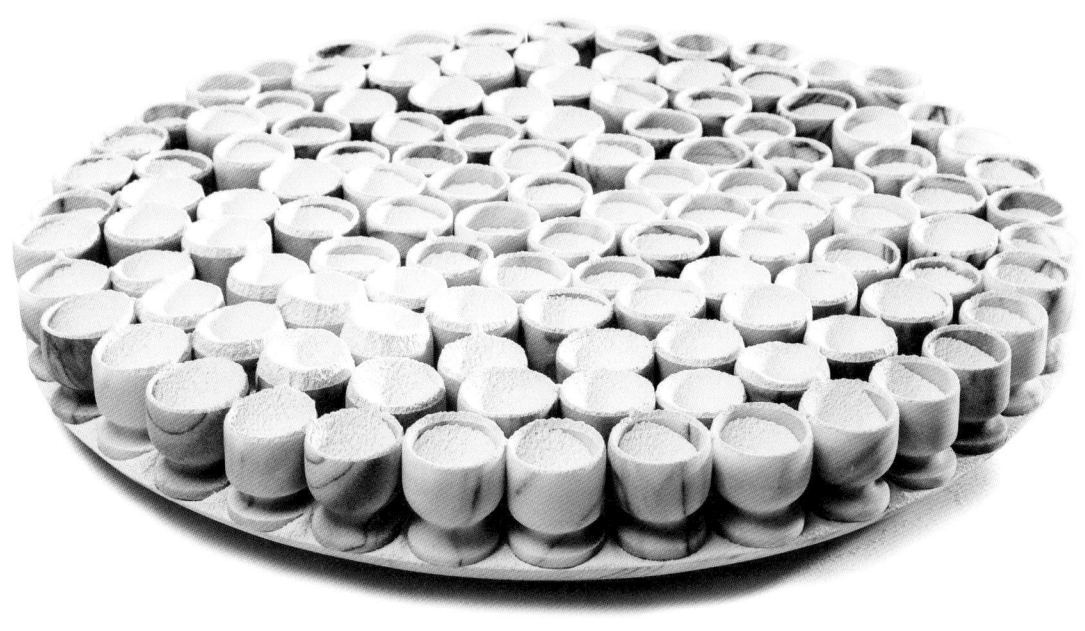

112
Objekt | Object
2017

Tarja Tuupanen

Lavish cakes, milk puddings, and molded and set jellies at the table. Plenty, excess, greed, and wonderful vulgarity. English gardens were flipped by royalty and the landed gentry inspired by the goings-on over on the Continent. The Baroque is quite literally a massive punch in the face, an overload of self-confidence, no apologies, no excuses. Can you have a Baroque thought? Irregular, overloaded, disruptive. The result would be a curated hoarding of meaningful elements, an ornate display of personality. This assemblage turning into a full frontal assault of the senses, a mash-up of stuff that no one really wants or uses anymore fits perfectly in the world of Misterclarke.

Üppige Torten, Milchspeisen, Formen mit fest gewordenem Wackelpudding auf dem Tisch. Überfluss, Exzess, Gefräßigkeit und wunderbare Ungeschliffenheit. Englische Gärten wurden vom Königshaus umgekrempelt und die Mitglieder des Landadels von den Vorgängen drüben auf dem Kontinent inspiriert. Der Barockstil ist buchstäblich ein schwerer Schlag ins Gesicht, ein überladenes Selbstbewusstsein, keine Ausrede, keine Entschuldigung. Kann man einen barocken Gedanken haben? Unregelmäßig, überfrachtet, zerstörerisch? Das Resultat wäre ein kuratiertes Horten aussagekräftiger Einzelteile, eine reich verzierte Zurschaustellung von Persönlichkeit. Diese Ansammlung, die zu einem Frontalangriff auf die Sinne wird, einem Durcheinander von Zeug, das niemand mehr haben oder benutzen möchte, passt perfekt in die Welt von Misterclarke.

STASH

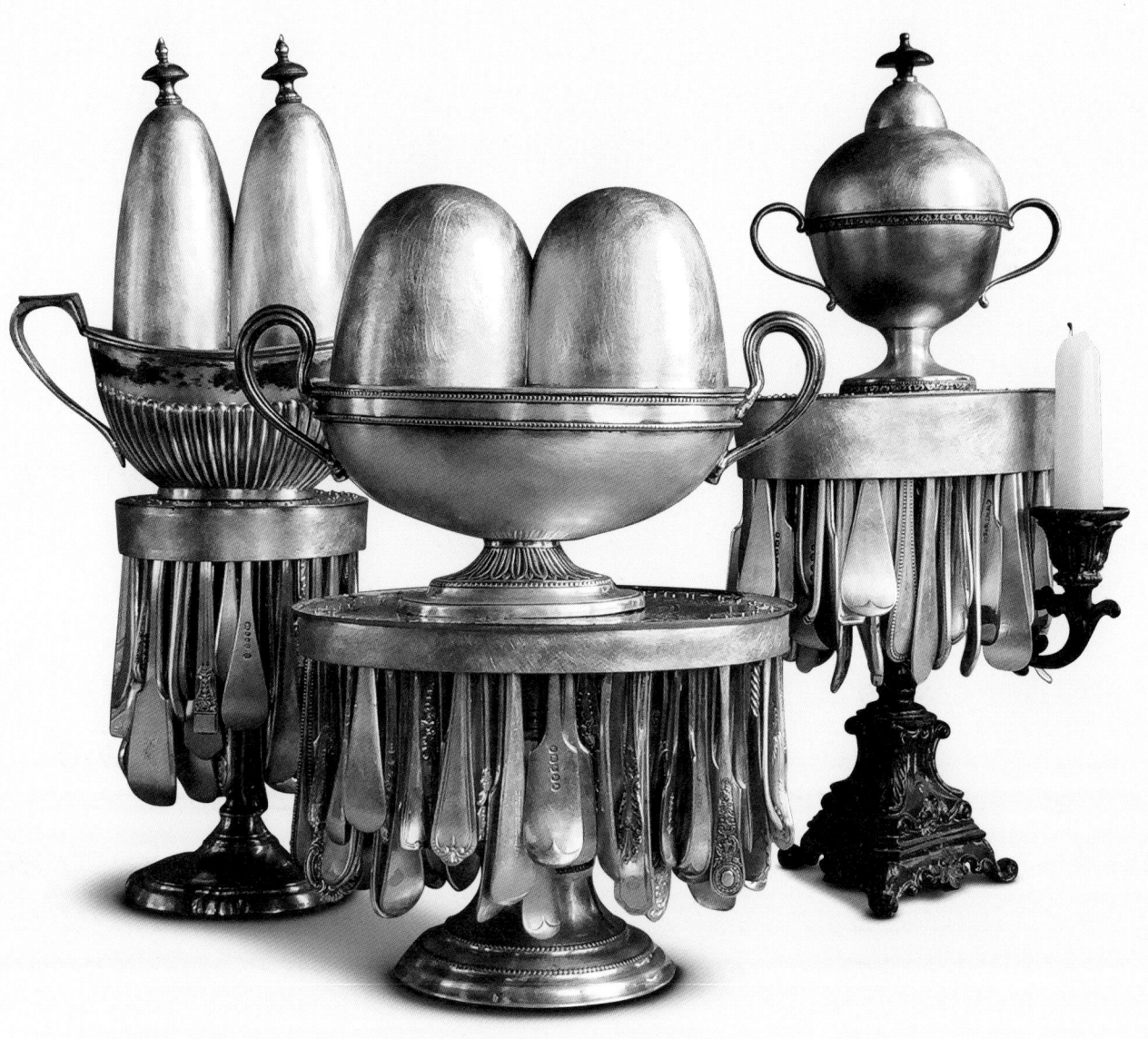

30
Objekte / Objects
2020

David Clarke

See no Evil

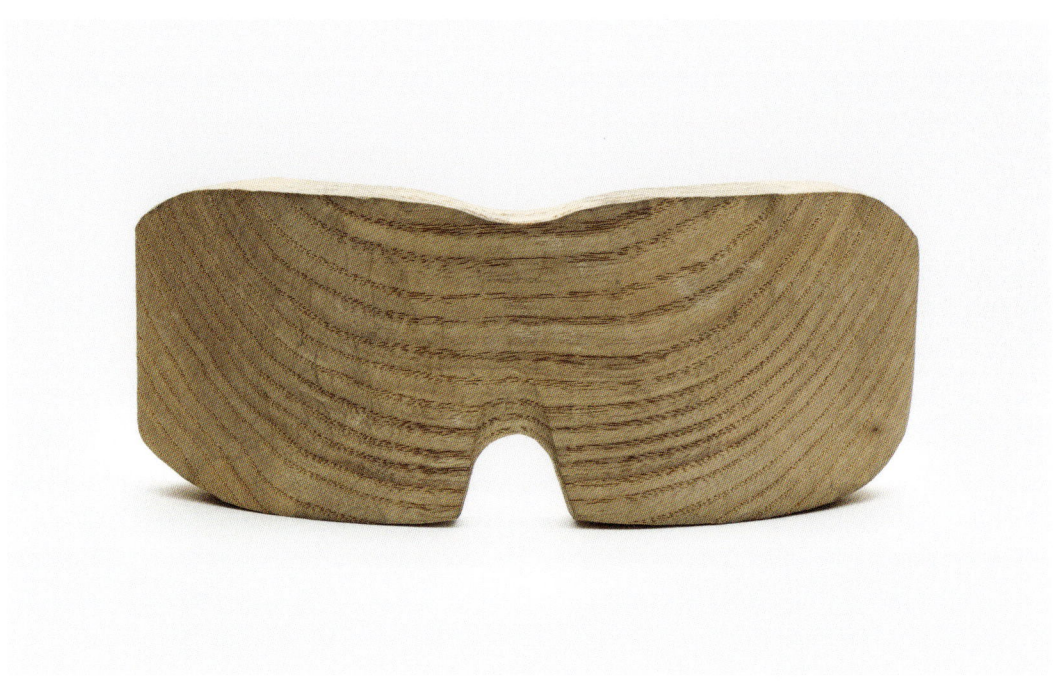

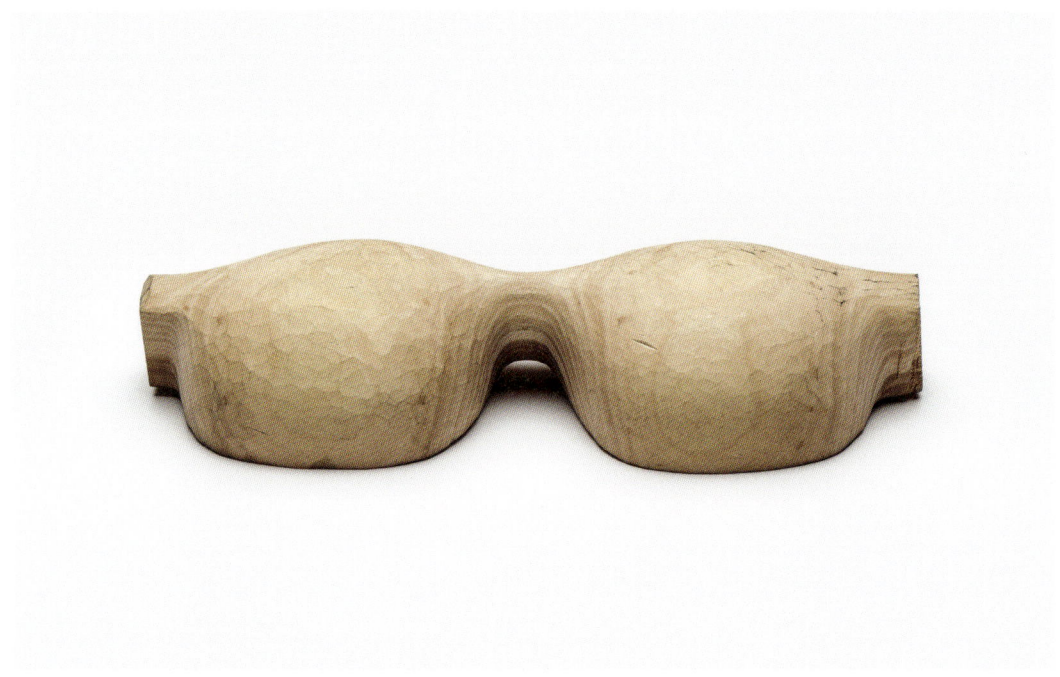

21
Objekte / Objects
2019–2020

Tobias Birgersson

9th Inning

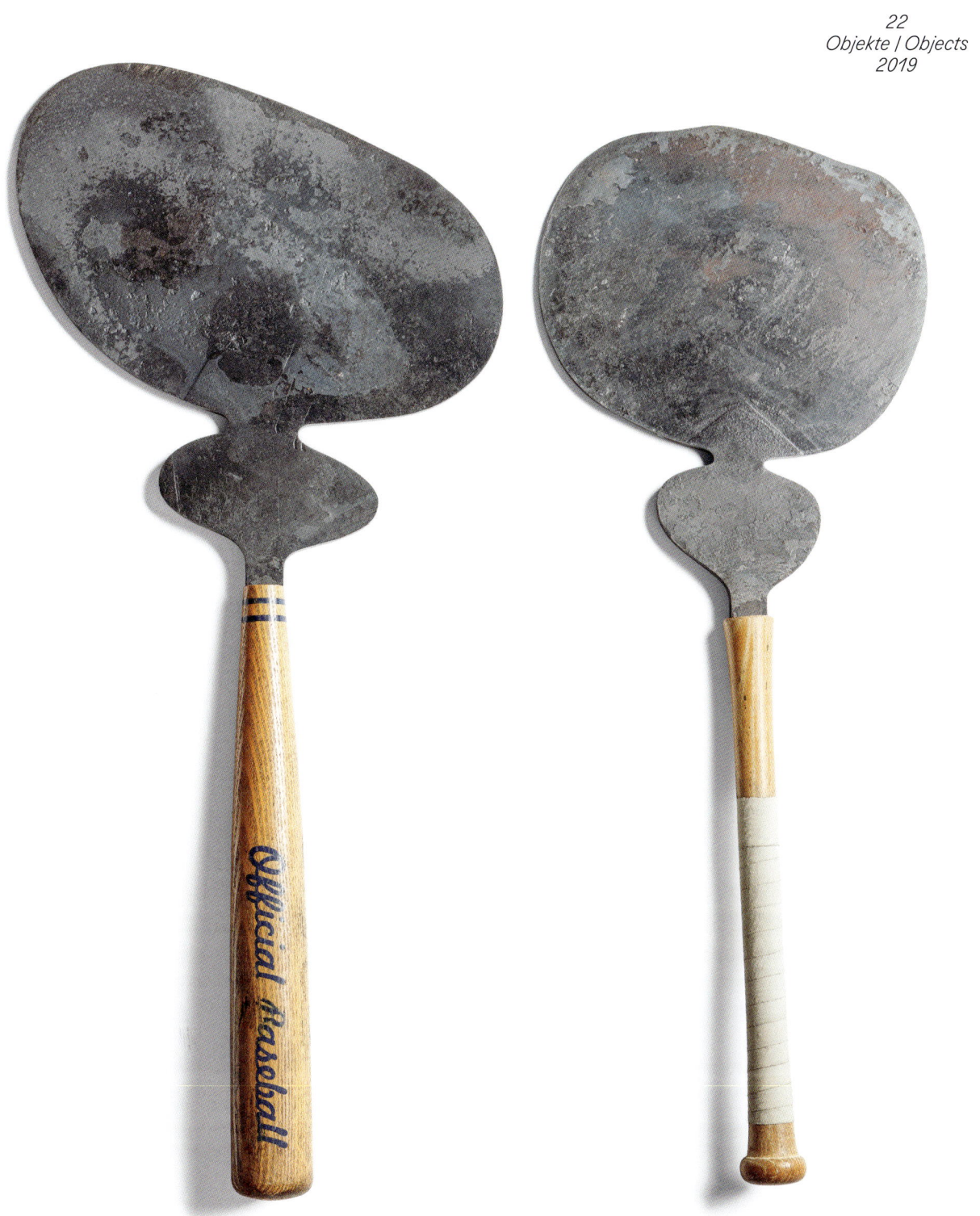

22
Objekte / Objects
2019

Tobias Birgersson

Darkness Falls

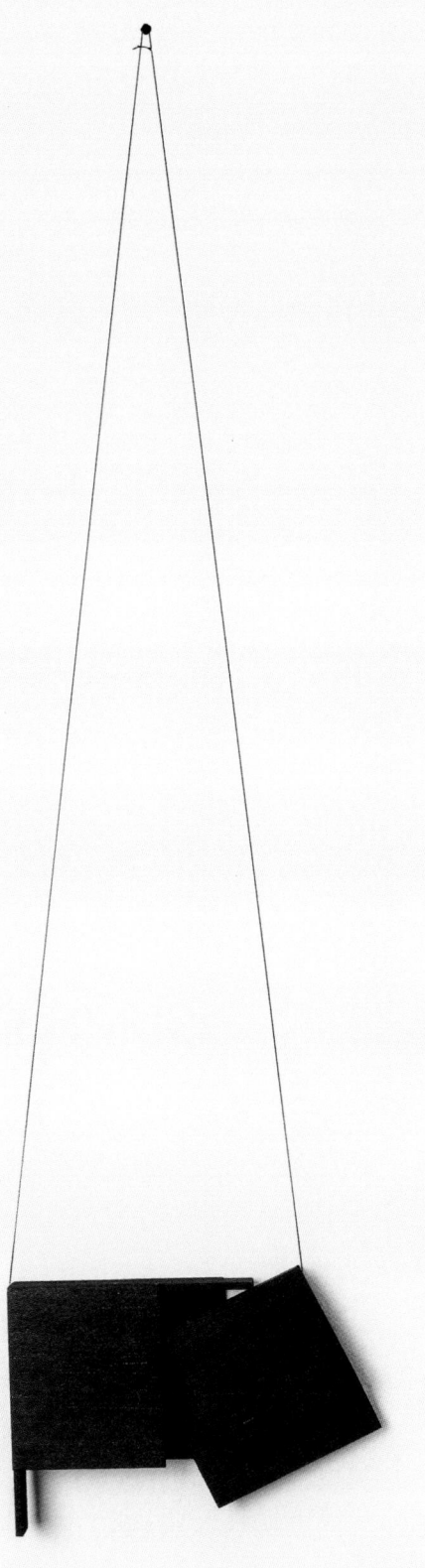

55
Halsschmuck | Necklace
2022

Kateřina Jirsová

Space of Home

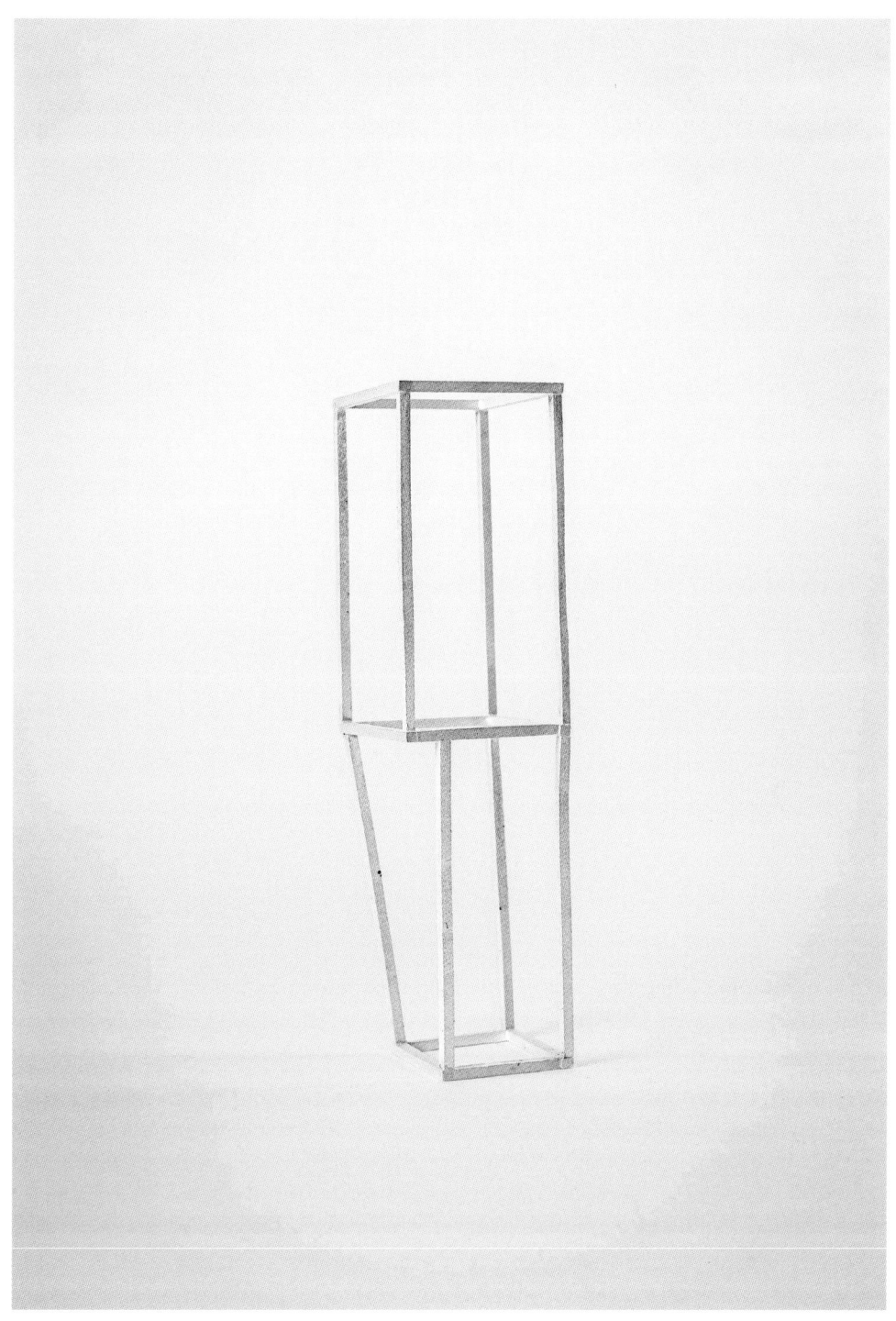

57
Brosche | Brooch
2009

Kateřina Jirsová

Singing in the Void (Green)

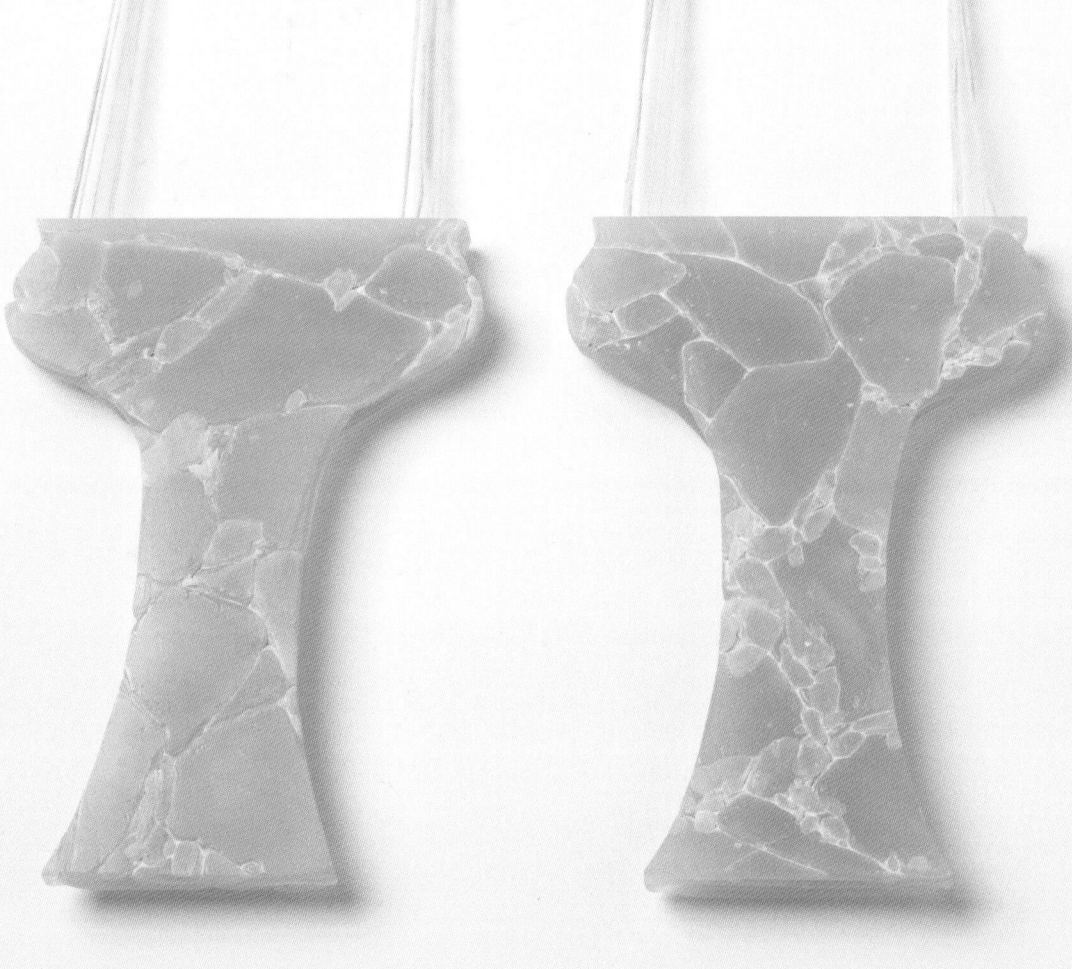

*31
Halsschmuck | Necklaces
2023*

Kanako Ebisawa

Blown up

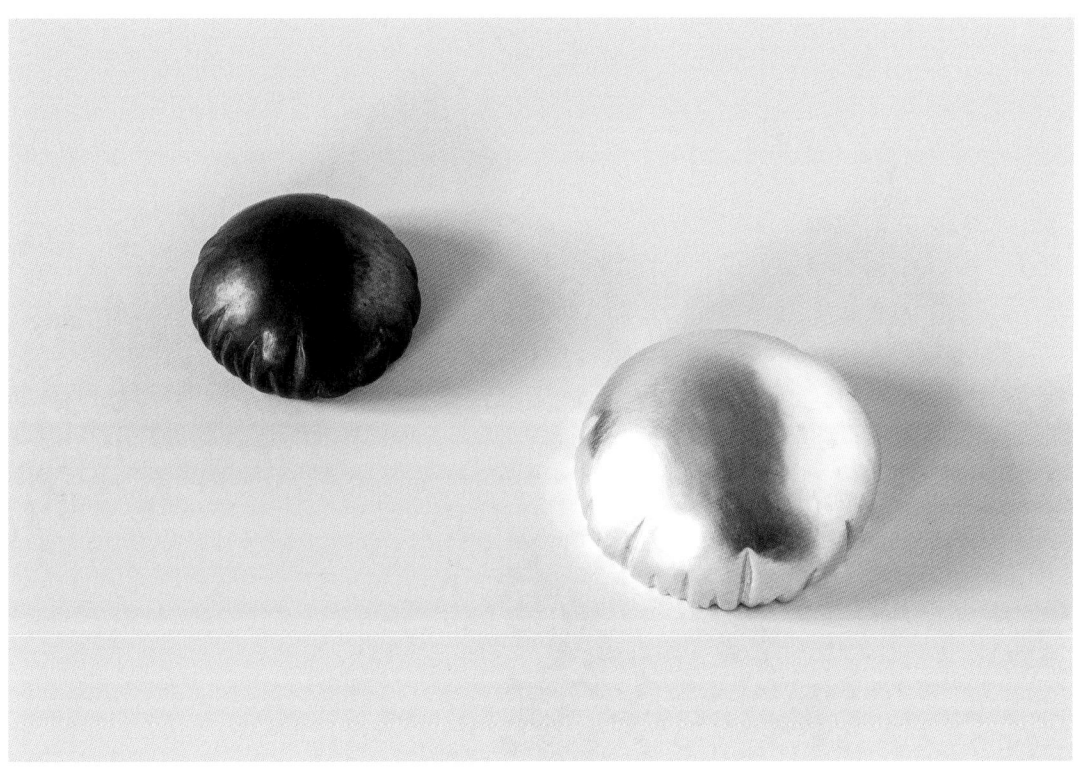

67
Broschen | Brooches
2022

Anders Ljungberg

Ebb #4

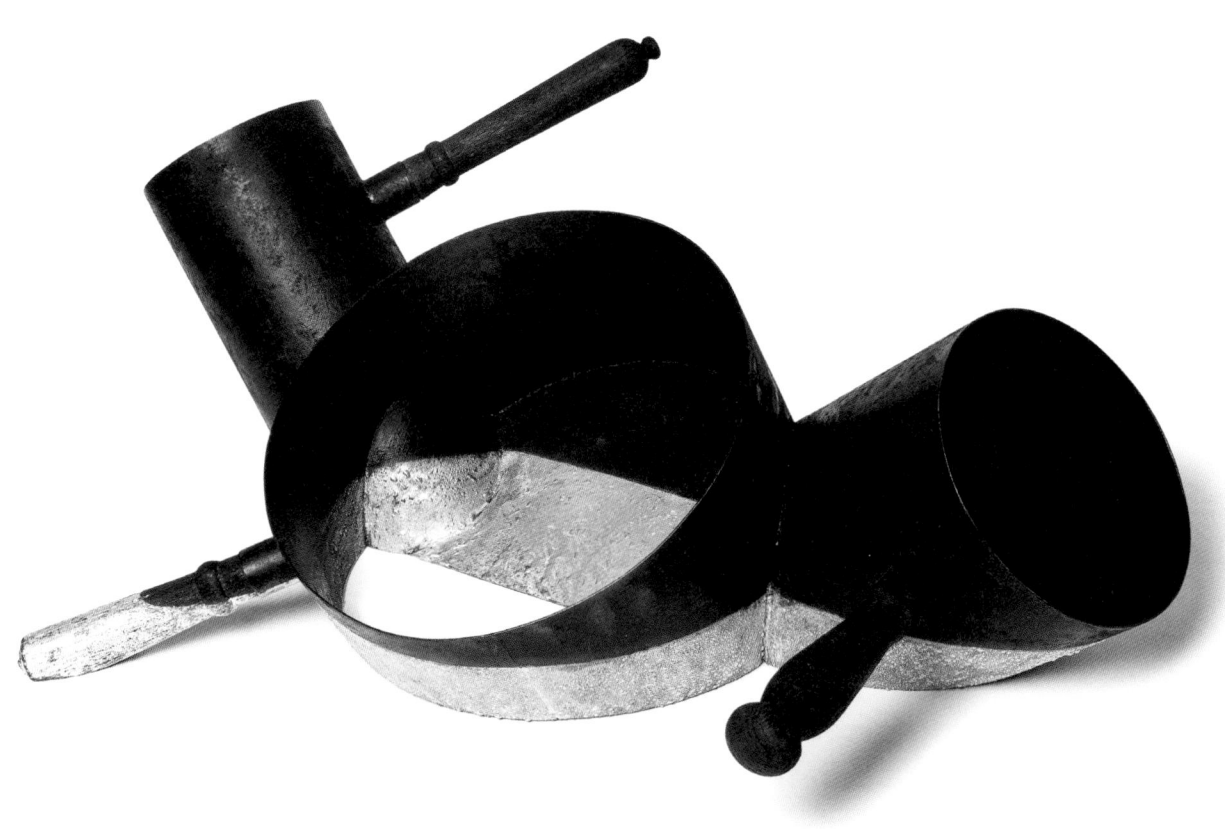

68
Objekt | Object
2022

Handled #4

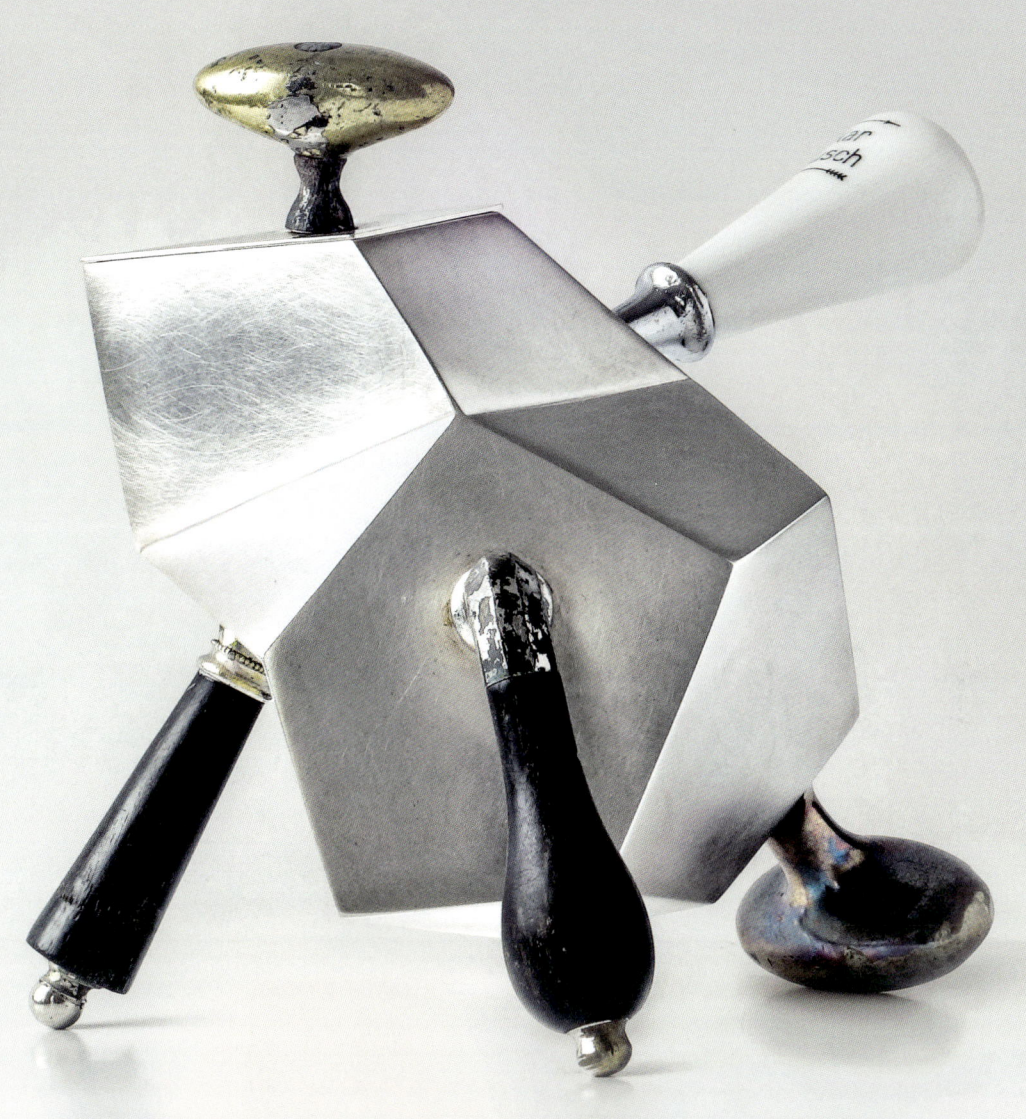

71
Objekt | Object
2016

Anders Ljungberg

Timeline

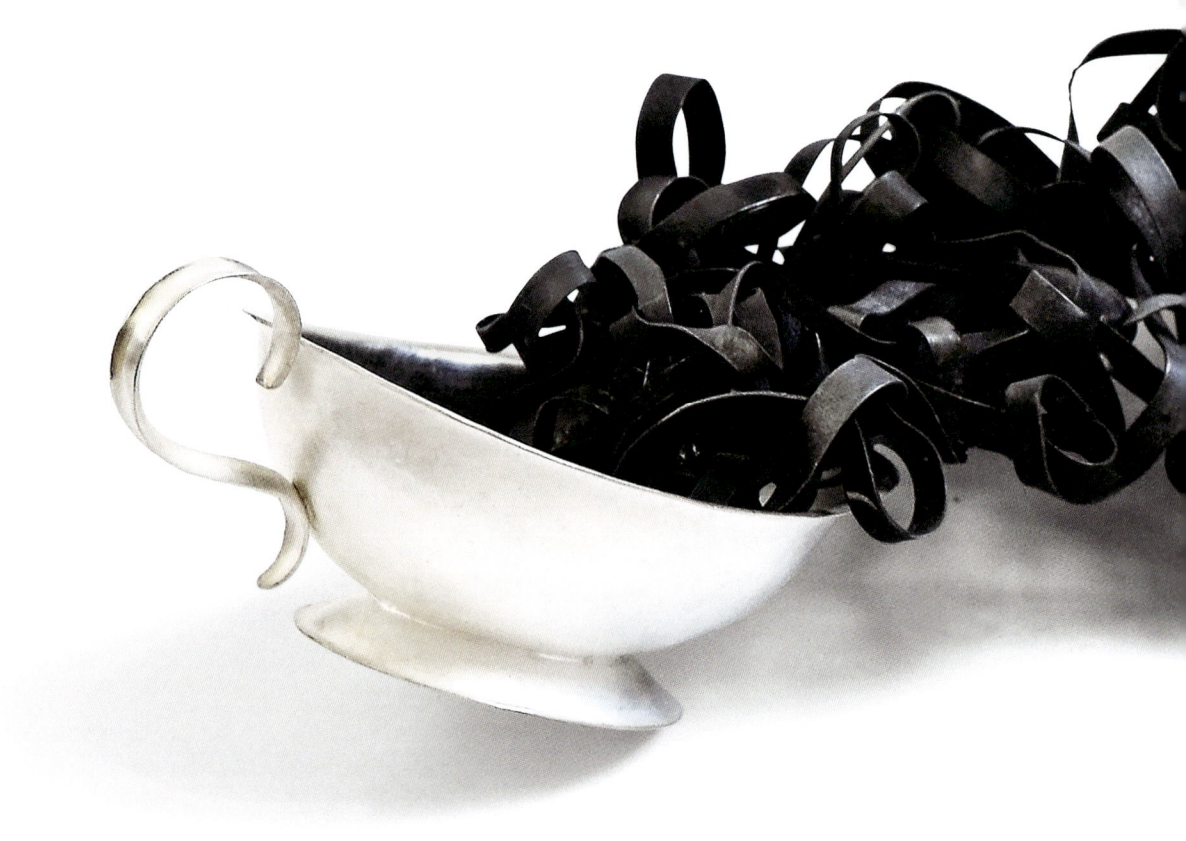

Anders Ljungberg

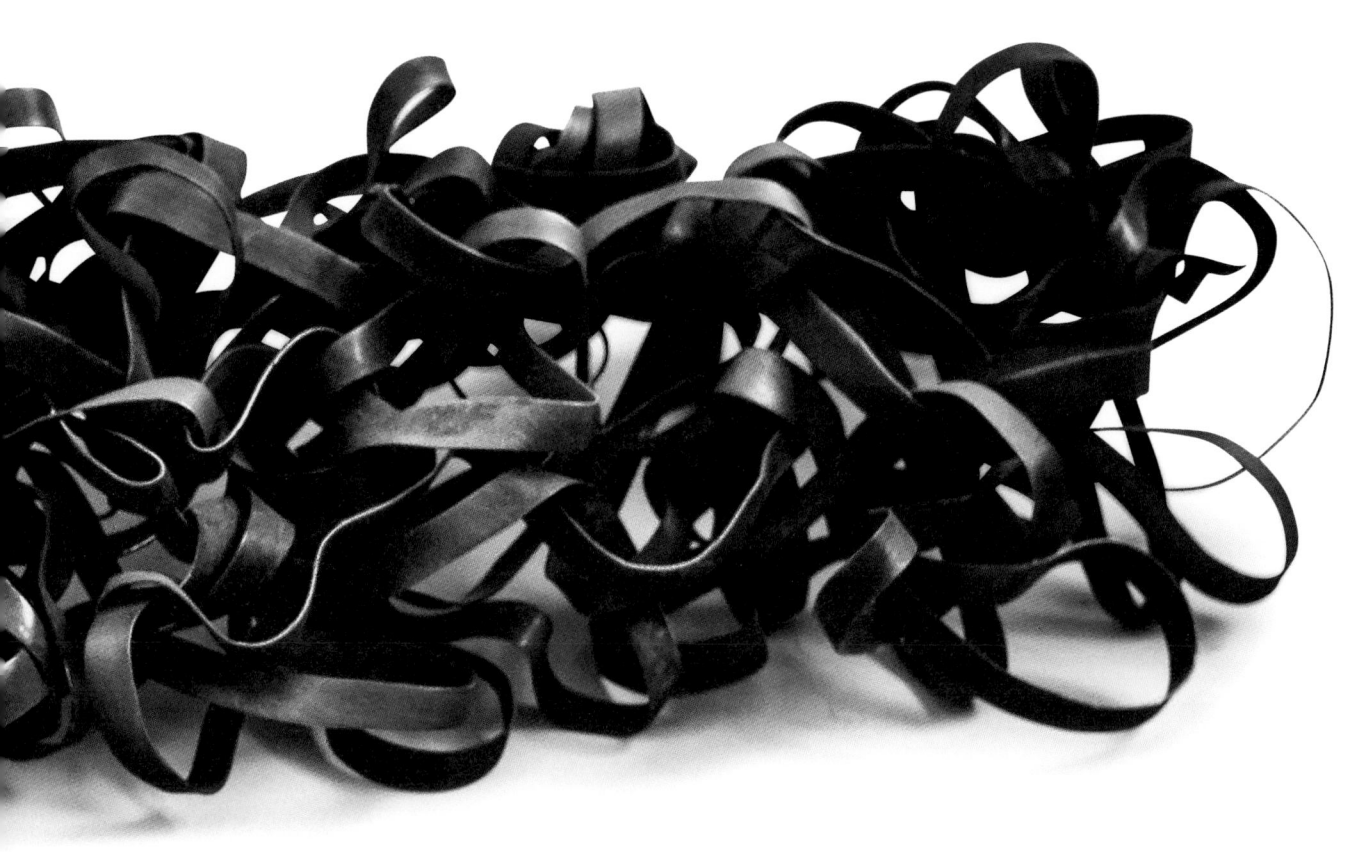

70
Objekt / Object
2019

Niche

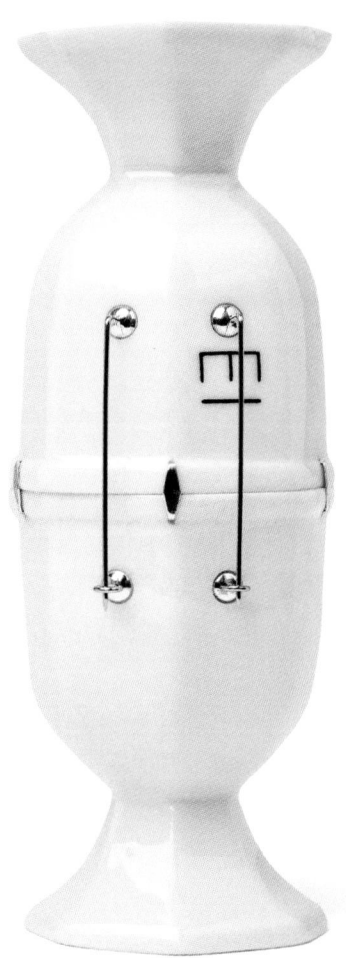

32
Brosche | Brooch
2021 | 2022

Kanako Ebisawa

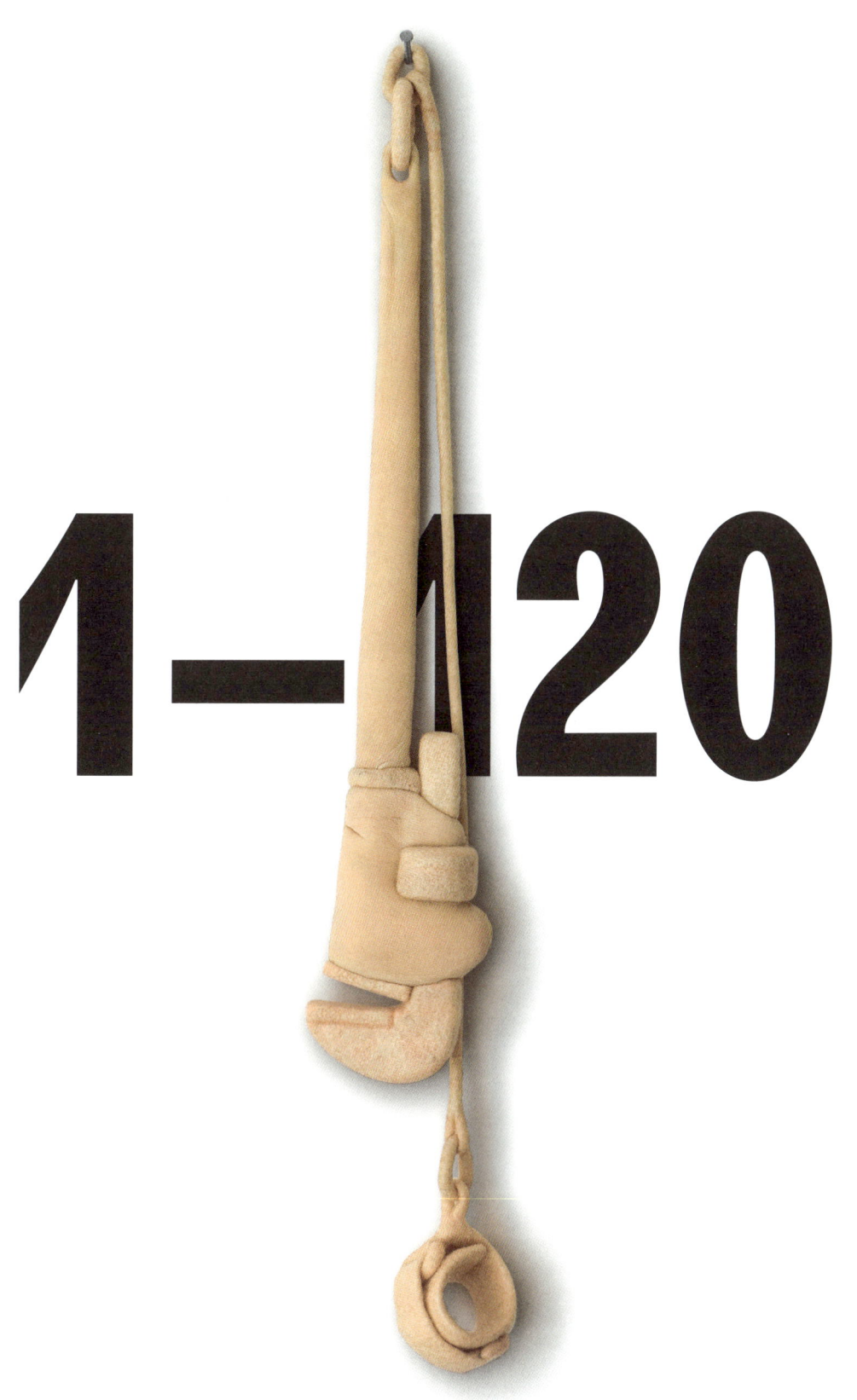

1—120

**The Pipe Wrench Lanyard
(Reißleine – Armband /
Lanyard—Bracelet)**
2018

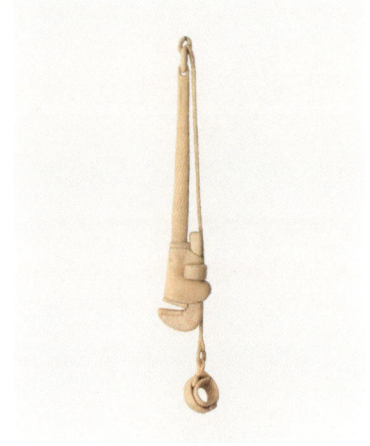

1
*Objekt | Object
Silikon, Wolle, Holz, Baumwolle, Stahl /
Silicone, wool, wood, cotton, steel
57 × 15 × 15 cm*
Seite | Page 129

**The Châtelaine
(Hammer- oder
Taschenlampengürtel /
Hammer or Flashlight Holder)**
2017

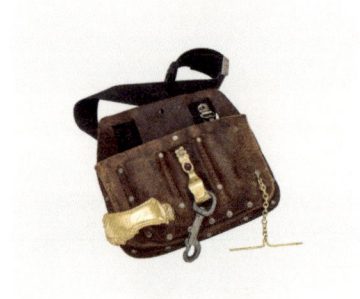

2
*Objekt | Object
Leder, vergoldetes Sterlingsilber, Rubin,
Stahl, Samt, Nylon /
Leather, gold-plated sterling silver, ruby,
steel, velvet, nylon
30 × 20 × 10 cm*
Seite | Page 86

**The Châtelaine
(Hammer- oder
Taschenlampengürtel /
Hammer or Flashlight Holder)**
2017

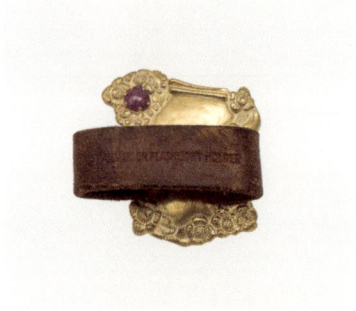

3
*Objekt | Object
Leder, vergoldetes Sterlingsilber,
Rubin, Stahl /
Leather, gold-plated sterling silver, ruby,
steel
9 × 9 × 5 cm*
Seite | Page 87

**The Châtelaine
(Quick Release Tool Snap)**
2017

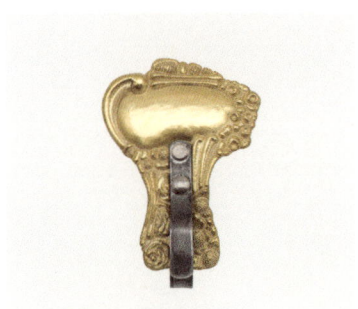

4
*Objekt | Object
Vergoldetes Sterlingsilber, Stahl /
Gold-plated sterling silver, steel
11 × 7 × 3 cm*
Seit | Page 87

Sawa Aso

5
Halsschmuck | Necklace
Aluminium, Baumwolle, Zaponlack, montiert, genietet, getrieben, lackiert, geflochten |
Aluminum, cotton, cellulose lacquer, mounted, riveted, embossed, lacquered, plaited
Eine Rolle | Each tube: Ø4,1 × 9,7 cm
Seite | Page 91

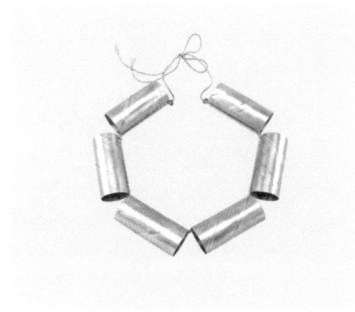

Alltagslöcher 1
2019

6
Halsschmuck | Necklace
Edelstahl, Edelstahldraht montiert, gelötet |
Stainless steel, stainless-steel thread, mounted, soldered
Fernglas | Binoculars: 7,3 × 9 × 3,5 cm

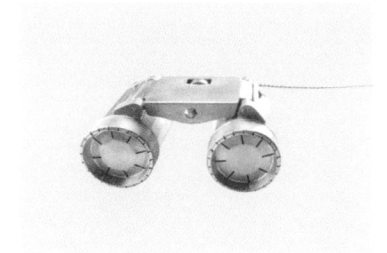

Fernglas
2017

7
Halsschmuck | Necklace
Stahl, Stahldraht, Eisendraht, Edelstahlkette, Edelstahldraht, Edelstahlseil montiert, gelötet |
Steel, steel wire, iron wire, stainless-steel chain, stainless-steel wire, stainless-steel rope, mounted, soldered
Brille | Glasses: 4,5 × 15 × 14 cm

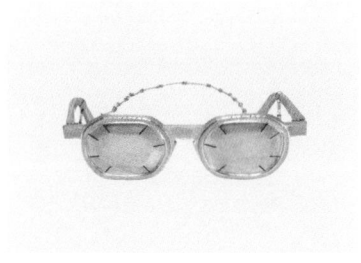

BRILLE – LE CLUB OPTIQUE
2013/2017

8
Kopfschmuck | Headdress
Stahl, Federstahldraht, Eisendraht montiert, gelötet |
Steel, spring steel, iron thread, mounted, soldered
21 × 21 × 8,6 cm
Seite | Page 90

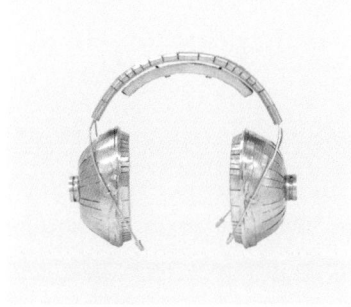

Ohrschützer
2012

9
Halsschmuck | Necklace
Silber, Seide, montiert, gelötet |
Silver, silk, mounted, soldered
6 × 21,5 × 5,5 cm
Seite | Page 89

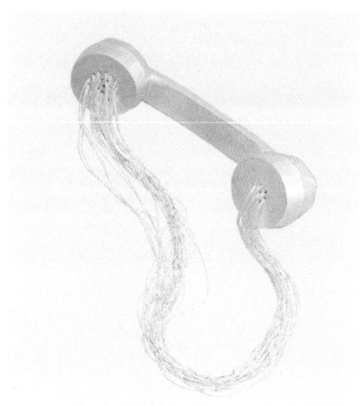

Telefonhörer
2011

Astrid Becksteiner-Rasche

Don't Forget the Voice of Peace
2023

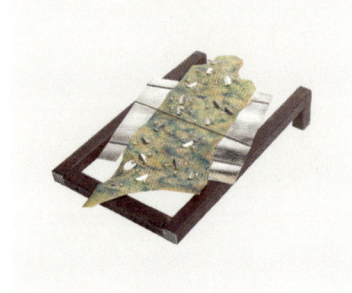

10
Tischobjekt | Table Object
Silber, Perlen, Pergament, Farbe;
Unterbau: Eisenrohr, Blei |
Silver, pearls, parchment, paint;
substructure: iron pipe, lead
ca. 55 × 34 × 3 cm

Für die kleine Messe
2023

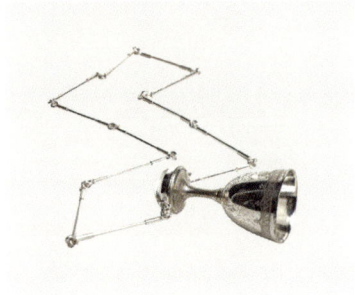

11
Halsschmuck | Necklace
Silberkette, kleiner Kelch, Bergkristall |
Silver chain, small goblet, rock crystal
ca. 49 cm
Seite | Page 112

Kelch
2023

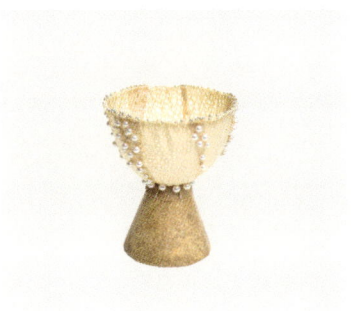

12
Objekt | Object
Pergament, Salzwasserperlen |
Parchment, saltwater pearls
16 × 14 cm
Seite | Page 111

Naama Bergman

13
Objekte | Objects
Gegossenes Salz | Cast salt
6,4–8,8 × Ø7,3–11,8 cm

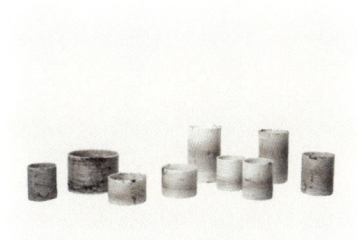

Casted Salt Glasses
2018–2019

14
Halsschmuck | Necklace
Aus der Serie | From the series
Salt Crystal Group
Salz, Eisendraht | Salt, iron mesh
Anhänger | Pendant: 4,5 × 11 × 6 cm
Faden | Thread: 78 cm
Seite | Page 83

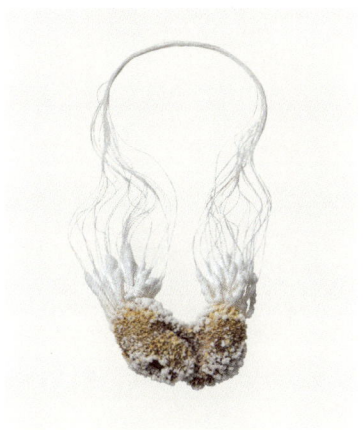

Salt Necklace 09
2017

15
Objekte | Objects
Aus der Serie | From the series
Salt Crystal Group
Salz, Eisendraht | Salt, iron mesh
18–23 × 18 × 18 cm
Seite | Page 85

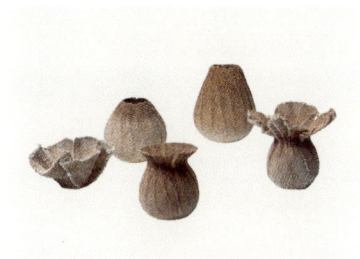

Salt Vessels
2016

16
Objekte | Objects
Gegossenes Salz | Cast salt
6,9–11 × 4,1–4,8 cm
Seite | Page 84

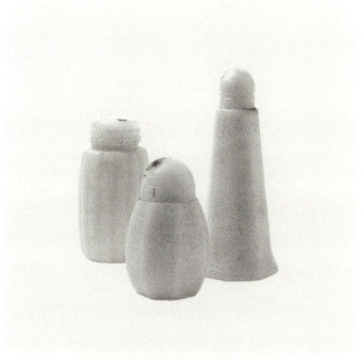

Salt Shakers
2002

Tobias Birgersson

Belly
2021

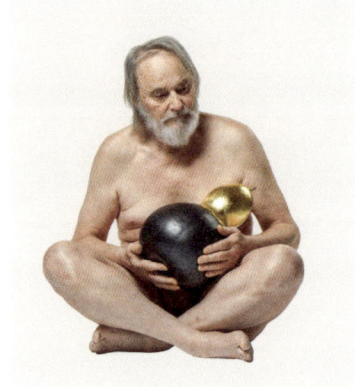

17
Objekt | Object
(in Zusammenarbeit mit Wolfgang Bremer |
Collaboration with Wolfgang Bremer)
Aus der Reihe | From the series
Enlightened
Kalebasse, Blattgold, Urushilack |
Calabash, gold leaf, urushi lacquer
ca. 30 cm

Black on Black
2021

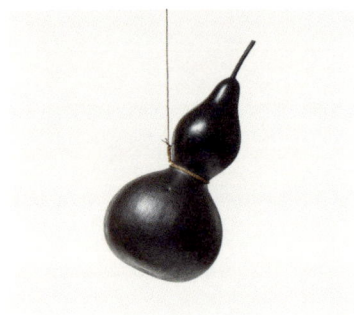

18
Objekt | Object
(in Zusammenarbeit mit Wolfgang Bremer |
Collaboration with Wolfgang Bremer)
Aus der Reihe | From the series
Enlightened
Kalebasse, Graphit, Urushilack |
Calabash, graphite, urushi lacquer
ca. 45 cm

Graphite Head
2021

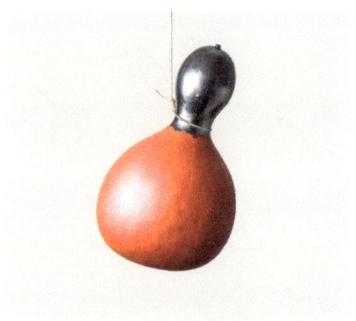

19
Objekt | Object
(in Zusammenarbeit mit Wolfgang Bremer |
Collaboration with Wolfgang Bremer)
Aus der Reihe | From the series
Enlightened
Kalebasse, Zinnober, Graphit handpoliert,
Urushilack |
Calabash, cinnabar, hand-polished
graphite, urushi lacquer
ca. 50 cm

The Toolness of Things
2021

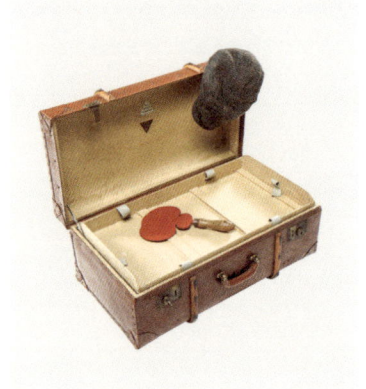

20
Objekt | Object
Geschmiedetes Eisen, Lack |
Hot-forged steel, lacquer
ca. 20 cm

21
Objekte | Objects
Esche, Apfel, Mahagony |
Ash, applewood, mahogany
ca. 10 × 17 cm
Seite | Page 118

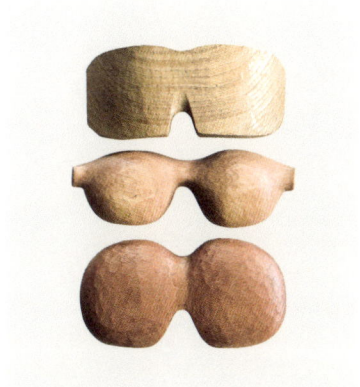

See no Evil (Tryptich)
2019–2020

22
Objekte | Objects
Geschmiedetes Eisen, Baseballschläger |
Hot-forged steel, baseball bat
90 × 40 cm
Seite | Page 119

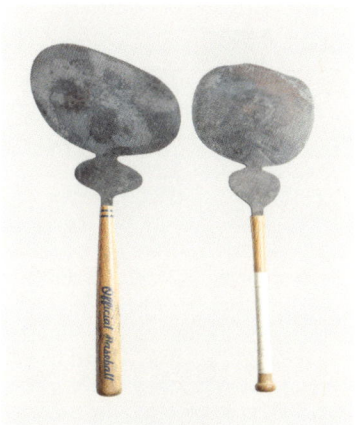

9th Inning
2019

23
Teekännchen | Teapot
Sterlingsilber | Sterling silver
ca. 17 × 10 cm

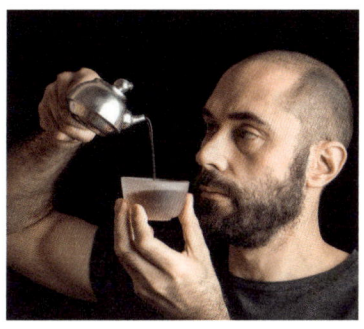

Poppy
2018

Beatrice Brovia / Nicolas Cheng

BEYOND REPAIR / LILIES VASE
2017

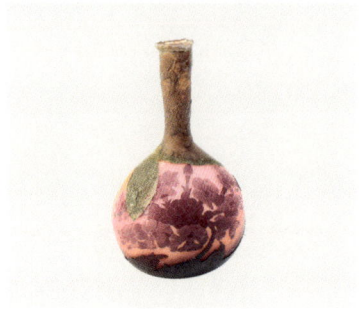

24
Objekt | Object
Originale gebrochene Vase von Émile Gallé, Nancy, um 1910, Rekonstruktion der fehlenden Teile: Metall aus E-Müll, 14 K Gold, 24 K Goldblatt |
Original broken vase by Émile Gallé, Nancy, ca. 1910, reconstruction of the missing parts: e-waste metal, 14k gold, 24k gold leaf
34 × 12 × 12 cm
Seite | Page 72

Ohne Titel / Untitled (Kino 12 & 13)
2014–2016

25
Broschen | Brooches
Kristall, Gold, optischer Film, Quarzkristall, Tantal |
Crystal, gold, optical film, quartz crystal, tantalum
ca. 8,6 × 5,2 × 1,2 cm

Ohne Titel / Untitled (Kino 11)
2014–2016

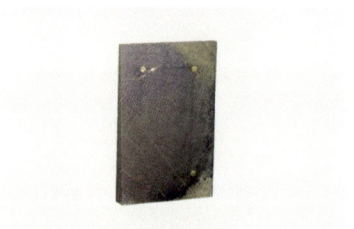

26
Brosche | Brooch
Kristall, Gold, optischer Film |
Crystal, gold, optical film
7,5 × 4,7 × 1,5 cm
Seite | Page 75

SOAP HANDLE
2013

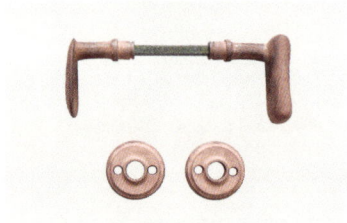

27
Objekt | Object
Aus der Reihe | From the series
Door Handles (edition of four)
Kupfer, Silberlegierung | Copper, silver alloy
7–8 × 3–4 × 6 cm

SOAP HANDLE
2013

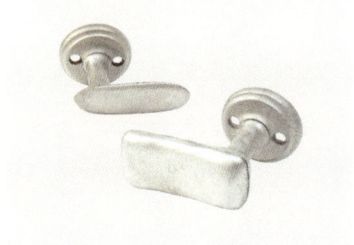

28
Objekt | Object
Aus der Reihe | From the series
Door Handles (edition of four)
Silber | Silver
7–8 × 3–4 × 6 cm
Seite | Page 73

TEXTILE HANDLE
2011

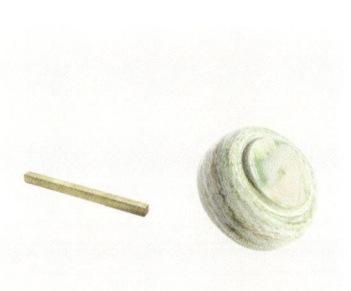

29
Objekt | Object
Aus der Reihe | From the series
Door Handles (edition of four)
Baumwolle, vergoldetes Messing, vergoldetes Silber |
Cotton, gold-plated brass, gold-plated silver
8 × 8 × 6 cm
Seite | Page 73

David Clarke

30
Objekte | Objects
Zinn, Silberplatte, Stahl |
Pewter, silver platter, steel
ca. 30 × 18 × 18 cm
Seite | Page 117

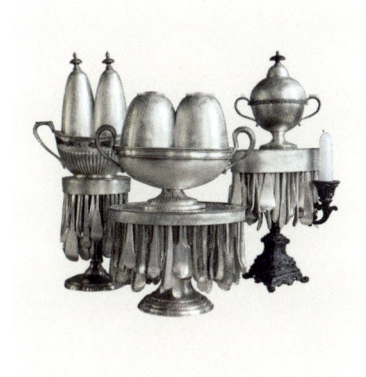

STASH
2020

Kanako Ebisawa

31
Halsschmuck | Necklaces
Glas, Schnur | Glass, cord
Anhänger | Pendant: 11,5 × 8 × 1,3 cm
Seite | Page 122

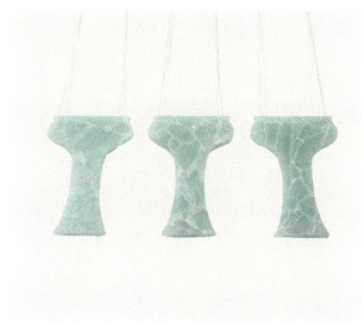

Singing in the Void (Green)
2023

32
Broschen | Brooches
Keramik-Eierbecher, Silber, Edelstahl |
Ceramic egg cup, silver, stainless steel
13 × 5 × 3,5 cm
Seiten | Pages 41 | 128

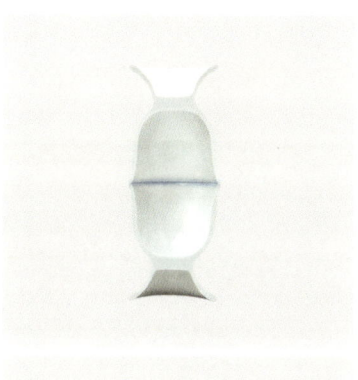

Niche
2021/2022

Ute Eitzenhöfer

Shalo boli duge
2022

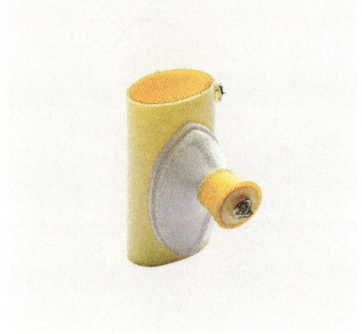

33
Ansteckobjekt | Pin-on Jewelry
Shampooflasche (HDPE), Körpermilchflasche (PP), Beryll, Silber 925 |
Shampoo bottle (HDPE), body-lotion bottle (PP), beryl, 925 silver
ca. 7,7 × 3,7 × 6 cm
Seite | Page 60

circle 02
2019

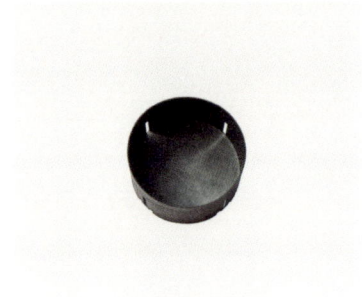

34
Brosche | Brooch
Silber geschwärzt | Blackened silver
5,8 × 5,8 × 3,9 cm
Seite | Page 62

circle 01
2019

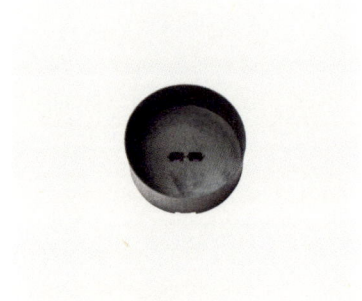

35
Brosche | Brooch
Silber geschwärzt, Amethyst |
Blackened silver, amethyst
5,1 × 5,1 × 3,3 cm

Roségoldblech mit Griff
2013

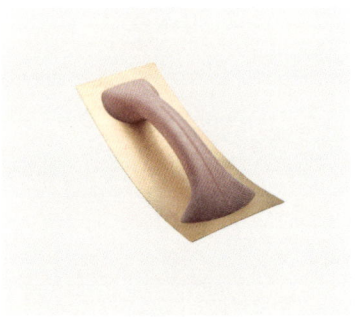

36
Objekt | Object
Roségold 750, Kunststoff (aus Verpackung) |
750 rose gold, plastic (from packaging)
ca. 15 × 6 × 3,5 cm

Deckel mit Pins 1–3
2002

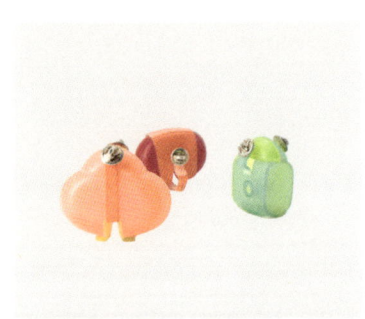

37
Ansteckobjekte | Pin-on Jewelry
Shampoodeckel (PE), Perle, Silber 925 |
Shampoo lids (PE), pearl, 925 silver
ca. 3,4–4,2 × 2,8–4,9 × 1,9–2,5 cm
Seite | Page 63

38
Ansteckobjekt | Pin-on Jewelry
*Shampoodeckel (PE), Perle, Silber 925,
teilweise rhodiniert |
Shampoo lid (PE), pearl, 925 silver, partly
rhodium-plated
ca. 3,3 × 4,5 × 3,7 cm*
Seite | Page 62

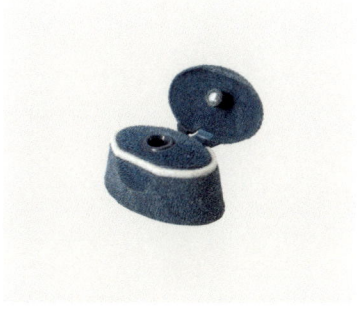

Ensha
2002

39
Objekt | Object
*Duschgelflaschen (HDPE) |
Shower-gel bottles (HDPE)
ca. 7 × 6,3 × 4 cm*

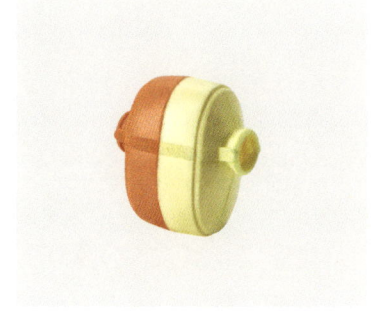

Entität
2002

Åsa Elmstam

40
Halsschmuck | Necklace
*Handgesägtes, vergoldetes Messing,
kommerzielle, vergoldete Kette |
Hand-sawn gold-plated brass,
pre-purchased gold-plated chain
40 × 15,5 × 0,5 cm*

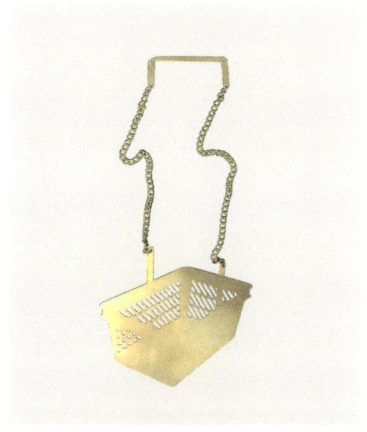

Things 21
2018

41
Halsschmuck | Necklace
Aus der Reihe | From the series
Möbelmässan
*Holz: Eiche, Zitterpappel, Pinie, Esche, Kork;
Rückseite: Terrazzo, Polymerlehm, Messing,
Farbspray, MDF, Kunstrattan;
Textil: Baumwolle, Wolle, Leinen, Hanf |
Wood: oak, aspen, pine, ash, cork; reverse:
terrazzo, polymer clay, brass, spray paint,
MDF, artificial rattan; textile: cotton, wool,
linen, hemp
43 × 26 × 5,5 cm*

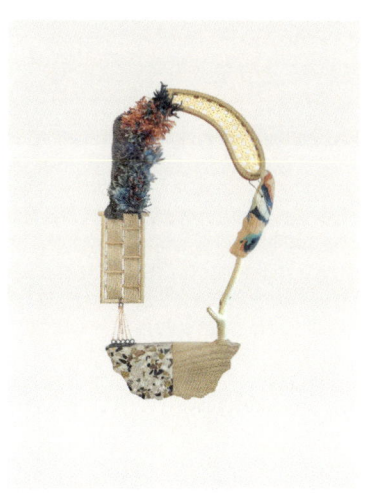

Things 23
2017

**Ohne Titel / Untitled
(Vessel / Hanging container)**
2016–2017

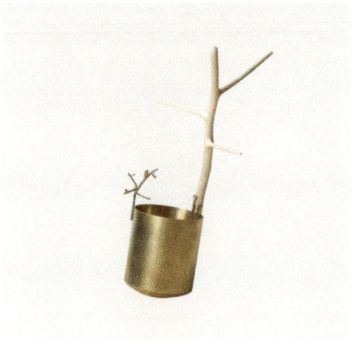

*42
Objekt / Object
Messing, Holz der Zitterpappel /
Brass, aspen wood
35 × 22 × 17 cm
Seite / Page 52*

Things 2
2010–2011

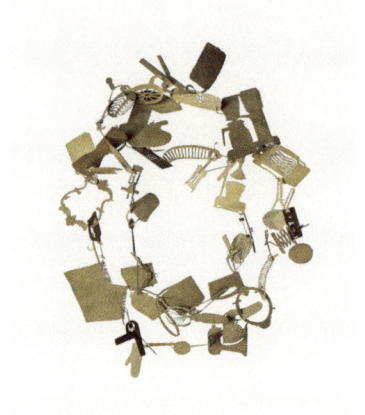

*43
Halsschmuck / Necklace
Hand gesägter, gelöteter,
sandgestrahlter Messing /
Hand sawn, soldered, sandblasted brass
100 × 40 × 5 cm
Seite / Page 53*

Anne Fischer

Gefäß / Vessel
2013

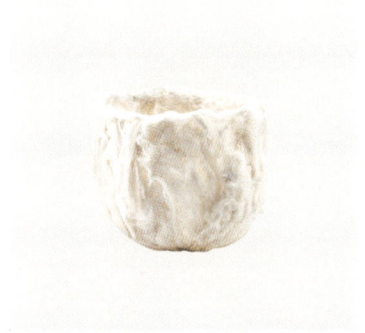

*44
Objekt / Object
Kardierte Wolle, Plastik /
Carded wool, plastic
45 × Ø45 cm
Seite / Page 68*

Gefäße / Vessels
2010

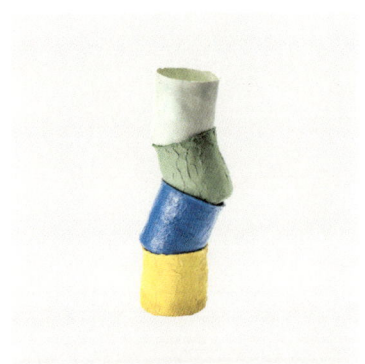

*45
Objekte / Objects
Acrylfarbe / Acrylic paint
Je / Each ca. 14 × Ø12 cm
Seite / Page 67*

Karolina Hägg

46
Objekte | Objects
Austernschalen, Silber, Zinn, Lack |
Oyster shells, silver, pewter, lacquer
ca. 10 × 5 × 4 cm
Seiten | Pages 48 | 49

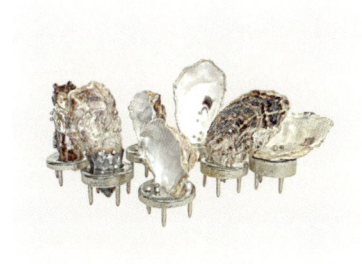

Spectacle Bread and Mother-of-Pearl
2023

47
Objekte | Objects
Silber, selbstgemachte Seife |
Silver, homemade soap
7,5 × 9 × 7 cm

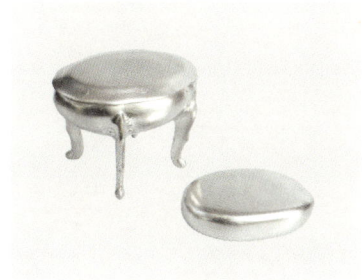

Soap
2020

48
Objekt | Object
Aus der Reihe | From the series
The Cocktail Effect
Zucker, Silber | Sugar, silver
ca. 26 × 15 × 20 cm
Seite | Page 47

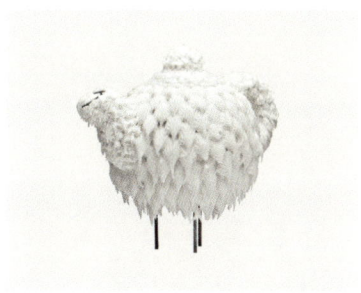

Teapot
2013

49
Objekt | Object
Aus der Reihe | From the series
The Cocktail Effect
Gelatine, Blei | Gelatine, lead
6 × 18 × 18 cm
Seite | Page 51

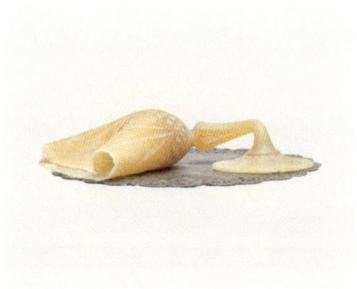

Vine Glass
2013

Nils Hint

oOOo
2017

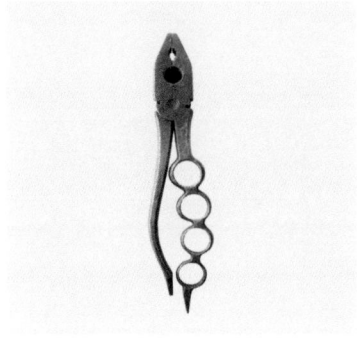

50
*Ring
Geschmiedetes Eisen, Fundobjekt /
Hot-forged iron, ready-made
ca. 22 × 8 × 2 cm*

Very Practical Necklace
2015

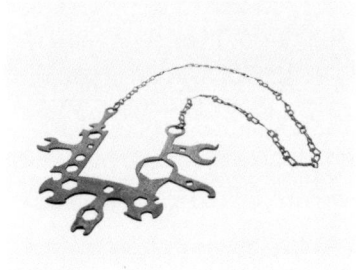

51
*Halsschmuck / Necklace
Geschmiedetes und verschweißtes Eisen,
Fundstück /
Hot-forged and welded iron, ready-made
78 × 25 × 20 cm*

Shadow
2014

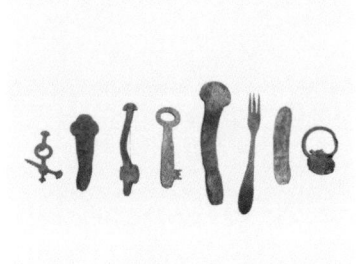

52
*Broschen / Brooches
Geschmiedetes Eisen, Fundobjekte /
Hot-forged iron, ready-mades
ca. 2 × 15 cm
Seiten / Pages 70 / 71*

Shadow
2014

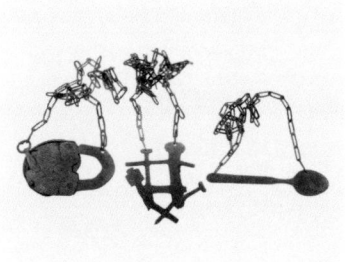

53
*Halsschmuck / Necklaces
Geschmiedetes Eisen, Fundstücke /
Hot-forged iron, ready-mades
ca. 14 – 21 × 47 – 75 × 1 cm*

Extraordinary Piece No. 2
2011

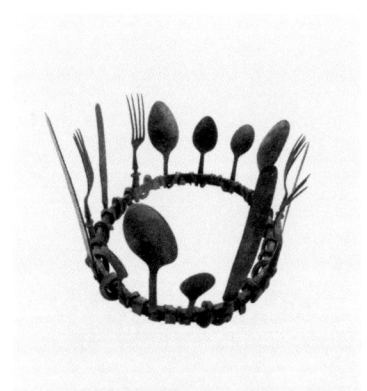

54
*Kopfschmuck / Headdress
Geschmiedetes Eisen, Fundstücke /
Hot-forged iron, ready-mades
20 × 25 × 25 cm
Seite / Page 69*

Kateřina Jirsová

55
Halsschmuck | Necklace
Balsa Holz, Baumwolle | Balsa, cotton
Anhänger | Pendant: 10 × 8,5 × 2 cm
Seite | Page 120

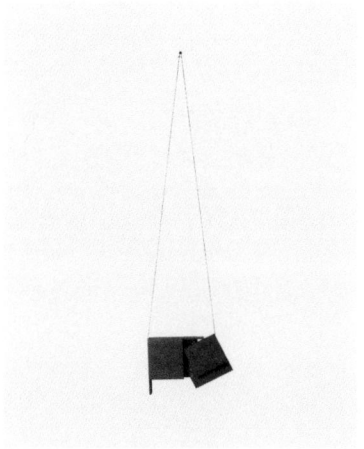

Darkness Falls
2022

56
Schalen | Bowls
Zucker | Sugar
4,3–7,2 × 6–16 cm

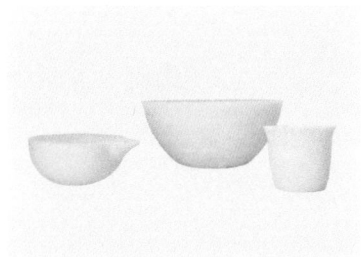

Preciouses
2009

57
Broschen | Brooches
Silber | Silver
3–9,5 × 2,5–3 × 2,5–5 cm
Seite | Page 121

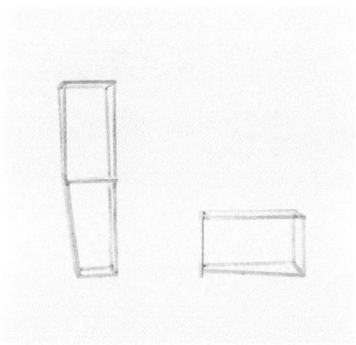

Space of Home
2009

Junwon Jung

ingrown
2023

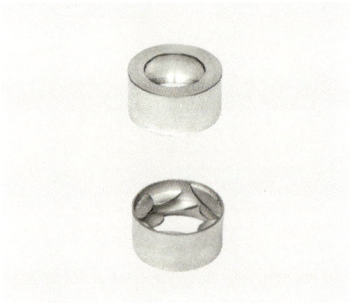

58
Ring
Silber | Silver
3 × 3 × 1,5 cm

box
2022

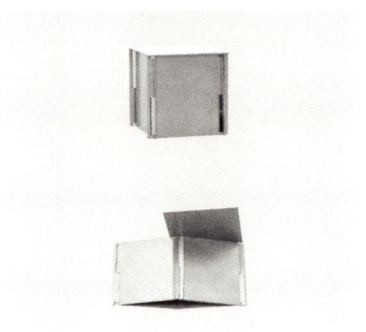

59
Brosche | Brooch
Titan, Holz | Titanium, wood
4 × 4 × 4 cm
Seite | Page 76

empty
2022

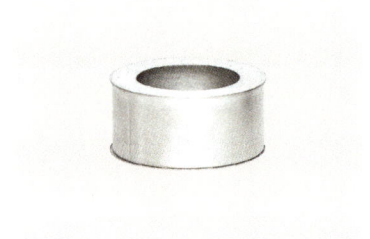

60
Ring-Box | Ring box
Silber | Silver
3 × 3 × 1,5 cm
Seite | Page 77

box
2020

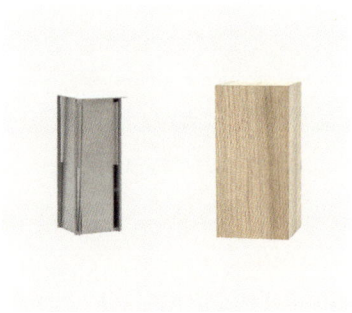

61
Brosche | Brooch
Galvanisierter Stahl, Holz |
Galvanized steel, wood
10 × 3,5 × 3,5 cm

box
2019

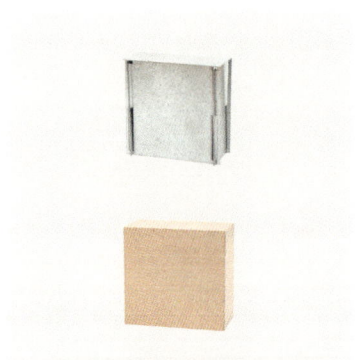

62
Brosche | Brooch
Galvanisierter Stahl, Holz |
Galvanized steel, wood
7 × 7 × 3,5 cm

63
Ring
Silber | Silver
3 × 2 × 2 cm

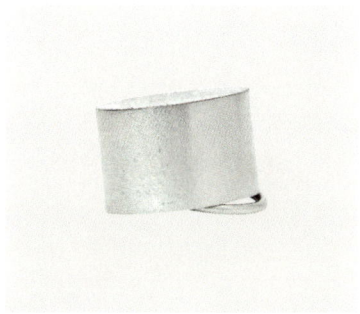

Ohne Titel / Untitled (oval)
2018

64
Ring
Silber | Silver
2,5 × 2,5 × 2,5 cm

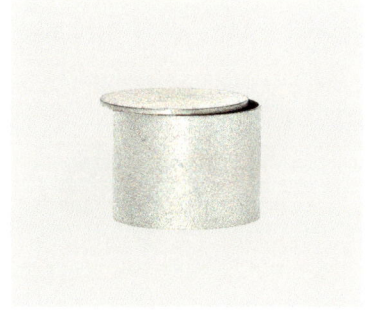

Ohne Titel / Untitled (rund / round)
2018

65
Brosche | Brooch
Silber | Silver
2,5 × 2,5 × 2,5 cm
Seite | Page 78

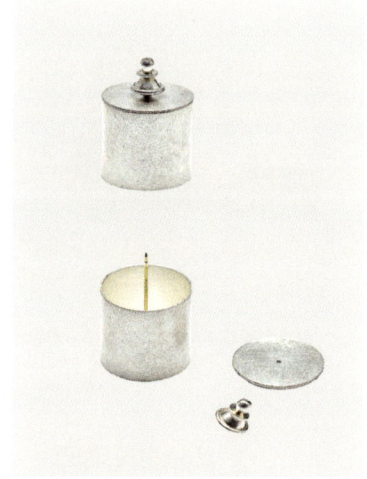

pawn
2018

66
Brosche – Objekt | Brooch—Object
Zink, Gold | Zinc, gold
10 × 5 × 5 cm
Seite | Page 77

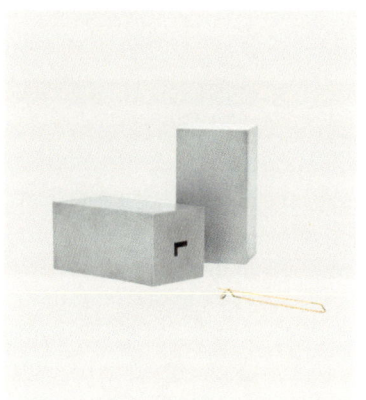

Nadel und Box / Pin and box
2016

Anders Ljungberg

Blown up
2022

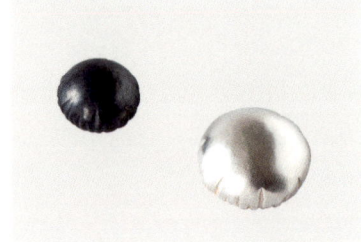

67
Broschen | Brooches
Silber, Stahl | Silver, steel
Ø 3,5–5 cm
Seite | Page 123

Ebb #4
2022

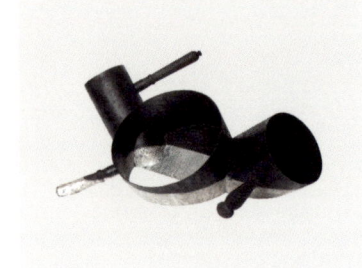

68
Objekt | Object
Patiniertes Messing, gebrannte Eiche, z.T. Zinn beschichtet |
Patinated brass, partly tin-plated burnt oak
52 × 36 × 25 cm
Seite | Page 124

Bag beneath #3
2019

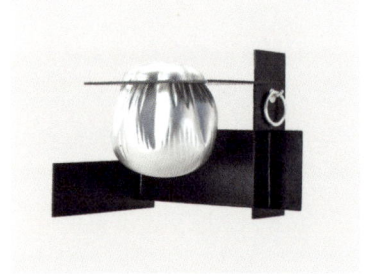

69
Objekt | Object
Silber, Stahl | Silver, steel
27,5 × 21,5 × 21 cm

Timeline
2019

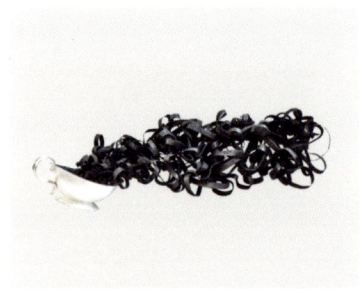

70
Objekt | Object
Silber, Zink | Silver, zinc
42 × 18,5 × 10 cm
Seiten | Pages 126 | 127

Handled #4
2016

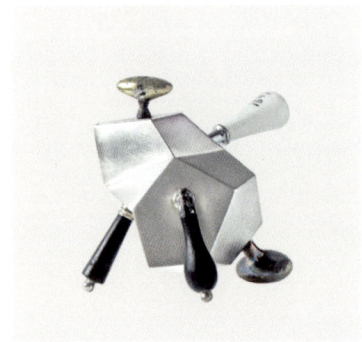

71
Objekt | Object
Silber, gebrauchte Griffe |
Silver, used handles
13 × 15 × 17 cm
Seite | Page 125

Kateřina Michálková

72
Objekte | Objects
Messing | Brass
10 × 7 × 3 cm
Seiten | Pages 54 | 55

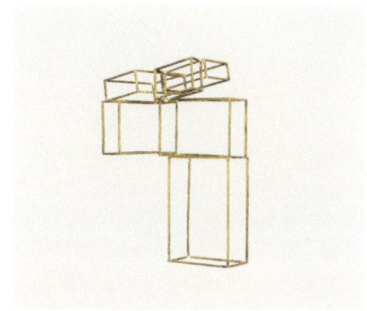

**Lure of Space Collection—
space sketches**
2018

73
Broschen | Brooches
*Verschiedene Hölzer: Esche, Buche,
Walnuss, Birne, Eiche, Messing- oder
Bronzenadeln |
Various woods: ash, beech, walnut, pear,
oak, brass or bronze pins*
4,5–13 × 5,5–10 × 2,5–3,5 cm

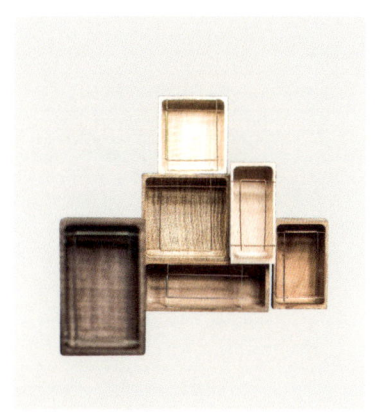

WITHIN
2017

Myra Mimlitsch-Gray

Double Cylinder Slide
2021

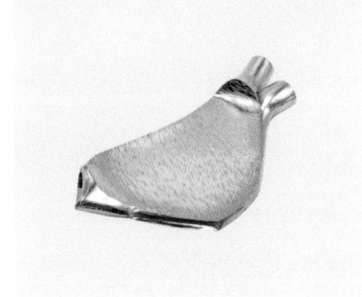

74
Tischobjekt | Table Object
Sterling Silber | Sterling silver
4,5 × 29,5 × 16,6 cm
Seite | Page 65

Antique White
2019

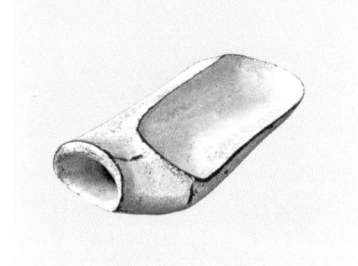

75
Objekt | Object
Porzellan, Emailglasur auf Stahl |
Porcelain, enamel on steel
6,3 × 32 × 15 cm

Penguin
2017

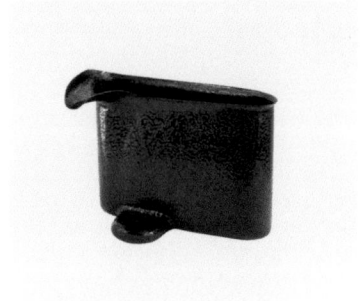

76
Objekt | Object
Porzellan, Emailglasur auf Stahl |
Porcelain, enamel on steel
16,5 × 19 × 18 cm
Seite | Page 65

Taped Pitcher
2017

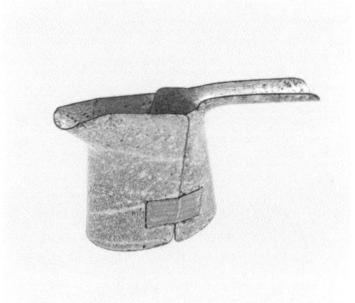

77
Kanne | Pot
Porzellan, Emailglasur auf Stahl |
Porcelain, enamel on steel
18 × 33 × 13 cm

**Freistehende Bratpfanne /
Freestanding skillet**
2007

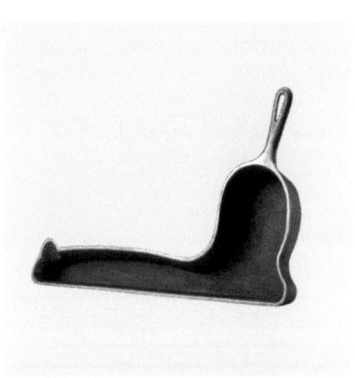

78
Objekt | Object
Gegossenes Eisen | Cast iron
33 × 58,5 × 6,5 cm
Seite | Page 66

Eija Mustonen

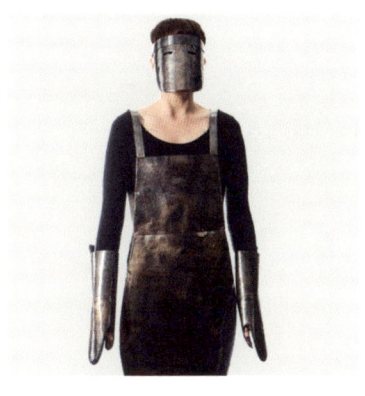

79
Ensemble
Nickelsilber, Kupfernieten /
Nickel silver, copper rivets
Schürze / Apron: 110 × 40 × 17 cm
Schutzhandschuhe / Protective gloves:
35 × 13 × 8 cm
Maske / Mask: 18 × 17 × 21 cm
Seite / Page 93

Apron, Mittens and Mask
2022

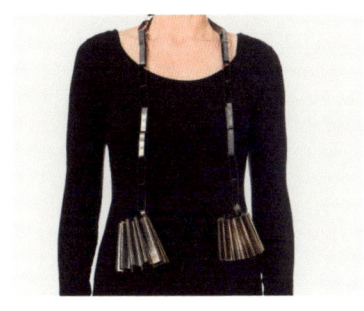

80
Halsschmuck / Necklace
Nickelsilber, Kupfernieten /
Nickel silver, copper rivets
128 × 14 × 10 cm

Ohne Titel / Untitled
2022

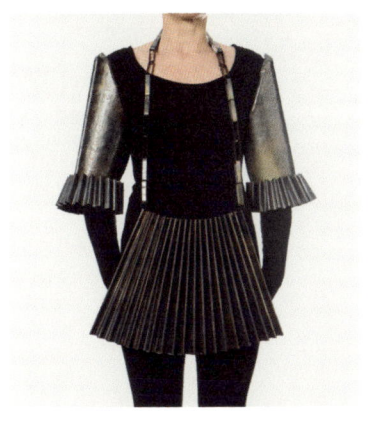

81
Ensemble
Nickelsilber, Kupfernieten /
Nickel silver, copper rivets
Ärmel / Each sleeve: 39 × 18 × 14 cm
Rock / Skirt: 87 × 44 × 3 cm
Seite / Page 95

Sleeves and Skirt
2022

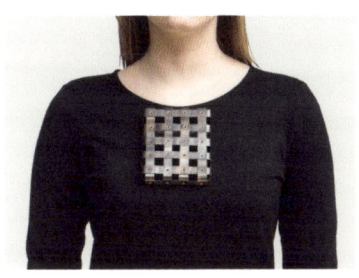

82
Brosche / Brooch
Nickelsilber, Kupfernieten /
Nickel silver, copper rivets
12,5 × 10 × 2 cm

Ohne Titel / Untitled
2016

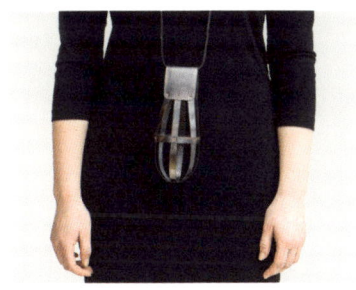

83
Halsschmuck / Necklace
Nickelsilber, Kupfernieten, Silberkette /
Nickel silver, copper rivets, silver chain
Anhänger / Pendant: 20 × 8 × 7 cm
Seite / Page 94

Ohne Titel / Untitled
2016

Markus Pollinger

Gefäß / **Container**
2020

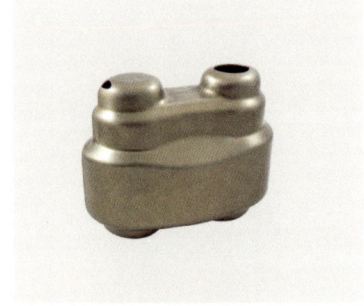

84
Objekt | Object
Edelstahl | Stainless steel
15,5 × 20 × 10 cm
Seite | Page 58

Gefäß / **Container**
2020

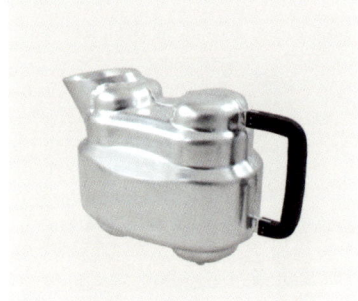

85
Objekt | Object
Kupfer versilbert, Stahl |
Silver-plated copper, steel
17,5 × 27 × 10 cm
Seite | Page 59

Gefäß / **Container**
2020

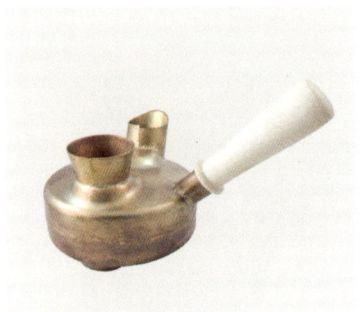

86
Objekt | Object
Kupfer gefärbt, Ahorn |
Colored copper, maple
13 × 28 × 31 cm
Seiten | Pages 56 | 57

Karen Pontoppidan

87
Brosche | Brooch
Aus der Reihe | From the series
innen
Leinwand, Acrylfarbe, Faden, Silber |
Canvas, acrylic paint, thread, silver
11 × 11 × 7 cm

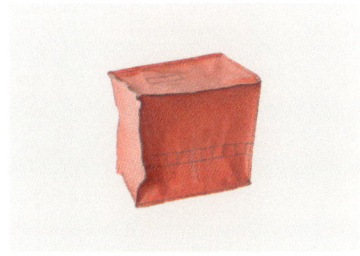

innen#7
2023

88
Brosche | Brooch
Aus der Reihe | From the series
innen
Leinwand, Acrylfarbe, Faden, Silber |
Canvas, acrylic paint, thread, silver
12 × 9 × 9 cm

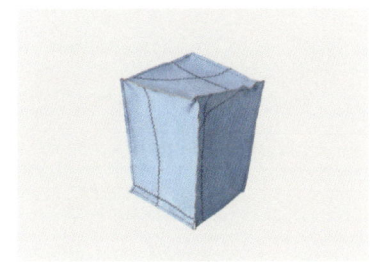

innen#5
2023

89
Brosche | Brooch
Aus der Reihe | From the series
innen
Leinwand, Acrylfarbe, Faden, Silber |
Canvas, acrylic paint, thread, silver
13 × 6 × 6 cm
Seite | Page 105

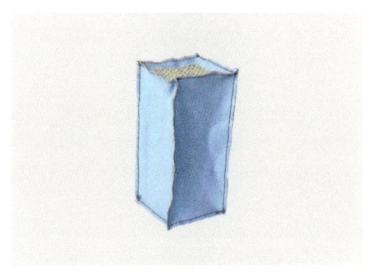

innen#2
2023

90
Objekt | Object
Aus der Reihe | From the series
KNELL II
Silber, Klebstoff | Silver, glue
3,8 × 43 × 37 cm

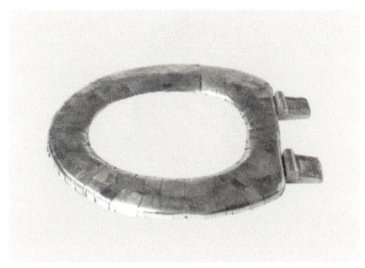

Klobrille / Toilet seat
2019

91
Objekt | Object
Aus der Reihe | From the series
KNELL II
Silber, Klebstoff | Silver, glue
7 × 44 × 7 cm
Seiten | Pages 100 | 101

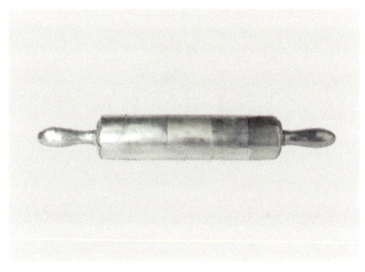

Nudelholz / Rolling pin
2019

92
Objekt | Object
Aus der Reihe | From the series
KNELL II
Silber, Klebstoff | Silver, glue
5,8 × 21 × 3,5 cm

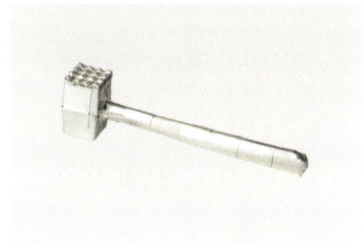

**Fleischhammer /
Meat tenderizer**
2018

Hammer
2018

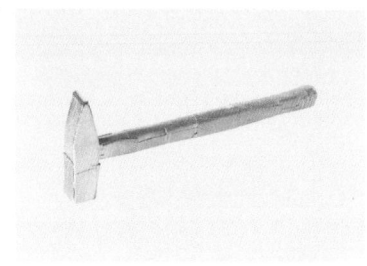

93
Objekt / Object
Aus der Reihe / From the series
KNELL II
Silber, Klebstoff / Silver, glue
11 × 29 × 2,3 cm

Pfanne / Pan
2018

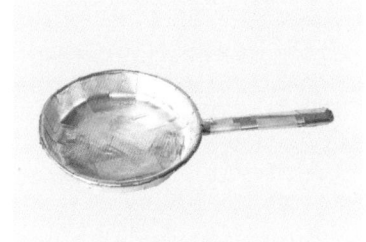

94
Objekt / Object
Aus der Reihe / From the series
KNELL II
Silber, Klebstoff / Silver, glue
8,7 × 39 × 22 cm

Bügeleisen / Flat iron
2017

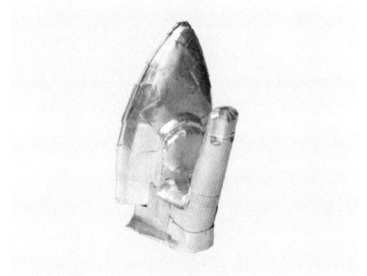

95
Objekt / Object
Aus der Reihe / From the series
KNELL II
Silber, Klebstoff / Silver, glue
27 × 15 × 14 cm
Seite / Page 103

KNELL – The Gender Bell#29
2018

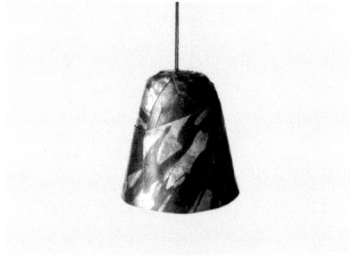

96
Halsschmuck / Necklace
Aus der Reihe / From the series
KNELL – The Gender Bell
Zinn, Faden, Holz, Aluminium /
Tin, thread, wood, aluminum
7 × 6,5 × 5,7 cm

KNELL – The Gender Bell#3X
2016

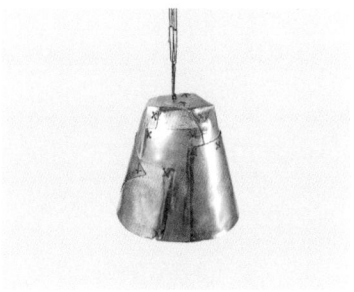

97
Halsschmuck / Necklace
Aus der Reihe / From the series
KNELL – The Gender Bell
Silber, Eisen, Holz / Silver, iron, wood
5,4 × 5,8 × 5,4 cm

KNELL – The Gender Bell#2
2016

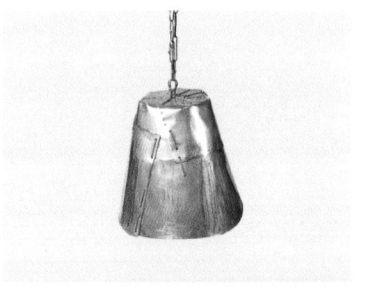

98
Halsschmuck / Necklace
Aus der Reihe / From the series
KNELL – The Gender Bell
Silber, Eisen, Penisknochen /
Silver, iron, penis bone
6,4 × 6,4 × 5,7 cm
Seite / Page 104

99
Halsschmuck | Necklace
Aus der Reihe | From the series
HOME
Zinn, Farbe, Faden | Tin, paint, thread
7 × 3,5 × 3,5 cm

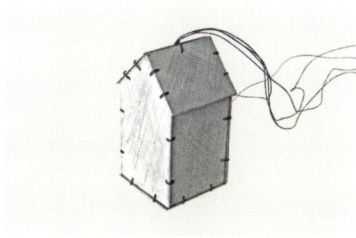

HOME#33
2010

100
Halsschmuck | Necklace
Aus der Reihe | From the series
HOME
Zinn, Faden | Tin, thread
5 × 3,4 × 3,2 cm

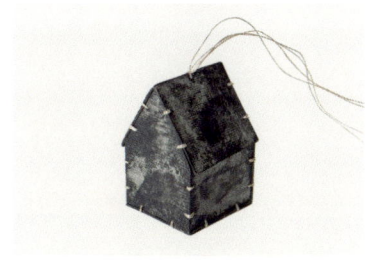

HOME#17
2009

Anna Rikkinen

101
Objekt | Object
Fundobjekt, Schmuckfragmente, Textil |
Ready-made object, jewelry parts, textile
ca. 20 × 60 × 20 cm
Seiten | Pages 42 | 43

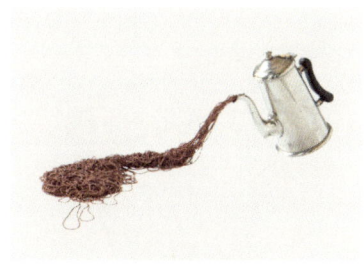

Hot Mess
2023

102
Objekte | Objects
Aus der Serie | From the series
Woods Baroque
Hölzerne Fundobjekte, Metallgerüst,
Textilband |
Wooden ready-made objects,
metal rods, ribbon
ca. 24–50 cm
Seite | Page 45

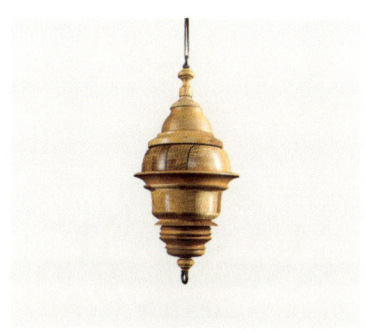

Woods Baroque 2
2022

103
Halsschmuck | Necklace
Fundobjekte, bemalte Holzobjekte,
Textilband |
Ready-made objects, painted wooden
objects, ribbon
50 × 40 × 12 cm
Seite | Page 46

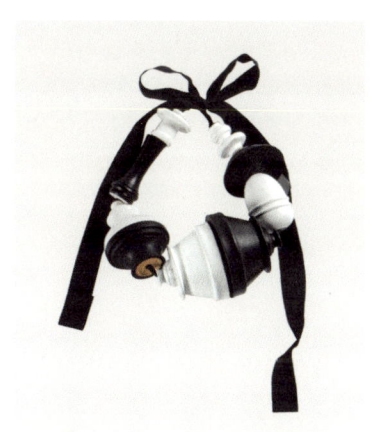

A Dutch Encounter VII
2011

Hans Stofer

String Theory – ST2
2014

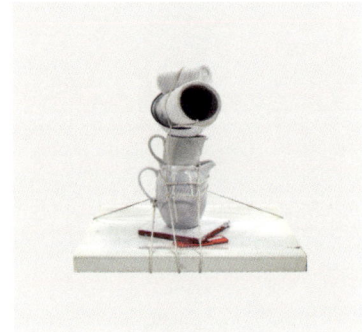

104
Objekt | Object
Mixed Media | Mixed media
30 × 17 × 17 cm
Seite | Page 98

Creation
2010

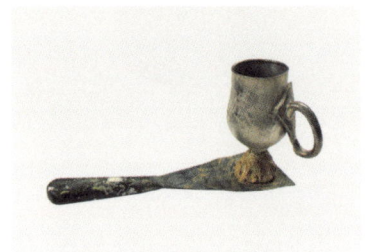

105
Objekt | Object
Stahl, Holz, Farbe, Silber |
Steel, wood, paint, silver
10 × 20 cm
Seite | Page 97

Off Balance
2010

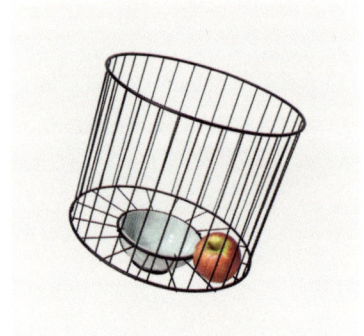

106
Objekt | Object
Beschichteter Stahl, Keramikteller |
Coated steel, ceramic dish
30 × Ø20 cm
Seite | Page 96

Hein-Ecken
2009

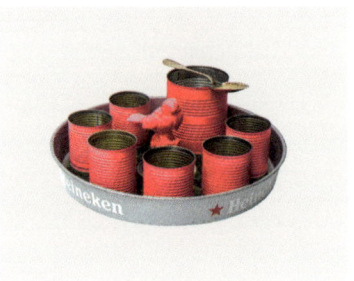

107
Objekt | Object
Bemalter Stahl, Silber, Keramik, Magnete |
Painted steel, silver, ceramic, magnets
16 × Ø40 cm

Vivi Touloumidi

108
Objekt | Object
Glas, Bronze, Kupfer, weiße Patina,
Edelstahl |
Glass, bronze, copper, white patina,
stainless steel
17 × 11 × 30 cm
Seite | Page 109

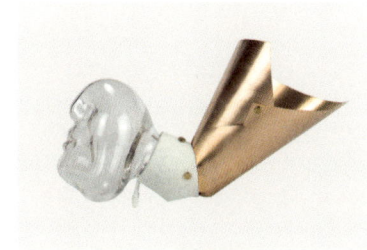

Hommage to Hannah Höch (Die Braut oder: Pandora 1924 / 1927)
2023

Tarja Tuupanen

109
Halsschmuck | Necklace
Gebrauchte Marmor-Tischobjekte,
Bänder, Messing |
Used marble tableware, ribbons, brass
Stein | Stone: 26 × 6 × 6 cm
Seite | Page 113

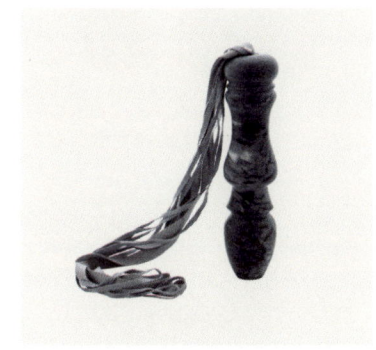

About Ornament II
2020

110
Halsschmuck | Necklace
Gebrauchte Marmor-Tischobjekte,
Baumwolle, Bänder |
Used marble tableware, cotton, ribbons
Stein | Stone: 14 × 10 × 5 cm

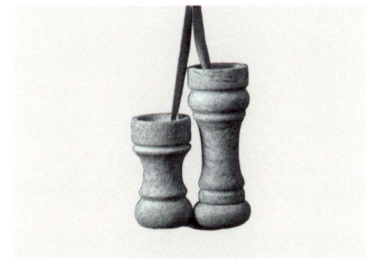

Ohne Titel / Untitled
2019

111
Objekt | Object
Gebrauchte Marmortischobjekte,
Holz, Kunststoff |
Used marble tableware, wood, plastic
120 × Ø6 cm
Seite | Page 114

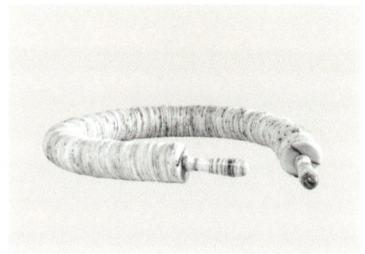

Baking Pin
2017

112
Objekt | Object
Gebrauchte Marmor-Tischobjekte,
Marmorstaub |
Used marble tableware, marble dust
7–9 × Ø60 cm
Seite | Page 115

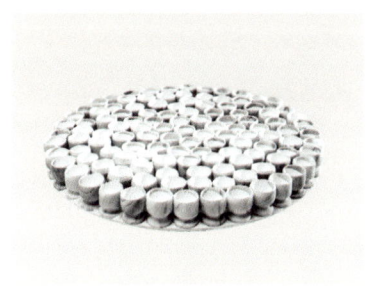

Table
2017

Luzia Vogt

Zuckerdose / Sugar bowl
2013

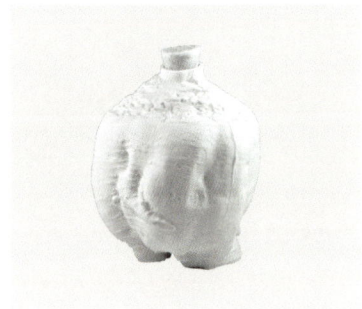

113
Objekt / Object
Bone-China-Porzellan, Carrara-Marmor
gegossen, innen glasiert, gebrannt;
Marmor: geschliffen /
Bone china porcelain, cast Carrara marble,
glazed interior, fired; marble: sanded
13,2 × 10,1 × 8,7 cm
Seite / Page 79

Rhythmus
2008–2011

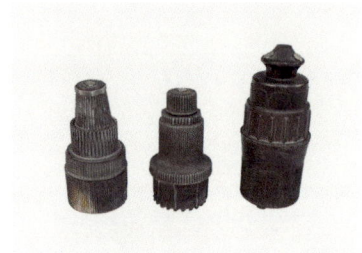

114
Salz- und Zuckerstreuer /
Salt and sugar shakers
Silber / Silver
ca. 6–4 cm
Seite / Page 81

I Am Hungry Nr. V
2008

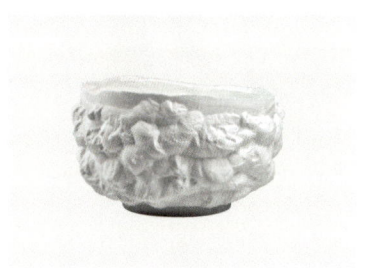

115
Schale / Bowl
Bone-China-Porzellan gegossen, innen
glasiert, gebrannt /
Cast bone china porcelain,
glazed interior, fired
7,3 × 12 × 12,4 cm
Seite / Page 80

Stella Wanisch

Presse
2021

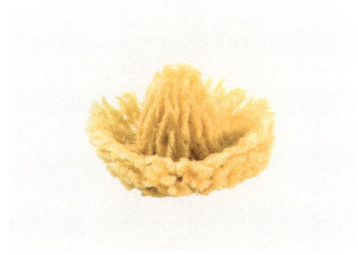

116
Objekt / Object
Naturschwamm / Natural sponge
8 × Ø12 cm
Seite / Page 99

Presse
2021

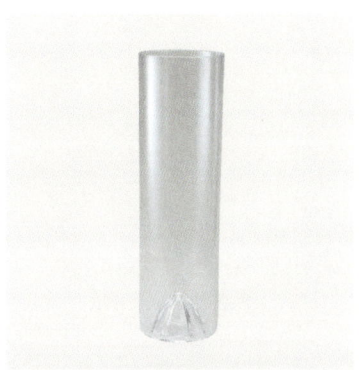

117
Objekt / Object
Glas mundgeblasen / Handblown glass
38 × Ø9 cm

Jing Yang

118
Halsschmuck | Necklace
Messing, Baumwolle | Brass, cotton
15 × 8 cm
Seite | Page 108

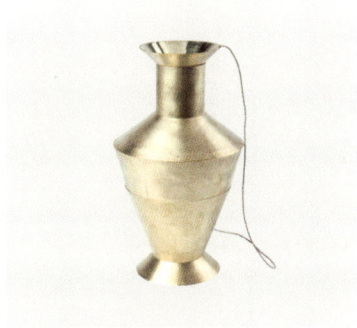

Ich bin keine Vase
2016

119
Halsschmuck | Necklace
Messing, Baumwolle | Brass, cotton
ca. 17 × 9 cm
Seiten | Pages 106 | 107

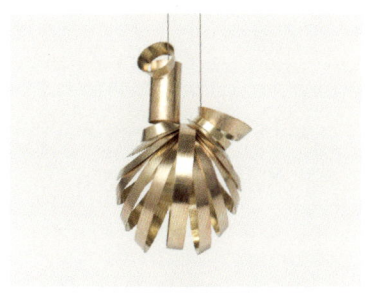

Ich bin keine Vase
2016

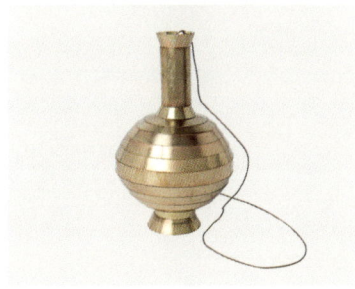

120
Halsschmuck | Necklace
Messing, Baumwolle | Brass, cotton
12 × 6 cm
Seite | Page 158

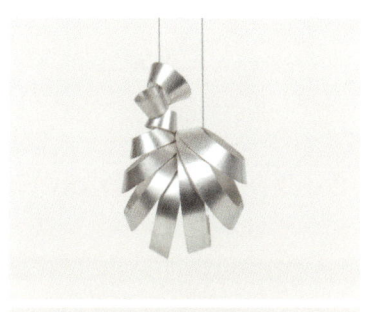

Ich bin keine Vase
2015

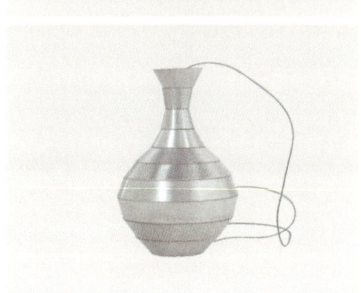

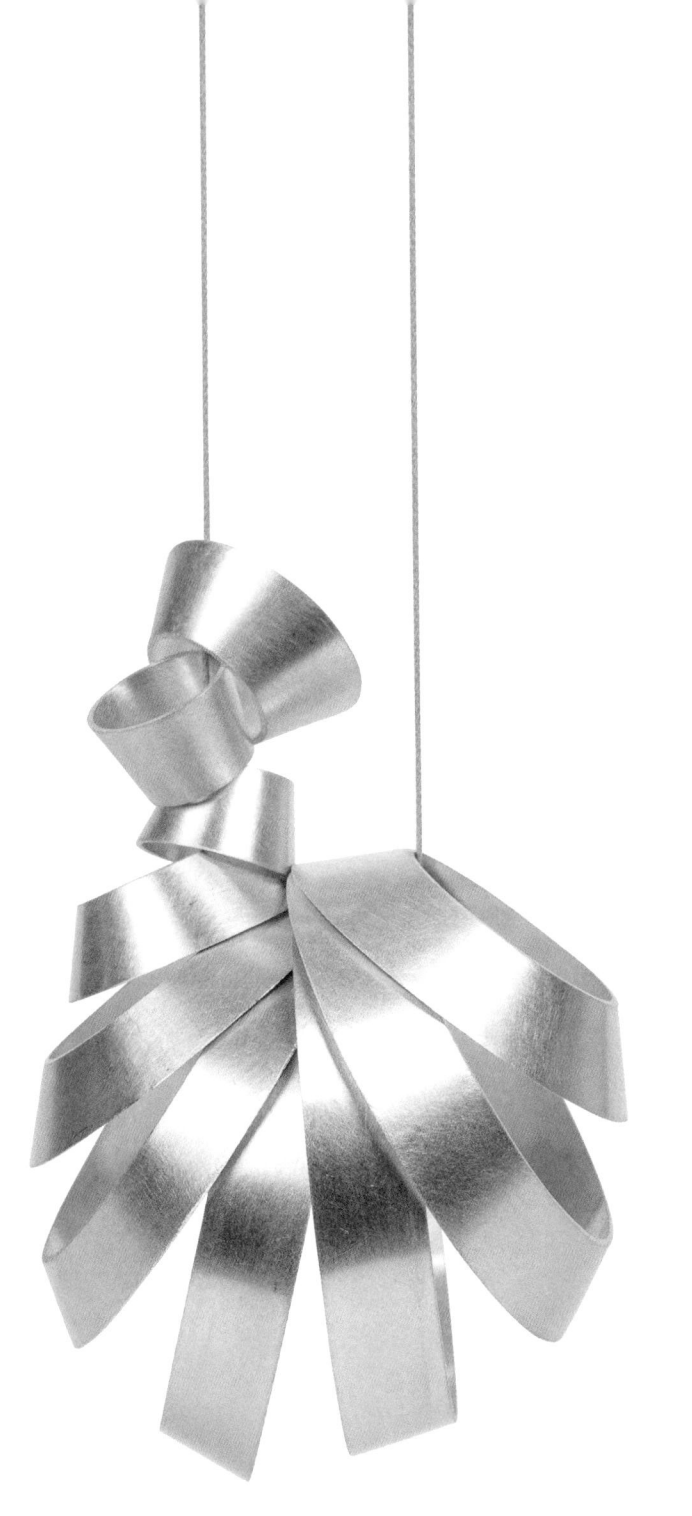

A–Y

Tobias Alm

born 1985 in Stockholm, SE

Education
2012–2014   Jewellery + Corpus, Master program, Konstfack, University of Arts, Crafts and Design, Stockholm, SE
2006–2009   Ädellab, Bachelor program, Konstfack, University of Arts, Crafts and Design, Stockholm, SE
2004–2006   Metallhantverk | Smide, Stenebyskolan, Dals Långed, SE

Teaching and Consultancy | Fabrication
Part time teacher in wood craft at Kristofferskolan, Stockholm, SE
2020   Guest teacher in chasing and repoussé course, BFA program, Jewellery Art, HDK Valand, University of Gothenburg, SE
• Guest teacher in chasing and repoussé course, Leksands Folkhögskola, SE
2019   External tutor, MFA program, Jewellery Art, Academy of Design and Crafts, University of Gothenburg, SE
• Guest teacher in Arts and Crafts, the Concepts course, Metal Art, Academy of Design and Crafts, University of Gothenburg, SE
2018   Final review critic, MFA program, Jewellery + Metalsmithing, Rhode Island School of Design, Providence | RI, US
• Guest teacher in Arts and Crafts, the Concepts course, Metal Art, Academy of Design and Crafts, University of Gothenburg, SE
2006–2016   Part time public art fabricator | technical consultant for Annika Oskarsson and Thomas Nordström, Stockholm, SE

Public Art Commissions
2019   The Hand and the Tool, Public art commission for preschool in Solberga, Stockholm, through Stockholm Konst, SE
2017   The Hand and the Tool, Public art commission for preschool in Kistahöjden, Stockholm, through Stockholm Konst, SE

Grants and Awards
2019–2021   Stockholm City Studio Grant, SE
2018–2019   Two-year working scholarship, Swedish Arts Grants Committee, Stockholm, SE
2016–2018   Stockholm City Studio Grant, SE
2015   Estrid Ericson stiftelse, Stockholm, SE
• Pronto!, Gothenburg City Culture Project Grant, SE
2014   Jubelfonden | Swedish Freemason Grant, Stockholm, SE
• Fabrikör J.L. Eklund scholarship, Stockholm, SE
2013   Estrid Ericson stiftelse, Stockholm, SE
• Fabrikör J.L. Eklund scholarship, Stockholm, SE
2006–2012   Fabrikör J.L. Eklund scholarship, Stockholm, SE
• One-year working scholarship, Swedish Arts Grants Committee, Stockholm, SE
• 3 × IASPIS international culture exchange scholarship Konstfack graduation award, SE
• Estrid Ericson stiftelse, Stockholm, SE
• Konstfack young student grant, Stockholm, SE

Artist in Residence
2016 | 17   IASPIS, Swedish Arts Grants Committee, Studio Residency, Stockholm, SE

Work in Public Collections
• CODA Museum, Apeldoorn, NL
• Nationalmuseum, Stockholm, SE

Sawa Aso

geboren 1983 in Tokyo, JP

Ausbildung
Seit 2014   Freischaffende Schmuckkünstlerin
2012–2014   Meisterschülerin Schmuck bei Prof. Daniel Kruger an der Burg Giebichenstein Kunsthochschule Halle, DE
2007–2012   Studium an der Burg Giebichenstein Kunsthochschule Halle, DE, Fachrichtung Schmuck, bei Prof. Daniel Kruger, Diplom
2002–2006   Studium Interkulturelle Wissenschaften an der Seikei Universität, Tokyo, JP

Auszeichnungen und Stipendien
2021   Kultur ans Netz II, Arbeitsstipendium für Kulturschaffende des Landes Sachsen-Anhalt, DE
2020   Kultur ans Netz, Arbeitsstipendium für Kulturschaffende des Landes Sachsen-Anhalt, DE
2019   Arbeitsstipendium der Kunststiftung des Landes Sachsen-Anhalt, DE
2013   1. Preis für Junges Kunsthandwerk des Bayerischen Kunstgewerbevereins, München, DE
2012   Anerkennung Kunstpreis der Stiftung der Saalesparkasse, Halle, DE
• Förderpreis der Justus Brinckmann Gesellschaft, Hamburg, DE

Arbeiten in öffentlichen Sammlungen
• CODA Museum, Apeldoorn, NL
• MAKK Museum für Angewandte Kunst Köln, DE

Astrid Becksteiner-Rasche

geboren 1964 in Graz, AT

Ausbildung
2014–2016   Studium der Schmuckkunst bei Wolfgang Rahs, Ortweinschule, Graz, AT
2007   Promotion, kunst_quantitativ: richard kriesche, drei Bände, erschienen bei Leykam 2008
1982–1992   Studium der Deutschen Philologie und Kunstgeschichte, Karl-Franzens-Universität Graz, AT

Lehraufträge
1999–2005   Meisterklasse für Szenografie bei Erich Wonder, Akademie der Bildenden Künste Wien, AT
1998 | 99   University of Aberdeen, UK
1996 | 97   École Nationale de Paris, FR
1996   Kulturelle Repräsentation im Fernsehfeature Alltagsgeschichten, Institut für Europäische Ethnologie, Karl-Franzens-Universität Graz, AT

Freie Arbeit 1993–2004:
Video, Performance
• Formiert aus Luft, mit Peter Pessl, Leseperformance, ImCubus, Graz, AT
• Diffusion, mit Petra Ganglbauer, Graz und Wien, AT
• When the landscape ceases, mit Dieter Sperl, Leseperformance, Aberdeen, UK und Wien, AT
• Fu Five, für Dieter Sperl
• IC 72, mit Wolfgang Becksteiner, Graz, AT
• check, mit Georg Zeitblom, Aberdeen, UK
• abgerissene flanken, mit Dieter Sperl, für Salon 13, echoraum Wien, AT

- uncommon bundle, *mit John Jasperse für die gleichnamige Tanzperformance, Graz, AT*
- Peri, *mit Klaudia Reichenbacher und Gerhard Nierhaus für die gleichnamige Performance, Graz, AT*
- Schmerz Raum Stille, *mit Klaudia Reichenbacher für die gleichnamige Tanzperformance, Graz, AT*
- sidestepper, *mit Franzobel und Dieter Sperl, Graz, Aberdeen, UK und Wien, AT*
- temptation, *Anerkennungspreis des Landes Steiermark*
- Echos und Masken, *mit Elfriede Jelinek, für die gleichnamige Ausstellung im Rahmen des steirischen Herbstes*
- unser wald, *mit G.R.A.M.*
kurzlebige alliancen, *mit Manfred Erjautz, Dieter Sperl, plazma*

Künstlerische Tätigkeit als Gold- und Silberschmiedin
2018   Einzelausstellung ich verreise in meinen garten hommage an hannah höch, *kunst.wirt.schaft Graz, AT*
Seit 2017   Ausstellungsbeteiligungen, *kunst.wirt.schaft Graz, AT*
Seit 2014   Freie Schmuckkünstlerin
Seit 2007   Entwurf und Anfertigung von Schmuckobjekten

Naama Bergman

born 1982 in Tel-Aviv, IL

Education
2013–2019   Master class student, Jewellery class, Prof. Otto Künzli, Prof. Karen Pontoppidan, Akademie der Bildenden Künste, Munich, DE
2009–2010   Stone setting course, Maziar School of Jewelry Craft, Ramat-Gan, IL
2007   Exchange student, Prof. Otto Künzli, Akademie der Bildenden Künste, Munich, DE
2004–2008   BFA Department of Jewelry and Fashion, Bezalel Academy of Art and Design, Jerusalem, IL

Working Experience and Teaching
Since 2021   Lecture, Department of Jewelry and Fashion, Bezalel Academy of Art and Design, Jerusalem, IL
Since 2019   Freelance goldsmith, Munich, DE
2009–2010   Goldsmith, Ruby Star's studio, Tel-Aviv, IL
2008–2011   Senior Teaching Assistant, Department of Jewelry and Fashion, Bezalel Academy of Art and Design, Jerusalem, IL
2008–2009   Goldsmith, Lee Bonk's studio, Tel-Aviv, IL

Awards and Scholarships
2019   Franz-Lothar Altmann Foundation prize for Diplom exhibition, DE
2018   Graduation grant from the STIBET program of DAAD, DE
- Finalist at the Mari Funaki Award for Contemporary Jewellery, Melbourne, AU
- Danner Foundation internal class competition prize, DE
- Upper Bavarian Award for Applied Art, Munich, DE
2017   Second prize of the Danner Foundation internal class competition, DE
- Finalist at Bayerischer Kunstgewerbeverein, Prize for young applied arts, Munich, DE
2015–2016   DAAD Study Scholarships for Foreign Graduates in the Fields of Fine Art, Film, Design/Visual Communication and Film, DE
2016   Third prize of the Danner Foundation internal class competition, Munich, DE
2015   Finalist at the BKV Prize for young applied arts, Munich, DE
2014   Jubilee Scholarship Foundation, Scholarship for portfolio design, Akademie der Bildenden Künste, Munich, DE
2008/09   America-Israel Cultural Foundation, Scholarship for metal design, IL
2008   Eithan Ron prize, Excellence award for Jewelry design, Bezalel Academy of Art and Design, Jerusalem, IL
- Third place of the annual International Graduation show 2008 at the MIDORA trade fair for watches and jewelry in Leipzig, DE
- Irit Strauss prize, Scholarship for excellence in the History and Theory Department, Bezalel Academy of Art and Design, Jerusalem, IL

Artist in Residence
2022   DIVA atelier, DIVA, Museum for Diamonds, Jewellery and Silver, Antwerp, BE

Work in Public Collections
Arkansas Arts Center, Arkansas, US

Tobias Birgersson

born 1973 in Visby, Gotland, SE

Education
1999–1901   MFA, Metallformgivning, Konstfack, University of Arts, Crafts and Design, Stockholm, SE

Teaching
Since 2016   Associate Professor and Senior Lecturer, University of Gothenburg, SE
Since 2007   Konstfack, University of Arts, Crafts and Design, Ädellab, Stockholm, SE

Founding member of LOD Gallery and Atelier and Kungsholmens Täljargille

Awards
2022   One-year working grant, Swedish Arts Grants Committee, Stockholm, SE
2004   Unga Konsthantverkare, Bengt Julins Fond, Stockholm, SE
2003   Two-year working grant, Swedish Arts Grants Committee, Stockholm, SE

Curatorship
2022   Extended Family *at Streitfeld during Munich Jewellery Week, DE*
2021   The Fourth Dimension, *Not Quite Fengersfors, SE*
2020   Sharing is Caring, *Orangerie, English Garden, Munich, DE*
- Andrew Hayes tour, *Gallery LOD, Steneby Art Hall, Wallénhallen, Gallery Sebastian Schildt, SE*
- Uncommon Element, *Gallery Konsthantverkarna, Stockholm, SE*
- Metal endeavours, *International Metal Art Exhibition, Gallery Sebastian Schildt, Stockholm, SE*
2018   HDK Steneby GBG Design Week, *Högskolan för Design och Konsthantverk, Gothenburg, SE*
- Adi Toch – Shifting space, *Israel/GB, Gallery LOD, Stockholm, SE*
- Forge Form Fabricate, *University Museum of Southern Illinois University, Carbndale/IL, US*
- Metall + Metall, *Steneby Art Hall, Gothenburg, SE*
- Äta Korpus, *Karolina Hägg, Gallery LOD, Stockholm, SE*
2017   WHATNOT, *Myra Mimlitsch Gray, Gallery LOD, Stockholm, SE*

Public Art Commissions
2021   Bon för stora småvarelser *with Simon Westling, Cothenburg, SE*

2018 Divider, *Kalmar, with Päivi Ernqvist, A Symbolic Cattle Grid, SE*
• Toolness of things II, *Ohrdruf, DE*
2016 Pathfinder, *Stockholm Art, MICASA Six Walkways, SE*

Artist in Residence
2018 AIR at Technisches Denkmal Tobiashammer, Ohrdruf, DE
2017 Southern Illinois University, Carbondale | IL, US (metalsmithing program)

Work in Public Collections
Nationalmuseum, Stockholm, SE

Beatrice Brovia

born 1985 in Modena, IT

Education
2020–2022 Högskolepedagogik (pedagogical course for higher education), Konstfack, University of Arts, Crafts and Design, Stockholm, SE
2007–2009 Jewellery + Corpus, Master of Fine Arts, Prof. Ruudt Peters, Prof. Karen Pontoppidan, Konstfack, Stockholm, SE
2004–2007 Interior Architecture, Bachelor of Science, Politecnico di Milano, IT

Working Experience
Since 2020 Senior lecturer specialising in jewelry and head of the BA program, Jewellery + Corpus, Ädellab, Konstfack, Stockholm, SE
2019–2020 Guest senior lecturer specialising in jewelry and deputy head of BA program, Jewellery + Corpus, Ädellab, Konstfack, Stockholm, SE
2013–2019 Lecturer specialising in jewelry, Jewellery + Corpus, Ädellab, Konstfack, Stockholm, SE
Since 2011 Cofounder, with Nicolas Cheng, of the collaborative artistic practice CONVERSATION PIECE, Stockholm, SE
2010–2013 Guest lecturer and tutor, BA and MA program, Jewellery + Corpus, Ädellab, Konstfack, Stockholm, SE
Since 2009 Self-employed artist and designer, active as practitioner and educator within the field of jewelry

Awards and Scholarships
2022 Herbert-Hofmann-Prize, Internationale Handwerksmesse, Munich, DE (with CONVERSATION PIECE)
2020 Two-year working grant, Swedish Arts Grants Committee, Stockholm, SE
2015 Bronze Price, Cheongju Craft Biennale, KR (with CONVERSATION PIECE)
2014 1st Prize (with CONVERSATION PIECE), New Traditional Jewellery Award, Sieraad Art Fair, NL
• Two-year working grant, Swedish Arts Grants Committee, Stockholm, SE
2013, 2015 Kulturbryggan (with CONVERSATION PIECE)
2013 Innovativ Kultur (with CONVERSATION PIECE)
2011, 2012, 2013, 2017 Estrid Ericson stiftelse, Stockholm, SE
2011 Konstnärsnämnden, Project Grant, Swedish Arts Grants Committee, Stockholm, SE
2010, 2011, 2012, 2013, 2014, 2017, 2018, 2020, 2022 IASPIS, Internationellt Kulturutbyte, SE
2010 Talente – Meister der Zukunft Design prize 2010, Internationale Handwerksmesse, Munich, DE

Artist in Residence
2020 Blumhardt Foundation International Artist in Residence, Objectspace, public gallery for design, craft and architecture, Auckland, Aotearoa, NZ

Work in Public Collections
• Cheongju Craft Biennale Foundation, KR
• Danner-Stiftung, Die Neue Sammlung – The Design Museum, Munich, DE
• Deedie Rose collection, promised to the Dallas Museum of Art, Dallas | TX, US
• Design Museum den Bosch, NL
• Die Neue Sammlung – The Design Museum, Munich, DE
• Françoise van den Bosch Foundation, Amsterdam, NL
• Museum Arnhem, NL
• Nationalmuseum, Stockholm, SE

Nicolas Cheng

born 1982 in Hongkong, CN

Education and Teaching
Since 2022 Professorship for Kontextuelle Praxis im Bereich Schmuck und Gerät, Akademie der Bildenden Künste, Munich, DE
2015–2019 PhD in Fine Arts in Jewellery & Crafts, University of Gothenburg, SE
2008–2010 MFA, Jewellery + Corpus, Konstfack, University of Arts, Crafts and Design, Stockholm, SE
2004–2006 BA in Design, Design Academy Eindhoven, NL

Awards and Scholarships
2022 Herbert-Hofmann-Prize, Internationale Handwerksmesse, Munich, DE
2021, 2022 IASPIS, Konstnärsnämnden, Internationellt Kulturutbyte, SE
2020 One-year working grant, IASPIS, Konstnärsnämnden, SE
• Göteborgs Slöjdförenings projektstipendier, SE
2019 IASPIS, Konstnärsnämnden, Internationellt Kulturutbyte, SE
2017 Wallenbergs Resestipendier, Gothenburg, SE
2016 Adlerbertska Stipendier, Gothenburg, SE
2015 Bronze Prize, Cheongju International Craft Biennale, KR
2014 1st prize, Confrontations – New Tradition Jewellery, Amsterdam, NL
2013 Innovativ Kultur and Kulturbryggans Project Grant, SE
• AFK – Amsterdam Fonds voor de Kunst Project Grant, NL
• Landeshauptstadt Munich, Kulturreferat and Danner-Stiftung Munich, DE
2011–2019 Estrid Ericson stiftelse, Stockholm, SE
2011–2013 Konstnärsnämnden Project Grant, SE
2011 YDTA, Young Design Talent Award, HK
• The Material of Poetry, Special Prize – Open Design Italia: Selected, IT
2010–2014 IASPIS, Internationellt Kulturutbyte, SE
2010 1st prize, Winner of Open Design Italia, IT
2009 Fabrikör JL Eklunds, Konstfacks Stipendium, SE
2008 40 under 40 Perspective Award, Outstanding Young Artists | Designers, HK

Artist in Residence
2020 The Blumhardt International Residency, Auckland, NZ
• Dunedin School of Art Residency, Dunedin, NZ
2007–2008 Artist in Residency, FABRICA Research Centre, Treviso, IT

Work in Public Collections
• Cheongju International Craft Biennale Foundation, Cheongju, KR
• Danner-Stiftung, Die Neue Sammlung – The Design Museum, Munich, DE
• Die Neue Sammlung – The Design Museum, Munich, DE
• Museum Arnhem, NL
• Stedelijk Museum's-Hertogenbosch, NL
• Stichting Françoise van den Bosch, NL
• The Metropolitan Museum of Art, New York/NY, US
• The Wallace Arts Trust, NZ

David Clarke

born 1967 in Nottingham, UK

Highs & Lows
1975 Arrived in London, UK
1976 Choirboy, St Andrews & Holy Trinity Church, Church of England, London, UK
1979 Paperboy, Madge's Corner Shop, London, UK
1982 Assistant to Cathy Hassell Fine Art Conservator, restoring old paintings, London, UK
1985 Dismissed from Peter Jones Department Store, London, UK
1989 Foundation Course Certificate, Sir John Cass School of Art, London, UK
1989 Unemployed, London, UK
1991 Potato shelf-filler, Marks & Spencer PLC, London, UK
1992 Camberwell College of Arts, Bachelor of Arts, London, UK
1993 Rejected application, Royal College of Arts, London, UK
1996 Store Manager, Marks & Spencer PLC, London, UK
1997 Royal College of Arts, Master of Arts, London, UK
1998 Misterclarke was hatched.

Listen & Guide
• UK: Royal College of Art, Glasgow School of Art
• Europe: Akademie der Bildenden Künste, Munich, DE; Alchimia School of Jewellery, Florence, IT; Konstfack School of Arts, Stockholm, SE
• Asia: The University of Arts Taipei, TW; Hiko Muzuno School of Jewellery, Tokyo, JP; Nanjing University of Arts, CN
• Australia and New Zealand: RMIT Melbourne, AU; Dunedin School of Art, Dunedin, NZ
• US: Rhode Island School of Design; University of Wisconsin-Madison & Milwaukee

Gathered & Share
• Birmingham Museum & Art Gallery, UK
• BR Collection Beijing, CN
• Brighton Museum & Art Gallery, UK
• Dallas Museum of Art, US
• Hiko Mizuno Collection, Tokyo, JP
• Röhsska Museum, Gothenburg, SE
• The Box, Plymouth, UK
• The Chipstone Foundation, Milwaukee/WI, US
• The Marzee Collection, Nijmegen, NL
• The National Museum, Oslo, NO
• The Worshipful Company of Goldsmiths, London, UK
• Ulster Museum Belfast, UK
• Victoria and Albert Museum, London, UK

Kanako Ebisawa

geboren 1986 in Akita, JP

Ausbildung
2015–2023 Akademie der Bildenden Künste, München, DE, Klasse für Schmuck und Gerät bei Prof. Karen Pontoppidan, Meisterschülerin
2013–2014 University of the Arts London, UK
• Central Saint Martins College of Art and Design, foundation course, Jewellery, Footwear & Fashion Accessories
2007–2009 Bachelor of Art, Engineering, Sapporo School of the Arts, JP
• Advanced course (Visual communication Design)
2002–2007 Associate Bachelor's Degree, Sapporo School of the Arts, JP
• Sapporo City Board of Education, Industrial design course (Visual communication Design)

Preise und Auszeichnungen
2023 Nominiert für den Rotary Kunstpreis NEUE WELTEN vol. 3, DE
• Finalist, SCHMUCK 2023 Internationale Handwerksmesse, München, DE
2021 Zweiter Preis, Interner Klassenwettbewerb, Danner-Stiftung, München, DE
2019 Stipendium zur Teilnahme an der Salzburger Sommerakademie, Bayerisches Staatsministerium für Bildung und Kultus, Wissenschaft und Kunst/Akademie der Bildenden Künste, München, DE/AT
• Finalist, Award Talente 2019
2018 Stipendium für ausländische Studierende des Bayerischen Kultusministeriums, München, DE
2016 Erster Preis, Interner Klassenwettbewerb, Danner-Stiftung, München, DE
2015–2017 DAAD-Studienstipendium für ausländische Graduierte in den Fachrichtungen Bildende Kunst, Design/Visuelle Kommunikation und Film, Bonn, DE

Ute Eitzenhöfer

geboren 1969 in Bruchsal, DE

Ausbildung und Lehrtätigkeit
Seit 2005 Professorin für Edelsteingestaltung an der Hochschule Trier, Fachbereich Gestaltung, Fachrichtung Edelstein und Schmuck, Idar-Oberstein, DE
2000–2004 Lehrtätigkeit an der Hochschule Trier, Fachbereich Gestaltung, Fachrichtung Edelstein und Schmuck, Idar-Oberstein, DE und an der Hochschule für Gestaltung Pforzheim, DE
Seit 1996 Freischaffend tätig in Karlsruhe, DE
1992–1996 Hochschule für Gestaltung Pforzheim, DE, Studiengang Schmuck und Gerät, Diplom
1990–1992 Goldschmiedelehre, Gesellenprüfung, Karlsruhe, DE
1988–1992 Berufsfachschule für Goldschmiede, Goldschmiedeschule Pforzheim, DE

Auszeichnungen
2001 Junge Schmuckkunst im Museum, ISSP-Förderankauf 2001, Schmuckmuseum Pforzheim, DE
2000 Marzee-prijs, Galerie Marzee, Nijmegen, NL
• Dritter Platz, Hessischer Staatspreis, DE
1998, 1999, 2001 Sonderschau FORM, Frankfurt/M., DE

Arbeiten in öffentlichen Sammlungen
- Alice und Louis Koch Sammlung, Landesmuseum Zürich, CH
- CODA Museum, Apeldoorn, NL
- Danner'sche Kunstgewerbestiftung, Dauerleihgabe Die Neue Sammlung – The Design Museum, München
- Jur and Thea van Lee-Ellis Collection, NL
- Museum für Angewandte Kunst, Frankfurt/M., DE
- Museum Turnov, CZ
- Rijksmuseum Amsterdam, NL
- Rotasa Trust Collection, Mill Valley/CA, US
- Schmuckmuseum Pforzheim, DE
- The Marzee Collection, Nijmegen, NL

Åsa Elmstam

born 1978 in Stockholm, SE

Education
2010   Three-month internship (sustainability in design), Open House company, Tokyo, JP
2006–2007   Tokyo Zokei University, Institution Sustainable projects, JP
2006   Stockholm School of Entrepreneurship, Design & Innovation, SE
2005   Ars Ornata – international workshop, Lisbon, PT
2004   International workshop, MassArt University, Boston/MA, US
2002–2007   BA, Konstfack, University of Arts, Crafts and Design, Metal department, Ädellab, Stockholm, SE
2000–2002   Metall & Wood, Nyckelviksskolan, Lidingö, SE
1999–2000   Konstskolan Basis, Stockholm, SE
1995   Exchange (Perry Court Waldorfschool), Canterbury, UK
1994–1997   Kristofferskolan (Steiner School, High School), Bromma, SE

Working Experience and Teaching
2022   Panel discussion and Artist talk, Svensk Form Gotland & GKF, Gotlands Museum, Visby, SE
- Lecture, Konstfack, University of Arts, Crafts and Design, Textile BFA, Stockholm, SE
2021   Klimatexistens *lecture*, Sigtunastiftelsen and CEMUS, Sigtuna, SE
2020–2021   Part-time teacher, Metal program, Nyckelviksskolan, Lidingö, SE
- Board member, KlimatAktion

2020   Vad är jag värd – värdet av det handgjorda *lecture*, Länsmuseet Gävleborg, SE
2019   Konsthantverkarna, Stockholm, SE Panel discussion, International Climate Conference, Stockholm, SE
2018   Artist lecture, The Biennal METALLophone, Vilnius, LT
2018–2020   Board member, Nutida Svenskt Silver (Contemporary Swedish Silver), Stockholm, SE
- Cultural producer and teacher, Sundbybergs stad, Kulturcentrum, Stockholm, SE
Since 2017   Pedagogue, Skansen open-air museum, Stockholm, SE
2014   Konsthantverkets vänner, Stockholm, SE
2010   Artist lecture, Tokyo Zokei University, JP

Awards and Scholarships (selection)
2022   Krisstipendium 4, Swedish Arts Grants Committee, Stockholm, SE
- Ateljéstöd, studio support, Cultural Department of Stockholm City, SE
2021   Krisstipendium 3, Swedish Arts Grants Committee, Stockholm, SE
2020   Krisstipendium 2, Swedish Arts Grants Committee, Stockholm, SE
- Nominated as one of four to Design S, Swedish Design Awards 2020
- Two-year working grant, Konstnärsnämnden/Swedish Arts Grants Committee, Stockholm, SE
2019–2021   Ateljéstöd Stockholm Stad, studio support, Cultural Department of Stockholm City, SE
2019   IASPIS, Konstnärsnämnden, Swedish Arts Grants Committee for international cultural exchange, Stockholm, SE
2018   One-year working grant, Konstnärsnämnden/Swedish Arts Grants Committee, Stockholm, SE
- Nominated as one of four to Design S, Swedish Design Awards 2018
- Estrid Ericson stiftelse, Stockholm, SE
2016–2018   Ateljéstöd Stockholm Stad, studio support Cultural Department of Stockholm City, SE
2016   Seven-day residency for artists in the Nordic Watercolour Museum, Nordiska Akvarellmuseet, SE
- Estrid Ericson stiftelse, Stockholm, SE
2013–2015   Ateljéstöd Stockholm Stad, Studio support, Cultural Department of Stockholm City, SE
2013   One of four finalists selected for The Art Jewelry Forum (AJF) Artist Award Competition, emerging artist
- KHV Konsthantverkets Vänners scholarship, SE

Work in Public Collections
- Danderyds Sjukhus – Logopedkliniken, Kulturförvaltningen Region Stockholm, SE
- Handelsbanken, SE
- Nationalmuseum, Stockholm, SE
- RIAN designmuseum, Falkenberg, SE
- Statens konstråd (Public Art Agency), SE

Anne Fischer

geboren 1980 in Nürnberg, DE

Ausbildung
2010–2012   Künstlerische Mitarbeiterin, Prof. Daniel Kruger, Burg Giebichenstein Kunsthochschule Halle, Fachgebiet Kunst, Fachbereich Schmuck, DE
Seit 2010   Atelier in Nürnberg, DE
2009   Meisterschülerin, Prof. Ulla Mayer, DE
2008   Auslandssemester, Konstfack, University of Arts, Crafts and Design, Stockholm, Ädellab, bei Prof. Karen Pontoppidan, SE
2004–2010   Akademie der Bildenden Künste Nürnberg bei Prof. Ulla Mayer, DE
2001–2004   Silberschmiedin, Berufsfachschule für Glas und Schmuck Neugablonz, DE

Vorträge
2008   Konkurrenz belebt das Geschäft, Plattform für DaNeben, Burg Giebichenstein, Halle, DE
2007   Students put their work on display, 40. Schmucksymposium Zimmerhof, Bad Rappenau, DE

Preise und Stipendien
2021   Investitionsförderung der Danner-Stiftung, München, DE
2017   Erster Preis, Handwerksmuseum Deggendorf, Wettbewerb Feuer und Flamme, DE
- Pott Award, Thema Besteck, Solingen, DE
2015   Einzelausstellung mit Katalog, Debütantenförderung des Bayerischen Staatsministeriums für Bildung und Kultus, Wissenschaft und Kunst, DE
2013–2014   Programm zur Realisierung der Chancengleichheit für Frauen in Forschung und Lehre, Bayerisches Staatsministerium für Bildung und Kultus, Wissenschaft und Kunst, DE
2011–2014   Atelierförderung der Stadt Nürnberg, DE
2010   Bayerischer Staatspreis, München, DE

2008 Danner-Stiftung, München, DE, zur Förderung der beruflichen Fortbildung
• Free Mover Stipendium, Konstfack, University of Arts, Crafts and Design, Stockholm, Ädellab, bei Prof. Karen Pontoppidan, SE

Kuratorische Tätigkeit
2018 Die Kanne – der Inhalt – das Objekt, Galerie Bayerischer Kunstgewerbeverein, München, DE

Arbeiten in öffentlichen Sammlungen
• Diözesanmuseum Bamberg, DE
• Klingenmuseum Solingen, DE
• Luftmuseum Amberg, DE

Karolina Hägg

born in 1986 Ljungby, SE

Education
Since 2019 Member of Nutida Svenskt Silver
2011–2013 Master of Fine Arts, Jewellery + Corpus, Konstfack, University of Arts, Crafts and Design, Stockholm, SE
2008–2011 Bachelor of Fine Arts, Metallformgivning/Ädellab, Konstfack, University of Arts, Crafts and Design, Stockholm, SE
2006–2008 Stenebyskolan, Metal art and silversmithing, Dals Långed, SE
2002–2005 Estetisk bild, Hammarskolan gymnasium, Ljungby, SE

Working Experience and Teaching
2023 Opponent, HDK – Academy of Design and Crafts, Jewellery Art, Gothenburg, SE
Since 2018 Lecturer in jewelry and metal techniques, Konstfack, University of Arts Craft and Design, Stockholm, SE
2018 Casting course, HDK Steneby Metallgestaltning, with Tobias Birgersson and Karl Engvall, HDK Steneby, Dals Långed, SE
2017 Casting Course, HDK – Academy of Design and Crafts, Jewellery Art, Gothenburg, SE
• Tuition of exam works, Bachelor in Metal Art, HDK Steneby, Dals Långed, SE
• External tutor, exam project at Bachelor level, Rémy Sorondo, HDK Steneby, Dals Långed, SE

Artist in Residence and Employments
2017 External tutor for Rémy Sorondo, bachelor project HDK Steneby, Dals Långed, SE
2016–2018 Responsible for gallery and shop Nutida Svenskt Silver, Stockholm, SE
Since 2016 Metal constructor and set-designer/costume for artist Nathalia Edenmont
2016 HDK Steneby Metallgestaltning, Dals Långed, SE
2015 Hjärta metal sculpture, public commission, Malmöfestivalen, SE
2013 Assistant to curator Karen Pontoppidan, exhibition State of Things, Pinakothek der Moderne, Munich, DE

Grants
2021 Studio Grant, Stockholm City, SE
2018 Studio Grant, Stockholm City, SE
2013 Grant, Vasakronan Konstfack, Stockholm, SE
• Workshop Grant, KKV Artist collective workshop, Farsta, SE
• Grant, Konstfack Flemmings och Färngrens stipendiestiftelse, Stockholm, SE
2012 Grant, JL Eklund Stipendium, Chamber of handicrafts, Stockholm, SE
2010 Grant, Ida och Gustav Undmans Stipendiefond, Stockholm, SE

Work in Public Collections
Nationalmuseum, Stockholm, SE

Galleries
• Galleri Sebastian Schilds, Stockholm, SE
• Nutida Svenskt Silver, Stockholm, SE

Nils Hint

born 1986 in Tallinn, EE

Education
2011–2013 Estonian Academy of Arts, Blacksmithing, MA, Tallinn, EE
2009 Escola Superior de Artes e Design, Porto, PT
2006–2010 Estonian Academy of Arts Blacksmithing, BA, Tallinn, EE
2005–2006 Vana-Vigala Technic School, Blacksmithing, Rapla maakond, EE

Teaching
2019 Workshop, together with Urmas Lüüs, HDK Steneby, SE
2018 BLACKSHOPWORKSMITH workshop, Oslo National Academy of Arts, NO
• Fundamental Forging workshop, Rhode Island School of Design, Providence/RI, US
2017 Workshop, Hiko Mizuno College of Jewelry, Tokyo, JP
2015 Workshop in HDK Steneby, SE
Since 2014 Associate Professor, Jewellery and Blacksmithing, Estonian Academy of Arts, Tallinn, EE
2012–2014 Blacksmithing teacher, Kopli Vocational school of Tallinn, EE

Grants and Awards
2016 Kristjan Raua nimeline kunstipreemia, Tallinn, EE
2014 Grant for creative work, Cultural Endowment of Estonia
2013 Competition winner, culture-friendly entrepreneur gift object, Estonian Ministry of Culture
2012 SA Noor Ehe special prize, The 6th Tallinn International Applied Art Triennial, EE
• Competition winner, Bocuse d'or 2013, ceremonial dishes design, Lyon, FR
2010 Contest winner with Rainer Kaasik-Aaslav, contest for the design of the ring of Estonian Academy of Arts Tallinn, EE

Artist in Residence
2013 art-st-urban, residence program by Gertrud and Heinz Aechlimann, Luzern, CH

Work in Public Collections
• art-st-urban Art Center, St. Urban, CH
• Estonian Museum of Applied Art and Design, Tallinn, EE
• Gallery of Art in Legnica, International Collection of Contemporary Jewellery, PL
• The Fund of Student Works of the Chair of Jewellery and Blacksmithing of Estonian Academy of Arts, Tallinn, EE

Kateřina Jirsová

born 1985 in Stod, CZ

Education
2009–2013   Academy of Arts, Architecture and Design Prague, Studio K.O.V., Prof. Eva Eisler, CZ
2006–2009 Academy of Fine Arts Prague, Conceptual studio, Prof. Miloš Šejn, CZ
2001–2005   High school of Applied Arts Zámeček, Pilsen, Sculpture department, CZ

Internships
2012   Konstfack, University of Arts, Crafts and Design, Jewellery + Corpus, Ädellab, Stockholm, SE
2008   Academy of Fine Arts Prague, Studio of Magdalena Jetelová, CZ (visiting from the Academy of Fine Arts, Munich, DE)
2007   Academy of Fine Arts Prague, Studio of Anton Čierný, CZ (visiting from the Academy of Fine Arts and Design Bratislava, SK)

Other Activities
Since 2019   Collaboration with GAMPA, dramaturgical and production-management, City Gallery of Pardubice, CZ
Since 2018   Member of OFFCITY, independent platform focused on arts in public space and architecture, Pardubice, CZ

Workshops
2022   MØLLEØY workshop, Studio 17, Stavanger, NO
2009   Artfest, Galery Klatovy | Klenová, studio of Jiří Kovanda, Klenová, CZ
2006   Artfest, Galery Klatovy | Klenová, studio of Martin Zet, Klenová, CZ
2005   Artfest, Galery Klatovy | Klenová, studio of Václav Fiala, Klatovy, CZ

Artist in Residence
2018   Atelierhaus Salzamt, Linz, AT
2017   OFFCITY AIR 2017 | Back to the Mills, Automatic Mills, Pardubice, CZ
2015   Střelnice, Divadlo 29, Pardubice, CZ

Work in Public Collections
UPM Museum of Decorative Arts, Prague, CZ

Junwon Jung

born 1978 in Sang-Ju, KR

Education and Working Experience
2010–2016   Diplom, Akademie der Bildenden Künste, Prof. Otto Künzli & Prof. Karen Pontoppidan, Munich, DE
2009–2010   Lecturer, Metalwork & Jewelry Department, Kookmin University, Seoul, KR
2008–2009   Researcher, Institute of Environmental Design, Kookmin University, Seoul, KR
2004–2007   MFA, Metalwork & Jewelry, Kookmin University, Seoul KR

Awards
2020   Friedrich Becker Prize, Düsseldorf, Gesellschaft für Goldschmiedekunst e.V., Hanau, DE
2019   Herbert-Hofmann-Prize, Internationale Handwerksmesse, Munich, DE
2016   Bayerischer Staatspreis, Bayerisches Wirtschaftsministerium, Munich, DE
2014   Anerkennung, Oberbayerischer Förderpreis für Angewandte Künste, Munich, DE

Work in Public Collections
• Bröhan Design Foundation, Berlin, DE
• Deutsches Goldschmiedehaus, Hanau, DE
• Die Neue Sammlung – The Design Museum, Munich, DE
• Museum of Contemporary Design and Applied Art, Lausanne, CH
• Schmuckmuseum Pforzheim, DE
• The Marzee Collection, Nijmegen, NL

Anders Ljungberg

born 1966 in Stockholm, SE

Education
1989–1994   National College of Arts and Design Konstfack, Metal Department, Stockholm, SE
1988–1989   Nyckelviksskolan, College for Arts, Crafts, Architecture and Design Lidingö, SE

Teaching
Since 2016   Professor at Konstfack, CRAFT! | Ädellab, Stockholm, SE
2014–2016   Professor and Head of Department, Oslo National Academy of the Arts, Metal and Jewellery, Oslo, NO
2006–2014   Opponent, Beckmans College of Design, Lidingö; Konstfack, Ädellab, Stockholm; HDK-Valand, Academy of Art and Design, Gothenburg, SE
2006   Guest Professor, winter session, Rhode Island School of Design, Providence | RI, US
2000–2014   Guest teacher, Beckmans College of Design, Stockholm, SE
• HDK-Valand, Academy of Art and Design (HDK Steneby), Dals Långed, SE
• Konstfack, Metal + Ceramic, Glass, Stockholm, SE
2000–2010   Senior Lecturer, National College of Art and Design, Konstfack, Ädellab, Stockholm, SE
Since 1995   Lecturer at different occasions, Sweden and abroad (US, KR, CN, UK, DE, NL, DK, NO, BE and others)

Grants and Awards
2010   Two-year grant, Konstnärsnämnden, Swedish Arts Grants Committee, Stockholm, SE
2005   Two-year grant, Konstnärsnämnden, Swedish Arts Grants Committee, Stockholm, SE
2003   Landstingets culture grant, Stockholm, SE
• Marianne och Sigvard Bernadottes culture grant, Stockholm, SE
2000   Bengt Juhlins craft grant, Stockholm, SE
1999   One-year grant, Konstnärsnämnden, Swedish Arts Grants Committee, Stockholm, SE

Work in Public Collections
• Engelbrektskyrkan, Stockholm, SE
• HKH Konung Carl XVI Gustav (Royal Collection Stockholm), SE
• Kunstindustrimuseet, Norwegian Museum of Decorative Arts and Design, Oslo, NO
• Nationalmuseum, Stockholm, SE
• Nordiska Museet, Stockholm, SE
• Röhsska Museum of Design and Craft, Gothenburg, SE
• The Marzee Collection, Nijmegen, NL

Kateřina Michálková

born 1990 in Havlíčkův Brod, CZ

2017–2018 Internship, Ceramics and Porcelain Studio, Academy of Arts, Architecture and Design (Head of the Studio Maxim Velčovský, Assistant Milan Pekař), Prague, CZ
2014–2018 Academy of Arts, Architecture and Design, Department of Applied Arts, K.O.V. Studio (Head of the Studio Eva Eisler, Assistant Eva Humlová, Peter Demek), Prague, CZ
2012–2014 Internship, Studio of Environment, FFA BUT Faculty of Fine Arts, Brünn University of Technology (Head of the Studio Barbora Klímová, Assistant Michal Moravčík), CZ
2011–2012 Internship, Akademia Sztuk Pieknych im. Jana Matejki w Krakowie, PL
2010–2016 FFA BUT Faculty of Fine Arts, Brünn University of Technology, Studio of Sculpture 2 (Head of the Studio Prof. Jan Ambrůz, Assistant Pavel Korbička), CZ
2006–2010 Study of Promotional Design/Exhibitions, Secondary School of Art and Design, Brno (Head of the Studio Jiří Sobotka), CZ

Myra Mimlitsch-Gray

born 1962 in Camden/NJ, US

Education
1986 Master of Fine Arts, Metalsmithing, Cranbrook Academy of Art, Bloomfield Hills/MI, US
1984 Bachelor of Fine Arts, Metal and Jewelry, Philadelphia College of Art, Philadelphia/PA, US

Fellowships, Awards and Honors
2020 Individual Artist Fellowship in Craft/Sculpture, New York Foundation for the Arts, US
2019 Masters of the Medium Award, James Renwick Alliance, Washington, DC, US
• Open Studios Residency, Haystack Mountain School of Crafts, US
2018 Chancellor's Award for Excellence in Scholarship and Creative Activity, State University of New York, US
2016 ACC American Craft Council Fellowship, Minneapolis/MN, and Induction into the College of Fellows, US
• Individual Artist Grant, Peter S. Reed Foundation, New York City/NY, US
• Interview entered into the Archives of American Art Oral History Collection, Smithsonian Institution, Washington, DC, US
2014 Individual Artist Fellowship in Crafts/Sculpture, New York Foundation for the Arts, US
• Artist-in-Residence, Ädellab, Konstfack, University of Arts, Crafts and Design, Stockholm, SE
2012 The United States Artists Glasgow Fellowship in Crafts and Traditional Arts, US
2007 Artist-in-Residence, Arts/Industry Program, Kohler Company, Wisconsin, US
2005 Individual Artist Fellowship, New York Foundation for the Arts, US
2001 Recipient, Silver Star Alumni Award, University of the Arts, Philadelphia/PA, US
1999 Funded Media and Visual Arts Residency, The Banff Centre for the Arts, Alberta/CA, US
1998 Recipient, Chancellor's Award for Excellence in Teaching, SUNY State University of New York, US
1997 Individual Artist Fellowship, New York Foundation for the Arts, US
1995 Individual Artist Award, The Louis Comfort Tiffany Foundation New York, US
1994 Individual Artist Fellowship, National Endowment for the Arts, Washington, DC, US
• Individual Artist Grant, Empire State Crafts Alliance, Fredonia/NY, US
1992 MacDowell Colony Fellowship, Peterborough/NH, US
1991 Regional Arts Fellowship, Arts Midwest/National Endowment of the Arts, US

Work in Public Collections
• Arkansas Museum of Fine Arts, Little Rock/AR, US
• Cooper Hewitt, Smithsonian Design Museum, New York/NY, US
• Cranbrook Art Museum, Bloomfield Hills/MI, US
• Detroit Institute of Arts, Detroit/MI, US
• Greater Lafayette Museum of Art, Lafayette/IN, US
• John Michael Kohler Arts Center, Sheboygan/WI, US
• Kohler Co., WI, US
• Lauren Rogers Museum of Art, Laurel/MS, US
• Metal Museum, Memphis/TN, US
• Metropolitan Museum of Art, New York/NY, US
• Mint Museum of Craft and Design, Charlotte/NC, US
• Mitsubishi Materials Corporation, Sanda-Shi, JP
• Museum of Arts and Design, New York/NY, US
• Museum of Fine Arts, Boston/MA, US
• Museum of Fine Arts, Houston/TX, US
• National Museum of Scotland, Edinburgh, UK
• Philadelphia Museum of Art, PA, US
• Racine Art Museum, Racine/WI, US
• Renwick Gallery, National Museum of American Art, Smithsonian Institution, Washington DC, US
• Rhode Island School of Design Museum, Providence/RI, US
• Samuel Dorsky Museum of Art, State University of New York, New Paltz/NY, US
• Tacoma Art Museum/WA, US
• University of Akron, Mary Myers School of Art, Akron/OH, US
• Victoria and Albert Museum, London, UK
• Yale University Art Gallery, New Haven/CT, US

Eija Mustonen

born 1961 in Polvijärvi, FI

Education
2000–2005 Master of Arts, University of Industrial Arts of Helsinki, FI
1983–1987 Silversmith, The Institute of Industrial Arts and Handicrafts in Lahti, FI
1981–1983 Stonesmith, The Craft Collage of Lappeenranta, FI

Working Experience
2019 Jury member, Susan Beech Mid-Career Artist Grant, US
2018 Jury member, Amber competition Aberif design Award, Gdansk, PL
2016–2017 Jury member, 7th Tallinn Applied Art Triennial Ajavahe. Time Difference, EE
2011 Coordinator, Spirit of Stone event, Lappeenranta, FI
2009 Jury member, Talente, Munich, DE
2006 Jury member of Innovation Prize, Inhorgenta 2006, Munich, DE
2005 Curator for KORU contemporary joieria finladesa, Barcelona, ES
2003–2012 Coordinator, international jewelry KORU1 2 3 & 4 events, Lappeenranta-Imatra, FI

Since 1997 Member of Hibernate-group
1997 Coordinator, international jewelry alchemy event, Lappeenranta, FI

Work in Public Collections
- CODA Museum, Apeldoorn, NL
- Collection of Finnish State Art Commission, FI
- Die Neue Sammlung – The Design Museum, permanent loan of the Danner Foundation, Munich, DE
- Montreal Museum of Fine Arts, CA
- Pahlman's Collection, Helsinki, FI
- Rotasa Collection Los Angeles, US
- The Marzee Collection, Nijmegen, NL
- The Museum of Fine Arts, Houston / TX, US

Markus Pollinger

geboren 1984 in Benediktbeuern, DE

Ausbildung
2016–2020 Akademie der Bildenden Künste, Diplom, Prof. Karen Pontoppidan, München, DE
2010–2016 Akademie der Bildenden Künste Nürnberg, Diplom bei Prof. Suska Mackert, DE
2008–2009 Meisterschule für das Gold- und Silberschmiedehandwerk, München, DE
2004–2005 Goldschmied, Berufsfachschule für Glas und Schmuck, Neugablonz, DE
2001–2004 Silberschmied, Berufsfachschule für Glas und Schmuck, Neugablonz, DE

Preise und Auszeichnungen
2022 Erster Preis, Silbertriennale / Ebbe-Weiss-Weingart-Preis, Hanau, DE
2020 Zweiter Preis, Oberbayerischer Förderpreis für angewandte Kunst, München, DE
2019 Förderpreis Kaufbeurer Künstler-Stiftung, DE
2017 Bayerischer Staatspreis, München, DE
- Finalist, BKV-Preis für Junges Kunsthandwerk, München, DE
- Artist in Residence, Hiko Mizuno College, Tokyo, JP
- Oberbayerischer Förderpreis für angewandte Kunst mit Ausstellung an der HM München, DE

2016 Meisterschüler bei Prof. Suska Mackert an der Akademie der Bildenden Künste Nürnberg, DE
2015 Erster Preis, Danner Klassenwettbewerb, Akademie der Bildenden Künste Nürnberg, DE
2013 Zweiter Preis, Danner Klassenwettbewerb, Akademie der Bildenden Künste Nürnberg, DE

Karen Pontoppidan

geboren 1968 in Kerteminde, DK

Ausbildung
1998 Diplom, Akademie der Bildenden Künste, München, DE
Seit 1997 Atelier, München, DE
1995–1997 Meisterschülerin
1991–1997 Studium bei Prof. Otto Künzli, Akademie der Bildenden Künste, München, DE
1988–1991 Ausbildung zur Formgeberin, Berufskolleg für Formgebung, Schmuck und Gerät, Schwäbisch Gmünd, DE
1986–1988 Praktikum, Gerda Lynggaard, Monies, Kopenhagen, DK

Lehrtätigkeit
Seit 2015 Professorin, Akademie der Bildenden Künste, München, DE
2006–2015 Professorin, Ädellab, Konstfack, University College of Arts, Crafts and Design, Stockholm, SE
2005–2006 Gastdozentin, Hochschule Pforzheim, DE
2003–2004 Gastdozentin, Fachhochschule Düsseldorf, DE
2000–2006 Assistentin von Prof. Otto Künzli, Akademie der Bildenden Künste, München, DE

Kuratorische Tätigkeit
2019 Ausstellung SCHMUCKISMUS, Die Neue Sammlung, Pinakothek der Moderne, München, DE
2015 Ausstellung LAGOMLAND, Galerie für Angewandte Kunst, München, DE
2014 Ausstellung The Talking Table, Galerie Rossana Orlandi, Mailand, IT
2012 Ausstellung Ädellab – The State of Things, Die Neue Sammlung – The Design Museum, München, DE
2007 Ausstellung Konnti, Helsinki, FI

Arbeiten in öffentlichen Sammlungen
- Alice and Louis Koch Collection, Landesmuseum Zürich, CH
- CODA Museum, Apeldoorn, NL
- Cooper Hewitt Museum, Smithsonian National Design Museum, New York / NY, US
- Die Neue Sammlung – The Design Museum, München, DE
- Grassi Museum, Leipzig, DE
- Hiko Mizuno College of Jewelry, Tokyo, JP
- Københavns Kunstforeningen, Kopenhagen, DK
- Nasjonalmuseet for Kunst, Arkitektur og Design, Oslo, NO
- Röhsska Museum, Göteborg, SE
- Schmuckmuseum Pforzheim, DE
- The Marzee Collection, Nijmegen, NL

Anna Rikkinen

born 1976 in Asikkala, FI

Education
2004 Bachelor of Design, Gerrit Rietveld Academie, Jewellery Department, Amsterdam, NL
2002 Bachelor of Arts, South Karelia Polytechnic, Jewellery and Stonework Design, FI

Artist Talks and Teaching
2023 Artist talk, Schmucksymposium, Haxthäuser Hof, DE
2021 Workshop leader & Artist talk, KORU7, International Contemporary Jewellery Triennial, Lappeenranta, FI
2018 Artist talk in Nordic Hands, HINT project, Godsbanen, Aarhus, DK
2017 Final work instructor, Saimaa University of Applied Sciences, Lappeenranta, South Karelia, FI
2015 Artist talk, KORU5, International Contemporary Jewellery Triennial, Lappeenranta, FI
2013 Artist talk, National Museum of Art, Architecture and Design, Oslo, NO
2012 Artist talk, KORU4, International Contemporary Jewellery Triennial, Saimaa University of Applied Sciences, Imatra, FI
2011 Artist talk, La Germinal project space, Barcelona, ES
2009 Nordic Jewellery – Yesterday and Today, Design Museum Helsinki, FI
2006 Artist talk with Nell Tanner, KORU2, International Contemporary Jewellery Triennial, Lappeenranta, FI

Grants
- Arts Council of Häme, FI
- Arts Promotion Centre Finland
- Frame Visual Art Finland
- National Council of Design
- Finnish-Swedish Cultural Fund
- Tellervo and Juuso Walden Fund, FI
- Finnish Cultural Foundation Päijät-Häme Regional Fund
- Willian and Ester Otsakorpi Fund, FI

Work in Public Collections
- Finnish State Art Deposit Collection, FI
- Jewellery Art Association Collection, FI
- The Marzee Collection, Nijmegen, NL

Hans Stofer

born 1957 in Baden, CH

Education
1981–1984   MA Schmuck & Gerät, ZHdK Zurich University of Arts, CH
1972–1976   Precision Engineering, Brown Boveri Technical College Baden, CH

Teaching
Since 2017   Professor Fachklasse Schmuck|Plastik, Burg Giebichenstein Kunsthochschule Halle, DE
2006–2017   Professor and Head of MA program, Jewellery & Metal, Royal College of Art, London, UK
2004–2006   Subject Leader 3D Design BA (Hons), Materials and Critical, Camberwell College of Art, London, UK
2000–2004   Acting Subject Leader BA (Hons), Silversmithing and Metalwork, Camberwell College of Art, London, UK
1999–2000   Appointed 0.6 Senior Lecturer BA (Hons), Silversmithing and Metalwork, Camberwell College of Art, London, UK
1994–1999   0.5 Lecturer, BA Hons, Silversmithing and Metalwork, Camberwell College of Art, London, UK
1987–1990   Production Unit Technician SMJG, manufacturing of multiples and small edition pieces, Royal College of Art, London, UK
- Part time Technical Assistant to David Watkins, artist, machining and manufacturing of hard-edged jewelry, London, UK
- Quinten Kynaston School, St John's Wood, Adult Education, Jewellery| Silversmithing, London, UK

1979–1981   Full time teacher at Brown Boveri Technical College, Baden, CH

Other
2016   Kistlein öffne dich, *Master class for executives*, Beratzhausen, DE
2015   Im Augenblick, *Art and disAbility Workshop No2*, Art and Frauenau, DE
2014   Anders und doch Gleich, *Art and disAbility Workshop No1*, Beratzhausen, DE
Since 2012   Member of the Danner-Stiftung Purchasing Committee, Munich, DE
2010   Master class Shenkar University for Design and Engineering, Ramat Gan, IL
2008|09   External Examiner, School of Applied Arts, Geneva, CH
2007   External Examiner, Phd Jack Cunningham, Glasgow School of Art, UK
2004–2007   External Examiner BA Hons, Jewellery|Applied Arts Middlesex University, London, UK
2000–2006   External Moderator, MA Applied Arts, Sandberg Institute, Amsterdam, NL
2000–2003   External Examiner BA Hons, DMJ and Jewellery, Buckinghamshire, UK
1999–2003   Setting up Grants Committee, Crafts Council, London, UK

Awards
2005   Shortlisted for the Jerwood Prize, Metal, UK
1995   Herbert-Hofmann-Prize, Internationale Handwerksmesse, Munich, DE
1989, 1991, 1994   Swiss Applied Arts Prize, CH
1987   Zurich Applied Arts Prize, CH

Work in Public Collections
- Birmingham Museums and Art Gallery, UK
- Danner-Stiftung, Munich, DE
- Die Neue Sammlung – The Design Museum, Munich, DE
- Musée Cantonal de Design et d'Arts Appliquées MUDAC, Lausanne, CH
- Nottingham Castle Museum, UK
- Swiss National Museum, Zurich, CH
- The Crafts Council Collection, London, UK
- The National Museum of Art, Architecture and Design, Oslo, NO
- The Potteries Museum, Stoke on Trent, UK
- Victoria and Albert Museum, London, UK

Vivi Touloumidi

born 1977 in Athens, GR

Education
2018–2022   PhD in the Arts, Antwerp Research Institute for the Arts (ARIA) & Royal Academy of Fine Arts Antwerpen, BE
2011–2013   MFA in the Crafts, Jewellery + Corpus, Konstfack, University of Arts, Crafts and Design, Stockholm, SE
2008–2009   Exchange studies on Jewellery & Ceramics, NSCAD University, Halifax, CA
2006–2010   BFA in Jewellery and Everyday Objects, University of Applied Arts Pforzheim, DE
2002–2004   Certificate in Goldsmithing, Professional Institute of Gold- and Silversmiths, Athens, GR
1997–2002   Diploma in Financial Management and Banking, Athens, GR

Research & Teaching Faculty Member
Since 2018   Lecturer focusing on artistic research, Royal Academy of Fine Arts Antwerp, BE

Lectures
2021   Anamma Lecture Series, Athens, GR
- Parse, 4th Biennial Research Conference, Faculty of Fine, Applied and Performing Arts, University of Gothenburg, SE
- Open Laboratory Weeks, Royal Academy of Fine Arts Antwerp, BE
- Zadan Lecture Series, HDK-Valand, Academy of Art and Design, Gothenburg, SE

2017   Research Lab CRAFT!, Konstfack, University of Arts, Crafts and Design, Stockholm, SE

Seminars and Workshops
2023   MA exam opponent, HDK-Valand, Academy of Art and Design, Gothenborg, SE
2021   BA exam opponent, HDK-Valand, Academy of Art and Design, Gothenborg, SE
2020   External tutor, HDK-Valand, Academy of Art and Design, Gothenborg, SE
2019   MA cross-disciplinary workshop with Mashid Mohadjerin, Royal Academy of Fine Arts Antwerp, BE
- External tutor, Academy of Design and Crafts at the University of Gothenburg, SE

2018 External tutor, Academy of Design and Crafts at the University of Gothenburg, SE
• Instructor, Hephaistos Summer School, Ilias Lalaounis Museum, Athens, GR
• BA workshop, Royal Academy of Fine Arts Antwerp, BE
2015 Co-teacher, Summer Academy Salzburg, AT

Acknowledgments and Awards
2023 Nomination Friedrich Becker Prize, Hanau, DE
2017 Herbert-Hofmann-Prize, Internationale Handwerksmesse, Sonderschau SCHMUCK, Munich, DE
• Friedrich Becker Prize, Hanau, DE
• ITAMI Award, JP
2014 Cominelli Foundation Award, IT
2011 TALENTE, Munich, DE
• Friedrich Becker Prize, Hanau, DE
• ITAMI Award, JP
• RRH (Ruth Reisert Hafner) Jewellery Award, Pforzheim, DE
2010 New Traditional Jewellery True Colors, Amsterdam, NL

Grants, Scholarships and Fellowships
2018–2022 PhD fellow, ARIA & Royal Academy of Fine Arts Antwerp, BE
2013 Konstfack grant, Jubel-Fond, Karl-Alex Rosenqvists, Stockholm, SE
2012 Ulla Fröberg-Cramérs scholarhip, Stockholm, SE
2008 Baden-Württemberg Auslandsstipendium, DE

Work in Public Collections
• Cominelli Foundation Permanent Collection, IT
• Ilias Lalaounis Jewelry Museum, Athens, GR
• Schmuckmuseum Pforzheim, DE
• The Marzee Collection, Nijmegen, NL

Tarja Tuupanen

born 1973 in Lieksa, FI

Education
2013 MFA, Konstfack, University of Arts, Crafts and Design, Stockholm, SE
2006 Teachers pedagogic studies, HAMK University of Applied Sciences, Hämeenlinna, FI
2003 Specialized program of jewelry art, South Carelia Polytechnic, Lappeenranta, FI
1999 College diploma, Jewellery and Stonework Design, South Carelia Vocational College, Department of Crafts and Design, Lappeenranta, FI

Workshops and Teaching
2021 Jury member, KORU7, International Contemporary Jewellery Triennial, Lappeenranta, FI
2020 STONE, two workshops organized by Magda Sa, Porto, PT
• Metamorphose, one-week workshop, Design d'objet, Cité scolaire Raymond Loewy, La Souterraine, FR
• Jury member, Amberif Design Award, Gdansk, PL
2016–2021 Thesis tutoring, LAB University of Applied Sciences, Imatra / Lappeenranta FI
2016, 2018, 2019 Stonework workshop, China Academy of Arts, Hangzhou, CN
2012 S-T-O-N-E, workshop with Nelli Tanner, KORU4, Imatra, FI
• Sense of stone workshop, Estonia Academy of Arts, Department of Jewellery and Blacksmithing, Tallinn, EE
2007 SEAL, workshop, Ravstedhus, Bylderup-Bov, DK
2006 Cameo today, workshop with Helena Lehtinen, KORU2, Lappeenranta, FI
2000–2022 Stonework teacher, LAB University of Applied Sciences (previously Saimaa University of Applied Sciences), Lappeenranta / Imatra, FI

Lectures
2023 Artist talk, Schmucksymposium Haxthäuser Hof 2023, DE
2022 Artist talk, China Academy of Arts, Hangzhou, CN
2021 AJF live with HIBERNATE, Tuupanen, Lehtinen, Mustonen, Sokura (online)
2020 Artist lecture, Axxell, Espoo, FI
2019 About stone – material, method and jewelry, HDK – Academy of Design and Crafts, University of Gothenburg, SE
2018 Artist talk, 25. International Jewellery Symposium Turnov, Muzeum Českého ráje v Turnově, CZ
2017 Artist talk, The WeeGee Exhibition Centre by the Finnish Museum of Horology, Espoo, FI
2015 Marbled, Body Alchemy-seminar, the Hangzhou Contemporary International Jewelry and Metal Art Triennial, China Academy of Arts, Hangzhou, CN
• I work with stone, Object & Jewellery, University College PXL-MAD, Hasselt, BE
• I work with stone, Jewellery Department, The Gerrit Rietveld Academie, Amsterdam, NL
2014 I work with stone, HDK – Academy of Design and Crafts, University of Gothenburg, SE
2012 I work with stone, Estonia Academy of Arts, Tallinn, EE
2011 I work with stone, Spirit of Stone symposium, Saimaa University of Applied Sciences, Lappeenranta, FI
2010 Coffee talk, La Germinal, Barcelona, ES
• Artist talk, Gemstone and Jewellery Campus Idar-Oberstein, Gemstone and Jewellery, Trier University of Applied Sciences, DE
2009 About Finnish Jewellery Art Association and Finnish Jewellery, KORU3-seminar, Imatra, FI

Memberships and Confidential Posts
2017–2018 Chairwoman of National Council of Architecture and Design in Arts Promotion Centre, FI
2015–2018 Member of Board for Public Display Grants to Visual Artists in Arts Promotion Centre, FI
2015–2016 Member of National Council of Architecture, Design and Environmental Art in Arts Promotion Centre, FI
2005–2013 and since 2020 Chairwoman of Finnish Jewellery Art Association, FI

Grants and Awards
2021 Artist grant, Arts Promotion Centre, Helsinki, FI
2020 Foundation for advancement of Karelian culture, acknowledgment, private fund
• Public Display Grant, Arts Promotion Centre, Helsinki, FI
• Grant for group for exhibition project (with Mia Maljojoki), Arts Promotion Centre, Helsinki, FI
2019 Travel grant for group (with Anna Rikkinen, Eija Mustonen), Frame Finland
2017 Grant for Hibernate-group for organizing exhibition (with Mustonen, Lehtinen, Sokura), The Finnish Cultural Foundation, South-Karelia, FI
2015 Five-year working grant, Arts Promotion Centre, Helsinki, FI
2014 Working grant, for Hibernate-publication (with Mustonen, Lehtinen), Arts Promotion Centre Finland
• Working grant, Arts Promotion Centre, Kymenlaakso and South Carelia, Helsinki, FI
2013 Working grant, Niilo Helander Foundation, FI
2010 Working grant, Arts Promotion Centre, Helsinki, FI

Work in Public Collections
- Collection of The Finnish Jewellery Art Association, Lapeenrenta, FI
- Design Museum, Helsinki, FI
- Die Neue Sammlung – The Design Museum, Munich, DE
- Françoise van den Bosch Foundation, Amstelveen, NL
- Regional Museum, Turnov, CZ
- Rhöska Museet, Gothenburg, SE
- The Collection of Finnish State Art Commission, FI
- The National Museum of Art, Architecture and Design, Oslo, NO

Luzia Vogt

geboren 1971 in Basel, CH

Ausbildung
2018   Master of Arts, Design / Product Design, Hochschule Luzern, CH
2003   Praktikum in Silberschmiedewerkstätten, Tokyo, JP
2002–2003   Austauschstudium, Nova Scotia College of Art and Design, Halifax, CA
2000–2004   Diplom, Hochschule für Gestaltung Pforzheim, Fachklasse Schmuck und Gerät, DE
1992–1996   Goldschmiedelehre, Basel, CH
1991–1992   Schule für Gestaltung, gestalterischer Vorkurs, Basel, CH

Berufliche Tätigkeit
Seit 2022   Lehrerin für Gestaltung, Goldschmiedeabteilung, Schule für Gestaltung, Basel, CH
2018–2020   Gastdozentin, Fakultät für Gestaltung, Hochschule Pforzheim, DE
Seit 2018   Lehrerin für Gestaltung, Goldschmiedeabteilung, Schule für Gestaltung, Bern, CH
2013   Gastdozentin, Universität Liechtenstein, LI
2012   Kuratorin der Ausstellung natural – artificial, Galerie Noël Guyomarc'h, Montréal, CA
2007–2020   Lehrerin für Gestaltung, Goldschmiedeabteilung, Berufsbildungszentrum, Luzern, CH
2006–2007   Lehrauftrag und externe Expertin, Schule für Gestaltung, Basel, CH
Seit 2006   Diverse Vorträge über die eigene Arbeit in der Schweiz, Deutschland und Kanada
Seit 2004   Schmuck- und Produkt-Designerin, eigene Werkstatt in Basel, CH
1996–2000   Designerin und Goldschmiedin in Montréal, CA, Basel und Zug, CH

Preise und Auszeichnungen
2009   Nominierung, Eidgenössischer Preis für Design Schweiz
2008   Nominierung, Eidgenössischer Preis für Design Schweiz
- Erster Preis Blickfang 2008, mit Nathalie Luder und Stephanie Hensle, Zürich, CH
2005   Eidgenössischer Preis für Design Schweiz
- Innovationspreis, Inhorgenta Europe 2005, Preis der Internationalen Jury, München, DE
2004   Erster Preis FormForum, Bern, CH
- Auszeichnung, Bertha Heraeus und Kathinka Platzhoff Stiftung, Frankfurt/M., DE

Arbeiten in öffentlichen Sammlungen
- BAK, Bundesamt für Kultur, Bern, CH
- Château Borély, Musée des Arts Décoratifs, de la Faïence et de la Mode, Marseille, FR
- Musée Cantonal de Design et d'Arts Appliquées MUDAC, Lausanne, CH
- DMA, Dallas Museum of Art, Dallas/TX, US
- The Marzee Collection, Nijmegen, NL
- Montreal Museum of Fine Arts, Montréal, CA
- Landesmuseum Zürich, CH
- Racine Art Museum, Racine/WI, US
- Städtische Sammlung, Jakob Bengel-Stiftung, Idar-Oberstein, DE

Stella Wanisch

geboren 1990 in Hagen, DE

Ausbildung
2023   Diplom Bildende Kunst, Schmuck und Gerät, DE
2015–2023   Bildende Kunst, Schmuck und Gerät bei Prof. Suska Mackert, Akademie der Bildenden Künste Nürnberg, DE
2013–2015   Schmuck bei Prof. Daniel Kruger, Burg Giebichenstein Kunsthochschule Halle, DE
2009–2013   Staatlich geprüfte Goldschmiedin, Zeichenakademie Hanau, DE

Auszeichnungen und Stipendien
2021–2023   Meisterschülerin, Bildende Kunst, Schmuck und Gerät, Prof. Suska Mackert, Akademie der Bildenden Künste Nürnberg, DE
2021   Erster Preis, Wettbewerb zur Gestaltung eines Andachtsraumes im Neubau August-Meier-Haus, Nürnberg, DE
2016–2023   Stipendiatin, Studienstiftung des deutschen Volkes, Bonn, DE
2015   Erster Preis, klasseninterner Danner-Wettbewerb, Klasse Grafikdesign und visuelle Kommunikation (in Kooperation mit Jonas Dorner), Akademie der Bildenden Künste Nürnberg, DE

Jing Yang

geboren 1987 in Hunan, CN

Ausbildung
Seit 2017   Freischaffende Künstlerin in München
2015–2017   Diplom, Meisterschülerin, Studium an der Akademie der Bildenden Künste, München bei Prof. Karen Pontoppidan
2010–2014   Studium an der Akademie der Bildenden Künste, München bei Prof. Otto Künzli
2006–2010   Studium an der Xiamen Universität, CN

Preise und Auszeichnungen
2017   Marzee Graduate Prize, Nijmegen, NL
2016   The 24th Legnica International Competition of Jewellery, Award of the Gallery of Art in Legnica, Legnica, PL
2015   TALENTE – Meister der Zukunft, Internationale Handwerksmesse, München, DE

© 2023 Schmuckmuseum Pforzheim | Pforzheim Jewellery Museum und | and arnoldsche Art Publishers, Stuttgart

Alle Rechte vorbehalten. Vervielfältigung und Wiedergabe auf jegliche Weise (grafisch, elektronisch und fotomechanisch sowie der Gebrauch von Systemen zur Datenrückgewinnung) – auch in Auszügen – nur mit schriftlicher Genehmigung der Copyright-Inhaber.
www.arnoldsche.com

All rights reserved. No part of this work may be reproduced or used in any form or by any means (graphic, electronic or mechanical, including photocopying or information storage and retrieval systems) without written permission from the copyright holders.
www.arnoldsche.com

Herausgeberinnen | Editors
Cornelie Holzach
Ellen Maurer Zilioli

Autorinnen | Authors
Cornelie Holzach
Ellen Maurer Zilioli
Carin E.M. Reinders

Die vorliegende Publikation erscheint anlässlich der Ausstellung
Auf Abwegen – Schmuck und Gerät am Rande der Vernunft
im Schmuckmuseum Pforzheim
(6.10.2023 – 14.01.2024)
und im CODA Museum Apeldoorn | NL
(19.05. – 22.09.2024). |
The present publication is published on the occasion of the exhibition
Gone Astray – Jewellery and Utensils on the Fringe of Reason
at Pforzheim Jewellery Museum
(6.10.2023 – 14.01.2024)
and at CODA Museum Apeldoorn | NL
(19.05. – 22.09.2024).

Kuratorin | Curated by
Ellen Maurer Zilioli

Übersetzung | Translation
Joan Clough, Castallack (EN)
Dr. Kurt Rehkopf, Hamburg (DE)

Lektorat | Copy editing
Wendy Brouwer, Stuttgart (EN)

Konzeption, Koordination und Lektorat im Schmuckmuseum | Concept, coordination and copy editing at Pforzheim Jewellery Museum
Isabel Schmidt-Mappes

arnoldsche Projektkoordination | Project coordination
Julia Hohrein

Grafische Gestaltung | Graphic designer
www.ina-bauer.studio

Offset Reproduktion | Offset reproductions
Schwabenrepro, Fellbach

Druck | Printed by
Schleunung Druck, Marktheidenfeld

Buchbinder | Bound by
Hubert & Co., Göttingen

Papier | Paper
Arena Natural Rough 140 g/m²
Arctic Volume 170 g/m²

Bibliografische Information der Deutschen Nationalbibliothek
Die Deutsche Nationalbibliothek verzeichnet diese Publikation in der Deutschen Nationalbibliografie; detaillierte bibliografische Daten sind über www.dnb.de abrufbar.

Bibliographic information published by the Deutsche Nationalbibliothek
The Deutsche Nationalbibliothek lists this publication in the Deutsche Nationalbibliografie; detailed bibliographic data are available at www.dnb.de.

ISBN 978-3-89790-700-3

Made in Germany, 2023

Umschlagabbildungen | Cover illustrations
vorne | front: Kanako Ebisawa, Niche, 2021/2022 (Seiten | Pages 128, 137). Foto | Photo: Mirei Takeuchi
hinten | back: Nils Hint, Shadow, 2014 (Seite | Page 142). Foto | Photo: Nils Hint

Zitate | Quotations

* Seite | Page 2: Erhart Kästner, Aufstand der Dinge. Byzantinische Aufzeichnungen. Frankfurt | M. 1985, S. | p. 179.

* Seite | Page 8: Monika Leisch-Kiesl, Wenn Gegenwartskunst und die Kategorie des Schönen aufeinandertreffen. In: Monika Leisch-Kiesl, Max Gottschlich, Susanne Winder (Hg. | eds.), Ästhetische Kategorien. Perspektiven der Kunstwissenschaft und der Philosophie. Linzer Beiträge zur Kunstwissenschaft und Philosophie, Bd. | vol. 7. Bielefeld 2017, S. | pp. 53–73; S. | p. 71.

Bildnachweis | Photo credits
© VG Bild-Kunst, Bonn 2023 für | for Tobias Birgersson, David M. Clarke, Åsa Elmstam, Anne Fischer, Anders Ljungberg, Vivi Touloumidi

Die Geltendmachung der Ansprüche gem. § 60h UrhG für die Wiedergabe von Abbildungen der Exponate | Bestandswerke erfolgt durch die VG Bild-Kunst.

Abb. | fig. 1: Courtesy of Archivio Storico della Biennale di Venezia, ASAC, Foto | Photo: Francesco Galli
Abb. | fig. 2: Courtesy of the artists and GALLERIA CONTINUA, Foto | Photo: Andrea Rossetti
Abb. | fig. 3: Gerhard Wolf, Die Vase und der Schemel. Ding, Bild oder eine Kunstgeschichte der Gefäße. Hg. | ed. Kunsthistorisches Institut. Florenz 2019, S. | p. 11

Tobias Alm: S. | pp. 86–87, 129; Kat. Nrn. | cat. nos. 1–4
Sawa Aso: S. | pp. 89–91; Kat. Nrn. | cat. nos. 5–9
Beatrice Brovia | Nicolas Cheng: S. | pp. 72–73, 75; Kat. Nrn. | cat. nos. 24–29
Courtesy of Galerie Zink, Waldkirchen & David Clarke: S. | p. 117; Kat. Nr. | cat. no. 30
Åsa Elmstam: S. | p. 53; Kat. Nrn. | cat. nos. 40–41, 43
Petronella Eriksson: S. | p. 52; Kat. Nr. | cat. no. 42
Natascha Frechen: S. | pp. 62 (oben | top), 63; Kat. Nrn. | cat. nos. 37–39
Adéla Fries: S. | pp. 120–121; Kat. Nrn. | cat. nos. 55–57
Ta Greta: Kat. Nr. | cat. no. 73
Christian Habetzeder: S. | pp. 47, 51, 118–119; Kat. Nrn. | cat. nos. 17–23, 48–49
Karolina Hägg: S. | pp. 48–49; Kat. Nrn. | cat. nos. 46–47
Nils Hint: S. | pp. 69–71; Kat. Nrn. | cat. nos. 50–54
Claudia Holzinger: S. | p. 99; Kat. Nrn. | cat. nos. 116–117
Junwon Jung: S. | pp. 76–78; Kat. Nrn. | cat. nos. 58–66
Gerhard Kassner: S. | pp. 111–112; Kat. Nrn. | cat. nos. 10–12
Julian Kirschler: S. | p. 60; Kat. Nr. | cat. no. 33
Anders Ljungberg: S. | pp. 123–127; Kat. Nrn. | cat. nos. 67–71
Rich Maciejewski|Kohler Co, WI | US: S. | p. 66; Kat. Nr. | cat. no. 78
Kateřina Michálková: S. | pp. 54–55; Kat. Nr. | cat. no. 72
Myra Mimlitsch-Gray: S. | p. 65; Kat. Nrn. | cat. nos. 74–77
Michael Müller: S. | p. 62 (unten | bottom); Kat. Nrn. | cat. nos. 34–36
Markus Pollinger: S. | pp. 56–59; Kat. Nrn. | cat. nos. 84–86
Karen Pontoppidan: S. | pp. 100–101, 103–105; Kat. Nrn. | cat. nos. 87–100
Jesse Pylsy: S. | pp. 93 + 95 (model: Pilvi Naakka), 94; Kat. Nrn. | cat. nos. 79 + 81 (model: Pilvi Naakka), 80, 82–83
Pia Maria Rautio: S. | p. 45; Kat. Nr. | cat. no. 102
Juhana Rikkinen: S. | pp. 42–43, 46; Kat. Nrn. | cat. nos. 101, 103
Lassi Rinno: S. | pp. 113–115; Kat. Nrn. | cat. nos. 109–112
Brigitte Sauer: S. | pp. 67–68; Kat. Nrn. | cat. nos. 44–45
Hans Stofer: S. | pp. 96–98; Kat. Nrn. | cat. nos. 104–107
Mirei Takeuchi: S. | pp. 41, 83–85, 106–108, 122, 128, 158; Kat. Nrn. | cat. nos. 13–16, 31–32, 118–120
Vivi Touloumidi: S. | p. 109; Kat. Nr. | cat. no. 108
Luzia Vogt: S. | pp. 79–81; Kat. Nrn. | cat. nos. 113–115

86–87 **Tobias Alm** *130*
88–91 **Sawa Aso** *131*
110–112 **Astrid Becksteiner-Rasche** *132*
82–85 **Naama Bergman** *133*
118–119 **Tobias Birgersson** *134–135*
72–75 **Beatrice Brovia / Nicolas Cheng** *136*
116–117 **David Clarke** *137*
41, 122, 128 **Kanako Ebisawa** *137*
60–63 **Ute Eitzenhöfer** *138–139*
52–53 **Åsa Elmstam** *139–140*
67–68 **Anne Fischer** *140*
47–51 **Karolina Hägg** *141*
69–71 **Nils Hint** *142*
120–121 **Kateřina Jirsová** *143*
76–78 **Junwon Jung** *144–145*
123–127 **Anders Ljungberg** *146*
54–55 **Kateřina Michálková** *147*
64–66 **Myra Mimlitsch-Gray** *148*
92–95 **Eija Mustonen** *149*
56–59 **Markus Pollinger** *150*
100–105 **Karen Pontoppidan** *151–153*
42–46 **Anna Rikkinen** *153*
96–98 **Hans Stofer** *154*
109 **Vivi Touloumidi** *155*

113–115 **Tarja Tuupanen** *155*
79–81 **Luzia Vogt** *156*
99 **Stella Wanisch** *156*
106–108 **Jing Yang** *157*

Cornelie Holzach
Ellen Maurer Zilioli
Herausgeberinnen

ABWEGEN

*Zeitgenössische
Gold- und Silberschmiedekunst
am Rande der Vernunft*

*Gefäß
Schmuck
Gerät*

AUF